# DRIVE IT!

## Life Lessons from Hollywood's Band

The Authorized Biography of Dr. Arthur C. Bartner

CHRISTY STANSELL

WINSOME ENTERTAINMENT GROUP LLC

**Drive It!** Life Lessons from Hollywood's Band



Christy Stansell
Nampa, ID
AuthorChristyStansell@gmail.com

Ordering Information:
Special discounts are available on quantity purchases by corporations, associations, educational institutions, and others. For details, contact Christy Stansell above.

Printed in the United States of America

First Edition

ISBN 978-1-5136-8987-6

Cover Photography Copyrighted By

Ling Luo
Los Angeles, CA
Lingluocontact@gmail.com

Publisher: Winsome Entertainment Group LLC

# CONTENTS

*For my daughters, Tylar and Rylee, and to future generations:*

*When you persevere through challenges and commit to excellence,*
*you develop confidence and know that you can do anything.*
*You, too, can DRIVE IT!*

# INTRODUCTION

My blood pressure went high-stepping when the idea for this book first occurred to me. My mind was immediately flooded with memories of my days in the band. I remember going to my first band camp as a college freshman and feeling incredibly intimidated and exhilarated all at the same time. Surrounded by a few hundred people I'd never met, all standing at attention to the command of one man, Dr. Arthur C. Bartner, I questioned if I was in the right place, and I also realized there was no place I'd rather be. When I was the solo twirler with the band in high school, we were known as "band geeks"—but not here. This college band wasn't just respected, it was treasured. I could tell something special was happening here. I may not have known then what I was getting myself into, but in hindsight, it was the most valuable college activity I could have ever done. The first thing I learned was how to march, how to *Drive It!* It's not your typical marching style—and it's not only about marching. It's an attitude. It's a passion. It's a tradition, a camaraderie, a connection unlike any other. It's a conviction that instills perseverance, excellence, and confidence with every step. And it's a philosophy that anyone can learn and apply to their own life as they strive for greater levels of success in any pursuit.

Something else I discovered is that music is a superpower. Music ignites our soul and unites our spirit. Every note has meaning and feeling, and every heart beats to a different drum. No matter what form it takes or what instrument it comes from, music has been bringing people together since the beginning of time. There's something about music that even when a song has ended, the rhythm lingers in our mind. Music activates our brain and allows us to experience a higher level of learning and apply new skills to other parts of our lives. Dr. Bartner has given his entire life to developing musicians. He taught students not only how to read notes or play an instrument, but more importantly how to evoke emotion in the tunes to bring an audience to life. The sounds of Dr. Bartner's musical direction have reached the ears of literally millions of people around the world—and that is not an exaggeration.

I was only one of several thousand USC students who benefited from Dr. Bartner's band leadership over five decades, learning much more than music and marching. Whether consciously or unconsciously, we also absorbed essential life lessons that helped us get through the college experience and continued to support our success in life after graduation. And we had a ton of fun along the way. The hundreds of celebrity-filled football game halftime shows, the international performance invitations, and the behind-the-scenes of making albums, movies, and television shows as Hollywood's Band are only part of Dr. Bartner's life story. His true legacy lies in the seventeen characteristics (one "High Note" per chapter) that build the three core principles (one per section) of his *Drive It!* philosophy outlined in this book. While it is not a how-to-play-music or how-to-march-in-a-band instruction manual, this book offers a how-to-*Drive It!* in all aspects of life, while being entertained and inspired along the way.

*Drive It!* is presented in three sections, similar to how the band goes through a game day: pregame, halftime, and postgame. During pregame, in developing the first *Drive It!* core value, we get insight into Art's personal life: where and how he grew up, his struggle to choose basketball or trumpet, where he went to school, got married, raised children, and how he became part of the Trojan Family. Pregame also details the beginning of the band, relationships with administrators and coaches, and what band members have to do if they want to become part of "The Greatest Marching Band in the History of the Universe." The halftime chapters are just as entertaining as a true halftime field show, because the band officially becomes Hollywood's Band—which contributes to the second *Drive It!* core value. We meet the celebrities, singers, actors, U.S. Presidents, and others who elevate the status of the organization and the man who runs it. The growing popularity of the talented band director and musicians led to incredible performance opportunities, including music videos, top-rated TV shows, and full-length feature films. Then, postgame evolves the third *Drive It!* core value. When they're not marching on the football field, Dr. Bartner takes Trojan Band members on international journeys that would make a travel agent jealous. Thousands of musicians performed under his direction of bands assembled for the Olympics, the Super Bowl, the World Series, World Expos, political national conventions, presidential library openings, and so much more. Hundreds of others were part of The All-American Marching

Band at Disneyland, which Dr. Bartner led for some twenty-eight years. Altogether, through countless pregame, halftime, and postgame experiences, Dr. Bartner's career spanned fifty years—that's five decades of commitment to inspiring perseverance, excellence, and confidence in musicians and audiences around the globe.

When I first met Dr. Bartner upon joining the band, I felt respectful appreciation toward him. Through my college years, that shifted to amused intimidation. Ultimately, some thirty years later, I feel awed admiration. It has been an honor and privilege to spend hours and hours visiting with him to tell the story of his life that is inextricably woven with the history of the band. What an adventure! Let's line up and get marching! It's time to *Drive It!*

# PREGAME

## PERSERVERANCE

Courtesy: Benjamin Chua

# 1

# BEGINNING OF A LEGEND

*Arthur C. Bartner loved playing his trumpet at age sixteen.*
Courtesy: Dr. Arthur C. Bartner

# CHAPTER ONE

## BEGINNING OF A LEGEND

"BAND! 'TEN-HUT!" From atop a ladder, Dr. Arthur C. Bartner calls the Trojan Marching Band to attention. All facing the same end zone, each section on its own yard line, he commands the musicians to stand tall. "Heels together! Stomach in! Shoulders back! Heads up! Who are we?" "Trojans!" "So, don't move," orders the band director. "DOMOOOOV!" No adjusting sunglasses or scratching noses or brushing hair off faces. Even if it tickles, too bad, leave it there. No flinching at attention. Wait in silence for the next command, because if it gets missed, the musician looks bad, and then the whole band looks bad, so stand still and pay attention. This drill was the beginning of instilling discipline in the ranks—and it worked, most of the time... sometimes. When too many members start messing around, look out: "TOOORTURE DRILLLLL!" Anytime a skill-building technique includes the word "torture," there must be a purpose behind it, and there was. Whether students realized it or not, drills were part of a greater plan, one that began decades before they marched their first step. The development of life skills and the *Drive It!* philosophy began when Dr. Bartner was just a boy.

Born August 30, 1940 in Maplewood, New Jersey, Arthur Charles was the second son of Mark and Bess. He had an older brother, a younger brother, and a baby sister: Robert, Peter, and Harriet. They were typical siblings with normal fun and regular fights. His father was rather distant and didn't have much of a role in raising the kids. He would go to work, come home, watch TV, eat dinner, go to bed, and start over in the morning.

Art's mother was the driving force in the family, the matriarch, and he remembers her as a workaholic. Teaching school and running the household didn't leave much time for anything else.

Art never felt like the bright one in the family. His older brother, Robert, didn't have to study to get A's. His younger brother, Peter, was smart, too, just less driven. His sister, Harriet, came along late and was way younger than them, so they weren't very close. They were all raised to be independent individuals. Art wanted to be smart, but he had to work hard to get ahead. He was very focused and had a strong desire to please everyone, so he did whatever he could to get attention and affection, and that came in the form of performances. Because one thing Art had that his siblings did not was a natural talent, love, and appreciation for music.

## The First Notes

Art's big brother, Robert, was the original trumpet player in the Bartner family, but he rarely picked it up to practice—he was just not interested. Neither were Peter or Harriet. They had all started instruments at one point and quit soon after. One day, Robert's unattended trumpet found its way into Art's hands (after he snuck into his brother's room), and a sudden blare of the horn both surprised and thrilled his mother. With her side of the family having a background in music and the arts, she seemed pleased that one of her children finally took an interest in music. He didn't care if his first note may have been slightly out of tune. "Well, it was awful," he said. "Totally non-recognizable note. Nothing to be proud of!" But it didn't matter. At the ripe age of nine, Art had found his thing. The trumpet ignited a spark in him that, up to that point, nothing else had. Except maybe basketball.

Art loved running around and shooting hoops. This kid could jump! And he could score! In fact, he could run much faster and jump much higher than his brothers and sister. About the same time he was fiddling around with the brass instrument, he was also toying with the brown ball. In his fourth-grade league, Art was impressed by an older player. "Here I was, a really skinny fourth grader, and here's this older, more mature, more developed, muscular guy who picked up the ball and drove through everybody to the other end of the court. And I'm thinking, man, I sure wish I could do that." Art now had a vision of how he wanted to play the game. He enjoyed the competition and the camaraderie of being part of a team. All those drills perfecting his skills put him in great physical shape. Making baskets came fairly easy to him, but it still took practice, and doing the same thing over and over again to build that muscle memory served him well in developing his ability to focus. He loved the game!

The challenge was finding time to practice both of his passions. Art balanced his time as best he could, but he credits his mother with dividing his days and guiding his talents. With a half-hearted chuckle, he recalled she would always ask him, "Have you done your homework? Have you practiced?" His mom liked good grades. Art liked sports and music. And he preferred to practice one more than the other. Before he could go out and dribble the ball, his mom insisted he get his schoolwork done and read through some notes with his trumpet. Art was getting pretty good, and his mom liked to show him off. She'd say, "Arthur, get your trumpet and play for Uncle Herman," even though as a kid, that's the last thing he wanted to do, and he was pretty sure it was the last thing Uncle Herman wanted, too.

Occasionally, Arthur and his mom would run through a number before a recital. She would accompany him on piano, although he would be center stage while she stayed behind the curtain, not wanting the spotlight. "When we'd practice, it was like a contest to see who would make the first mistake. Inevitably, it was me. It was a fun thing to do with her."

Whether it was on the court or on a stage, Art thrived on the crowd response. He remembers playing "Oh Holy Night" at his first Christmas Concert when he was eleven and feeling the audience's appreciation with their loud, enthusiastic applause—even though he took the wrong ending. "I forgot to take the repeat, and that confused everyone who was singing. I basically rewrote the Christmas carol. It was the beginning of my career," he laughed. Soon after, his interest in the trumpet hit a new level when he heard the United States Marine Band play "Bugler's Holiday." Art recalled, "It was the first real band I ever heard, and I was blown away. These were real trumpet players, and it was awesome. And I thought, hey, I might want to do this as a career." Except, there was still his affinity for basketball.

In junior high (which in those days in New Jersey covered seventh, eighth, and ninth grades), Art could hit notes in band class and make baskets after school. During summers off school, he'd practice trumpet in the evenings so he could spend his days dribbling his basketball the full mile down the road to the community house to sink some shots at the indoor court. That is, Art could shoot hoops when he wasn't on a train to his private lessons at Radio City Music Hall. His schoolteacher recognized Art's raw talent and connected him with Frank Venezia, who was a trumpet player in the NBC Symphony Orchestra under famed Italian conductor, Arturo Toscanini. Once a week, here was a thirteen-year-old boy catching a train, a ferry boat, and the New York subway to get the twenty-five miles from Maplewood to midtown Manhattan. Art's desire to please caused him to use his time wisely. Even though he did not like to practice, he would "play" in silence on the train. "I would put my music on my lap, sing, tap my toes, and move my fingers as if they were on the valves. That's how I would practice because you don't waste Venezia's time. You come prepared or you don't come at all."

Those private lessons and train-playing sessions paid off, because in ninth grade, Art made the New Jersey All-State Orchestra. The musicians played the fourth movement of *Tchaikovsky's Fourth Symphony* to finale their recital. Art claimed it as, "My first real music experience, and I was hooked." He was also getting jazzed about jazz. His first music idol was Harry James, who played lead trumpet with the Benny Goodman band. Art loved to listen to the full-length recording of their 1938 concert at Carnegie Hall. Music seemed to be taking over, but his heart was still set on basketball—he lived to play day and night.

By the time he got to high school, he was fully entrenched in both pursuits. He had made the junior varsity basketball team and was on his way to becoming a star player. Art admits he struggled with his priorities, and again, his mother did her best to keep him in line, and a little fate didn't hurt either. Sophomore year, with only three weeks' worth of basketball games left, he got injured. His sprained ankle put him out for the rest of the season. On the bright side, he had extra time on his hands that allowed him to try out for the All-State Band, and he made it. That meant he had the opportunity to play under Frederick Fennell, the world-class Eastman Wind Ensemble conductor in Rochester, New York. The group played *Pictures at an Exhibition,* composed by famed Russian pianist Modest Mussorgsky. The composer wrote the score in 1874 as a musical tribute to the artwork of a dear friend who had died suddenly. "That experience was a big deal! Because I was exposed to this big piece of music, and I realized this is what a band can sound like." Art couldn't have known then that his continued exposure to highly talented, influential music mentors would serve him well in the future.

## High Hopes for Hoops

While music had a tendency to take center stage, it was still the court that drove him. As a junior, Art made the varsity basketball team and was leading the team offensively. He was averaging fifteen points per game and making 73 percent of his free throws. He was the team hot shot, and he ate it up. But since his mother would not let him quit music, he decided to go ahead and try out for All-State Band again. With his talent, he made first chair, and then left tryouts early for a basketball game—so he wasn't there for callbacks, and he got cut. Fortunately, his school band director convinced the All-State judges to let him back in, but they put him in his place. "I went from first chair to last chair, because I chose to go to my varsity basketball game—and then we lost the game by only one point anyway."

Art wasn't about to make the same mistakes, so his senior year, he skipped all the extra band stuff and focused solely on basketball. Well, except for the jazz band group he and some high school buddies had formed. They would go out and get paid to play music for a dance, and then they'd sit in the drummer's car and listen to a late-night jazz radio station. Art loved that his friends were so into jazz, too. Art liked it so much that he wanted to get his feet wet in show business, so he got a job at a resort in the Catskills, known at the time as a high-end vacation spot in New York. These acts were full of comedians, jugglers, and singers who needed musical backup. Art would sight-read a piece of music and get the job, only to lose it once they found out he was only seventeen. That broke his heart, so he would turn his attention, once again, to basketball.

Art had had enough ups-and-downs and back-and-forths for one kid. The time had come for him to decide what he wanted to be when he grew up—a pro basketball player or a professional musician, either playing with a jazz group or conducting an orchestra. He could have gone to Eastman or Julliard, but he chose the University of Michigan, where he would study music education—and play basketball! Of course, basketball tryouts weren't until October, so Art thought he'd give it a go with the University of Michigan Marching Band. It was an entirely different experience than his high school band. "Face it, in high school, the marching band was not respected," Art said. "I started to play football my freshman year in high school, and I was good. I was tall, fast, and played wide receiver. And then I told my coach that I also wanted to be in the band—and he laughed at me. He said, 'That's not a choice. That's an excuse so you don't get hit.' But I loved playing my trumpet. And in college, the band was actually respected and esteemed. In college, marching band was a big deal!"

Art chose University of Michigan because he had a generous scholarship from his high school for a music education major, and all along he had "a crazy idea" that he could also play basketball for Michigan. By the time tryouts came around, he hadn't played in a while, and he looked around the room and realized, "I am out of my league here." As much as he loved running the court, he knew in his heart that he'd never cut it.

"Everyone was taller, faster, better shooters. These guys were here on scholarships. I knew I'd never make the team." So, it just made sense to focus on his music. "Decisions were made for me, if you will." And Art was on his way to becoming a band director—even if his college professors didn't believe he could or would do it.

## Well-Meaning Mentors

Art made his family proud and got through his four years of college with very good grades. He graduated magna cum laude, with above a 3.5 grade point average, and membership in the music school honor society, Pi Kappa Lambda. He loved the music theory and history studies, even if he didn't necessarily enjoy the non-music education parts. He could have skipped anthropology and astronomy. If it wasn't music related, he wasn't interested. Even with his music education degree, he felt unprepared to go out and teach, so he decided to stick around and get his master's. In the graduate school, three of the four required classes Art would get to take were taught by William Revelli, known by those in the field as the "Godfather of Collegiate Bands." He was also known for being a very fierce and intense perfectionist dedicated to excellence in every aspect of music performance. As the director of the University of Michigan Marching Band, Revelli initiated innovations in the industry, including synchronizing music and movement, using an announcer to support the performance, and playing a postgame concert for the crowds. He even invented High School Band Days, in which he would direct a massed band consisting of scores of the best students from the local schools. Art thought this sounded like a pretty good gig, so in class, when Revelli asked Art what he wanted to do after graduation, Art answered that he wanted to be a college marching band director. Revelli scoffed. Then, Revelli said, "Forget it. That's not going to happen," and moved on to the next kid. Art looks back on that moment to realize that Revelli didn't take him seriously. "He didn't view me as a serious musician because I still loved basketball and I loved jazz—and he didn't. I played in an underground jazz band that was not affiliated with the university. I still did the dance band, playing every weekend. I was president of my Sigma Alpha Mu fraternity and led its Glee Club. He didn't think I was being serious enough about music, and he was probably right." But Art didn't let Revelli's comments stop him.

## The First Steps

A master's in music education from the University of Michigan goes a long way on a resume. After his graduation in 1963, he easily got his first job at North Adams High School, not far from Ann Arbor, Michigan. With his expecting wife, Barbara, by his side, "Mr. Bartner" took over the music program. In those days, they wouldn't dare call him by his first name! Anything that had to do with music from fifth grade through twelfth grade, Mr. Bartner was in charge of. Daunting as that may have seemed—especially as a brand-new father with a newborn son, Steven, born a month into Art's new job—he was thrilled. Even at a rural school with no football field other than a clearing on a bluff in town, he had sixty kids performing in his first marching band. With only 225 students total at the school, he felt that was a pretty good ratio. Fall weather in Michigan could get more than a little chilly, so given that, plus the lack of any bleachers, parents would watch the team and the band from the warmth of their cars. Instead of applause, they gave honks of the car horns for approval. Parked in the drive-in audience one foggy Friday night were his wife and grandmother-in-law. Barbara's grandmother came in from New Jersey to visit and watch Mr. Bartner and his band perform. It's hard to say how much she could see through the thick mist and the dark, but after the show, grandma came up to her granddaughter's husband and said, "You know what, I think you're the second coming of Leonard Bernstein!" Mr. Bartner more than appreciated the encouragement with the comparison to one of his idols, because maybe he actually earned it. He had taken this Class D school and taught them to play Class B music and even received a first division rating at the state music festival from William D. Revelli, by the way, who happened to be judging that day. (Although "judging" really meant pointing out all the things they did wrong, but still!) Mr. Bartner took two years in North Adams to learn how to play every instrument—and how not to make mistakes. He looked at it as part of his own on-going education and the first rung on the ladder of success. Then, it was time to move on. Besides, they needed a bigger apartment, because he and Barbara had now welcomed their second child—a daughter, Debbie—to the family.

The Bartner family moved one hour north and made their new home in Flint, Michigan so he could teach in the nearby suburb of Davison. This new apartment had a little more space, and it while it wasn't wonderful, it was home. This new Class A school had more students and the opportunity for more bands. During his five years at Davison Senior High School, Mr. Bartner created and grew three new bands at the high school level: Beginning Band for ninth graders who were just starting to learn music; Cadet Band for tenth and eleventh graders who were better but not quite ready to perform; and the Wind Ensemble/Marching Band for the best and most dedicated music students. When he started, the marching band had sixty students, and he doubled that during his tenure. The program was considered one of the best in the state, as it was recognized for marching in parades, earning awards, and winning field show competitions. He had these kids playing AA music! Mr. Bartner was immersing himself in the world of marching bands, attending clinics and band festivals, and even judging with the top leaders and groups in the state. He was starting to make a name for himself, and he was having the time of his life.

Running the high school music program and raising a young family weren't the only responsibilities Art had in the late 1960s. Mr. Bartner was in the process of becoming *Doctor* Bartner—doing all the coursework, prelims, and tests for his doctorate from the University of Michigan. Balancing work, school, and life was challenging, to say the least. Sleep was not high on the list of priorities. "Thank goodness I had a wife who was wonderful with raising these two kids!" Because Mr. Bartner had a crazy schedule. For the first four years at Davison, he had a full-day teaching schedule, going 8 a.m. to 3 p.m., plus band rehearsals. His fifth year, his principal helped him out so Bartner could claim residency at the University of Michigan. That year, he would teach an hour to each of his three bands in the morning from 8 a.m. to 11 a.m., and then two days a week, he'd hop in the car and drive an hour to Ann Arbor for classes at U of M. After class, he'd drive back to Davison in time to rehearse the marching band after school. Tuesdays were instrument sectional practices, and Thursdays were full band dress rehearsals on the field. During all those years, on Mondays and Wednesdays, he'd teach private trumpet lessons, too. Bartner was also part of a jazz dance band that would play at Barton Hills Country Club on Fridays and Saturdays. Then came Sundays: Barbara's day off and Art got to take care of the kids. When the weather was nice, he would take them to a nearby park and let them play while he studied—and tried not to fall asleep. The joke was he wouldn't look up until he heard one crying. He loved his kids, though, and has fond memories of treating them to Der Wienerschnitzel. Hot dogs, a bag of popcorn, and root beer all around made for a typical Sunday treat. "It's amazing those kids survived," he reminisced. But the soon-to-be Dr. Bartner was ambitious—and he'll personally admit, perhaps even a bit arrogant—and he was getting ready to go for the big time. He was preparing to make the leap from high school to college bands. It was time to move up that ladder. While he believed he had what it takes, Art really had no idea what he was getting himself into.

## High Note: Be Decisive

As a boy, Art was passionate about two things: basketball and music. While it is certainly possible to do more than one thing really well, it takes a firm decision in order to excel. Because of his passion for both, Art's focus bounced back and forth like a metronome in his youth, and the results he experienced demonstrated the instability of his choices. He earned trumpet first chair in All-State Band, but he left try-outs early to play a basketball game. His team lost the game, and he lost his chair. When he was doing one thing, he was often thinking about the other. It was when Art decided to combine his passions and become a college marching band director—and stated it out loud to his professor—that his world began to shift. ***Stick to your decision, even when others may not believe it's possible. When you decide, you commit—no more back and forth***. You drive it forward anyway. It's the first step in developing perseverance that leads to success. *Be decisive.*

# 2

# CLIMBING THE LADDER

*Mr. Bartner calling the drills on the field in Michigan, 1969.*
Courtesy: Dr. Arthur C. Bartner

# CHAPTER TWO

## CLIMBING THE LADDER

Most guys he knew didn't like the work that goes into building a marching band, but Mr. Bartner did. He genuinely enjoyed the drills and discipline. He liked the arrangements and the rah-rah, and yes, even the students. Other band director colleagues only put up with the marching band until they could get to the concert season in the second semester. But, as a jock his whole life, Mr. Bartner loved the athleticism of the marching band, and he knew he could excel with it. "I got to looking around the state and I thought, 'Well, what can I do better than anyone else? Better than any other high school band director? If I want to climb the ladder and get to the college level, what can I do?'" He confessed that other trumpet players were better than him. He knew there were other ensemble directors who could conduct as well, if not better, than him. But he looked around and thought, "You know what? I like this marching band stuff. I always played sports. If it wasn't basketball, it was golf or tennis, even that short stint in football. I have this jock-coach-athletic attitude. I can apply that experience to marching band, and I can be really *good* at this." And he set out to prove it.

### The Next Rung

Mr. Bartner had paid his dues in public high schools for seven years. He felt ready to take on a new challenge, so he started searching for opportunities. He billed himself as a multi-faceted professional: a marching band director with a jazz background who could also conduct concert band and teach trumpet. Plus, he had a master's in music education and was well on his way toward his doctorate. He was a package deal. He applied everywhere he could and would have been content to take a job at a junior college as another rung on the ladder closer to the top. Mr. Bartner found out about a directorship opening at West Virginia University, so he applied, as did another slightly older University of Michigan alum, a guy Art knew. Bartner was a freshman when Don Wilcox was a senior, and they had both marched together in the University of Michigan Marching Band. That same spring of 1970, the band director at the University of Southern California resigned, and now Mr. Bartner had two big opportunities to consider—and the one in California had him wide-eyed, but he did not quite have his eyes wide open.

The USC football team had just beat his alma mater in the Rose Bowl—in front of more than a hundred thousand people in the stands and millions more on television! USC had a fancy mascot, the white horse named Traveler. Art couldn't ignore the lure of the warmer weather in the Golden State, and neither could his wife. Barbara and their two kids could spend time at the beach while he rehearsed with the band on the football field in the middle of campus. USC had a huge following, loyal fans, and a real stadium—which meant the marching band would have people in the audience who weren't trying to stay warm in their cars. He liked this idea. A lot. So, he put off West Virginia University, not telling them no, but also not telling them that he was entertaining another possibility on the other side of the country.

Mr. Bartner waited. He had submitted his resume to USC and heard nothing for weeks, a month, six weeks. Turned out, West Virginia University got tired of waiting and gave the job to the other guy. (Don Wilcox wound up being the marching band director at WVU for 34 years!) So, here's Art. He lost WVU. He didn't even have an interview for the 'SC job. He had no other prospects—and he needed an income to support his wife and two little kids. Fortunately, he had not yet resigned his high school band director position, so he could go back to his old job. But he wanted something new and different, and he didn't want to go to another school in the district. So, he waited.

Finally, the leaders of the USC School of Performing Arts invited Mr. Bartner out to Los Angeles at the end of April to attend the band's year-end concert and meet the staff for an interview. The university had a long-established reputation for bringing on faculty with stellar careers, so Art would be meeting with some of the best of the best. The USC Wind Ensemble Director was William A. Schaefer, a legendary conductor, arranger, and educator. He's the guy who called Art for the interview after one of Art's Michigan classmates brought up his name. Bob Wojciak happened to be at USC working on his doctorate and recommended Art for the job. Also on the panel was Professor Robert Marsteller, who was a mover and shaker as a prominent symphonic trombonist who performed with the Navy Band during World War II, before spending twenty-five years with the Los Angeles Philharmonic Orchestra. Marstellar graduated from Eastman School of Music, where Art had played with the All-State Band back in high school. Then, the dean. The dean of the School was Dr. Grant Beglarian. He also came from Michigan, earning his bachelor's, master's, and doctorate in Ann Arbor in the 1950s. Beglarian himself had only arrived at USC a year earlier, so he was still close with the Michigan faculty—which may or may not bode well for Mr. soon-to-be Dr. Bartner.

Time for the interview, and sitting in Beglarian's office, Art had his resume ready. It would seem that all of these Michigan connections would land on the plus side of the pros and cons. But Art was cold-sweat nervous. He had already been given a bad time from Marsteller, who didn't have a nice thing to say about William D. Revelli—a name that appeared all over Art's application. Then with Mr. Bartner facing him across his desk, Beglarian said, "I know Revelli personally. I think I'll give him a call right now." And Art thought, *Oh man, I'm in trouble.* He tried to hide his racing heart. "I played pretty bad third trumpet. I was not a guy who really put band first. I was president of my fraternity and president of the music school honor society Kappa Kappa Psi. I played forty games of intramural basketball. I was doing all these things, and Revelli didn't think I made the commitment to serious music. I took all his courses, but I did not ask him for a recommendation. Because I knew I did all the things he despised—dance, jazz—and I was never one of his guys."

Truth be told, Art completely respected Revelli. He believed his director and mentor was brilliant, calling him a founding father of modern collegiate bands. Art learned a lot from him, and he appreciated Revelli's approach, how he was consistently demanding. Really demanding. Always expecting excellence. Art still remembered the conversation in class when he said he wanted to be a college marching band director, and Revelli said, "Forget it." Of course, at this moment, he could only hear one side of the conversation, and he didn't know Beglarian well enough to read his expression. On the other end of the line, Art could not hear that Revelli said, "Well, Bartner will do a good job for you. But I have half a dozen other guys who could do it better." Beglarian hung up the phone and related this part of the conversation to Mr. Bartner, whose stomach was in a knot.

To Art's surprise and delight, Dean Beglarian reached across the desk to hand Bartner a contract and offer him the job. In one of those moments one never forgets, Bartner heard him say, "You're hired!" Art was to be in Los Angeles to start on August 1 as the new director of the University of Southern California Trojan Marching Band—or USC TMB, for short. His contract was as a Lecturer, not on a tenured track yet, so he'd have to prove himself and hope they liked him, but he wasn't worried about that. Art was jazzed! Barbara was thrilled! The Bartner family would become Southern California residents during the hottest part of the year, but they didn't care, because they were getting out of Michigan—something for which Barbara had been holding out hope for years. Her parents in New Jersey were kind enough to take care of little Steven and Debbie for a while so she and Art could pack up and move west—and literally drive halfway across country.

In what he later admitted was a "typical guy move," Art sold their newer, practical Buick station wagon and drove their used, older—but sporty—Chevy Camaro. He was in the driver seat for most of the miles, but he remembers Barbara took the wheel while he slept for a bit, and he said when he woke up, she was going so fast he was surprised she didn't get a ticket. Plus, they nearly ran out of gas. They decided to stop in Las Vegas, about four hours east of Los Angeles, because Barbara was sick to her stomach. It was too hot, and they were too exhausted to play in the city. They just wanted to get to California!

After several days on the road and in and out of motels, they were ready to settle in somewhere . . . somewhere near the beach! And in Southern California, there were plenty to choose from: Venice Beach, Manhattan Beach, Hermosa Beach—hey, how about Redondo Beach? They found an ad for an apartment about a mile from the ocean, but unfortunately, it was quite old and dingy—nothing that would work for a young family. Trying not to be too disappointed or discouraged, Art and Barbara walked out to continue their search, and just across the street they noticed some brand-new apartments. BRAND-NEW! Not wanting to miss an opportunity, they hustled over to find the manager and get more information about the complex. Like it was meant to be, there was an apartment available within their budget—even three bedrooms, so the kids could have their own spaces. They signed a lease and moved right in!

While Barbara and the kids settled into their new digs, Mr. Bartner got organized in his new office, if one could call it that. In a building called Booth Hall, he had a desk in a very small room, with one chair to share with the opera manager. (Yes, they shared the chair.) And fortunately, Art liked opera! It wasn't much, but it was his, and he was excited. He didn't even mind the forty-five-minute commute through the L.A. freeways. He occupied his mind with memorizing his music and being grateful because this was the something-new-and-different he was looking for.

## Battle of the Bands

As much as Mr. Bartner wanted it to be great, his first year at USC was rough and very eye-opening. Art was a naive high school teacher from a Michigan suburb, so there were a few things he didn't see coming that would prove to make the fall of 1970 one of the most taxing periods of Mr. Bartner's life. First, he took over the band as it was coming out of the 1960s hippie culture. It's hard to teach kids to play music and march when they're undisciplined—and certainly neither he, nor anyone, could control what they did away from campus. Then there was the protester crowd who did not want to be told what to do. At all. Neither did the older kids who were fresh out of the Army and just starting college at age twenty-three, twenty-four, or even twenty-five. They were fresh out of the military structure and sure didn't want to be disciplined by some thirty-year-old hotshot band director. Bartner was beginning to realize that he more than had his work cut out for him.

It wasn't just the students or the long commute that made for a bumpy first year in Southern California. Mr. Bartner was also still working on his requisites to finish his doctorate. He'd managed to get most of the components taken care of before he left Michigan, including his foreign language requirement—barely! He had taken French in high school, but even then, it wasn't his forte, so passing a college exam was no small feat. Art had to choose two books written in French, and the proctor would select a chapter from one of the books, and he'd have to translate the whole thing—by hand! Art chose wisely in picking something that interested him—music history, of course—but consulting the French dictionary to translate every few words was time-consuming, and he only had a couple of hours. As it so happened, the day he was taking his test, there was a massive Midwest thunderstorm—the kind with the brightest lightning and loudest thunder claps he'd ever experienced, causing the lights to flicker off and on. Bartner doesn't remember if he actually finished translating the chapter or not—so whether the proctor had mercy or pity, Art's not sure. All he knows is a week or so later, he got a postcard in the mail saying he'd passed the language requirement. What a relief. That was one more step up the ladder. Another was statistics.

While he was still teaching high school in Davison, Mr.

Bartner was commuting an hour to Ann Arbor for classes. The statistics teacher made his expectations very clear: "You miss a class, you don't pass." His lectures were taught 8 a.m. to 11 a.m. on Saturday mornings. That was fine, until it came time for Michigan Band Days. Not only was Mr. Bartner's ensemble one of the one hundred bands playing for a halftime performance, Davison High School was also one of only four selected to be featured after the game as well. It was a privilege to receive that invitation. Mr. Bartner needed to pass this statistics class, but he also couldn't not do his job. All he could think to do was be honest with the professor. As luck would have it, the instructor said he was a big fan of the Michigan Marching Band, so if Bartner was bringing his band to perform, he'd "love to stay after the game and watch. Oh, and don't worry about missing class." Phew!

Bartner's high school band blew it out of the water! They played "Aquarius" from the Broadway show, *Hair,* while the very intimidating Michigan Marching Band looked on from the sidelines. The Michigan band went wild during Davison's drum feature. Mr. Bartner remembers feeling immense pride that the college band, under the direction of William D. Revelli, loved his high school group's performance. It may not have been direct praise from Revelli himself, but the indirect accolades went a long way for Bartner and his students. So having passed statistics and French, Art was on his way to his doctorate, working on his dissertation in Los Angeles, all the while trying to make something out of this University of Southern California marching band.

Perhaps Bartner's rudest awakening that first year came when he took the Trojan Marching Band to Northern California for his first USC-Stanford football game. Student behavior and attitudes aside, it was the TMB's performance that really opened Art's eyes. He had the USC band play Broadway showtunes, a-la his alma mater, and like his high school band had done to rave reviews. But it was old-fashioned—and the crowd hated it. Stanford, on the other hand, played contemporary rock tunes that appealed to a younger crowd—and they loved it! Art lost the battle of the bands badly, and he realized that the way things were going, he needed to shake things up or he'd be finished before he even got started. But before he could do that, he had to make a trip back to his old stomping grounds.

## Doctoring It Up

Mr. Bartner was *this close* to becoming Dr. Bartner. He'd been working on his two-hundred-page dissertation while trying to get the new band in order. He would send a chapter or two every so often to his U of M dissertation mentor, Eugene Troth, for editing and review. Midway through the process, Troth left Michigan to become a dean at the University of Maryland School of Music—leaving Bartner high and dry. They kept in touch a little bit, though, and when Art found out Troth was coming for a convention in San Diego, California, Art asked if he'd mind getting together and looking over his paper. He agreed, they sat down, and Troth marked up most of the first chapter and said, "Start over." So, with red ink all over the first draft, Art had to rewrite pretty much the whole thing. It was a struggle, but he persevered and got it done. Now, all he had left to do to receive his doctorate was pass his orals.

Mr. Bartner returned to Michigan for the exam. He got to choose the panel of professors who would fire questions at him about his field of expertise. Art had spent more than two years working on his topic, "The Charles Stewart Mott Foundation: Its Contribution to the Musical Environment of Flint, Michigan." He knew his paper and he knew everyone in the room, so he felt confident. Until it came time for the dean's interrogation. The dean, Allen Britton, asked Art a question about the 15th century indigenous music of the Inca Tribe—or maybe it was the Aztec tribe—he can't remember anymore. But Art does remember his mental response: "I'm going like . . . What?! What does an ancient Indian tribe in South America have to do with the Mott Foundation's contribution to the musical environment in Flint, Michigan?" He had to admit he had no idea. Then they took a restroom break.

Mr. Want-to-be-Dr. Bartner was taking care of business, and who walked in but his old Michigan Marching Band Director, William D. Revelli. Art stood there thinking, *This is my worst nightmare.* After typical pleasantries, Revelli said to Art, "You know, you made a big mistake taking that USC job. Your high school band was a lot better." All Bartner could think was that he was probably right. His high school band had one hundred twenty excellent musicians who wanted to be on the field and loved to perform. They were an All-State Band! His college band had about eighty grumpy guys who were there only because they had to be, or they'd forfeit their scholarships. But he certainly didn't need the Godfather of Marching Bands pointing this out to him, in the restroom, right in the middle of his dissertation oral board. "Of all the people to run into in the bathroom."

Art finished in the restroom, completed his exam, and waited. Everyone on the panel was all for passing Art, except for the dean. Dean Britton said he couldn't pass this guy because he's not well-read and hadn't even read a book on the Incas—or was it Aztecs? Luckily for Art, one of the panelists was a friend who used to play piano in his college jazz dance band, and he asserted that they'd be foolish to dismiss Bartner. He said they should advance him because he had already landed a great job at a great music school. So, they passed him, and there were hugs and handshakes all around as Mr. Bartner became Dr. Bartner. His dissertation is on file in the Library of Congress.

Getting his doctorate did not mean that things got any better back in Southern California. "Not to be negative, but it really was a pretty miserable program." It was something the starry-eyed Art had not realized when he took the job. Once he got settled on campus, it became clear that the Trojan Marching Band was not very well-respected or supported, and no one in California—or even the West Coast—was interested in the job because of that lack of vision. But the now-Dr. Bartner believed he could fix it, even if his high school band budget was bigger than the university band budget. After all, he took a Class D high school band and had them playing Class B music within two years, and his Class A high school band was getting first division awards playing AA music—including recognition from the one and only Michigan Marching Band. Surely, Dr. Bartner could turn this band around, too. But, how?

## High Note: Be Supportive

Throughout his career, Dr. Bartner experienced what it was like to have support and to NOT have support from those around him. The professor at his alma mater was blatant about his lack of support, telling Bartner to "forget it" and then claiming—during Bartner's job interview—that there were several others who could do a better job at USC than Bartner would, and then saying to his face—during his oral boards—that he should have stuck to high school bands. The mentor who was assigned to help Bartner with his dissertation told him to "start over." When all Bartner wanted to do was build a great band, some students responded with disdain and unruliness. The lack of support can feel frustrating, discouraging, and disheartening, but it doesn't have to stop you. ***Remember your decision and commitment and turn your focus to the support you do have, and then drive it forward and pay it forward.*** Bartner's French and statistics teachers passed him in the presence of extraordinary circumstances, and a music-loving colleague sung his praises so he could pass his orals and complete his doctorate. Dr. Bartner's wife, Barbara, was behind him one hundred percent. And soon, he would build relationships with trusted mentors who would provide much needed support. Continuing to drive it forward, with or without support, is how you further develop the perseverance required for success. *Be supportive.*

# 3

# BUILDING A BAND

*When Dr. Bartner invited women to be part of the band, many joined as Silks, circa 1975.* Courtesy: Jeannine Zakaryan

# CHAPTER THREE

## BUILDING A BAND

There were all of fifty-five guys—no girls—at the first band camp in early September of 1970. Dr. Bartner had only just arrived himself in August, so there wasn't a lot of prep time, and he was on his own to get them organized. Band members check in on campus about a week before classes kick off to attend the week-long music and marching intensive. The purpose of the training, besides teaching foundational Trojan Pride principles, is to give them time to learn the pregame show and be ready to perform when football season started two weeks into the semester. That first year, about thirty members didn't bother to show up to camp, and the lack of fundamental skills was obvious during the season. It didn't help that Dr. Bartner (still Mr. Bartner at the time) was bringing the Big-10 style to the Pacific conference. As the year progressed, he discovered that what worked in the Midwest with high school kids did not work on the West Coast with college students. So, the second year, the new band director decided to shake things up.

### Attention, Ladies and Gentlemen

The first thing Dr. Bartner did was welcome women to the band. His high school bands were co-ed, so it only made sense to have the female influence in the TMB, as well. USC had added the "Song Girls" a few years before Dr. Bartner arrived. Not to be confused with cheerleaders, the dance squad of talented young women began as a way to encourage attendance at basketball games in 1967, and then they joined the band on the football field in 1968. Those first seven women would no longer be the only ladies on the football field, with Dr. Bartner's invitation for women to join the band. The gals could play an instrument if they wanted, or they could join the color guard and twirl tall flags, which in the drum and bugle corps industry and the TMB are called "Silks." Maybe a dozen women joined that first year, and maybe half of them were Silks. It would take some time for the word to get out. "Adding women to the ranks was a natural progression," Bartner said. "I didn't get too much kickback from the guys. I think it was a positive thing, especially since I had cleaned house of the disgruntled bandsmen."

The second thing Dr. Bartner did in his effort to build a better band was to gain control of the music scholarships. Up until that point, the School of Performing Arts oversaw the financial aid given to musicians, and so many of the band members were only in the group because they "had to be" as a condition of their scholarship. Bartner felt that being "required" to be in the band was not an incentive, so he wanted to weed out the ones who didn't want to be there. The USC Ensemble Director, Bill Schaefer, was who invited Dr. Bartner to apply for the job. They had become friends and the band director got the feeling that Schaefer wanted to see him succeed. So, they had a sit-down discussion about the status of the financial aid situation, and Schaefer agreed to give Bartner management of the money for his own musicians. Now there were two sets of scholarships. The music department had its own for its musicians, and the band director had band grants he could award to deserving students, rather than guys being in the band to get paid. Unfortunately, the addition of women and money didn't fix the band. "I had gotten what I wanted, but the band had only grown a little. It was disappointing because nobody was buying in, and the band wasn't growing." Bartner realized something was missing and it was going to take a lot more effort. He knew he had to address the very culture of the organization, and he needed help strategizing how to do that.

Art had been building the TMB program from the field up, starting with the basics: how to march. He didn't want the Trojans to follow the old-fashioned traditional marching style. He didn't want the same ol' high step of any other university band anywhere in the country. Dr. Bartner developed a new marching tradition, in which band members *"Drive It!"* down the field. The technique is impressive to watch and a challenge to learn. It takes practice to master the moves. Dr. Bartner recruited a handful of the best guys in the group to help him teach the style at band camp. He taught them the step and showed them what to watch for to make sure the step was consistent down the line. Every leg must be level for the best effect, and it's the "SNAP!" of the leg that makes the style. Bartner learned through the years that breaking down each element of a move into individual pieces helped to perfect the march.

"STUTTER CHAIR, BY THE NUMBERS!" Dr. Bartner alerted the band about the next drill. "Ready! ONE!" The left heel pops up off the ground, leaving the left toe touching the turf (or dirt on some practice fields.) "Ready! TWO!" Now the toes drive up sharply and halt in pointed position, with the thigh parallel to the ground and the calf perpendicular. "Ready! THREE!" The foot returns to the grass, but only the toes touch the ground. "Ready! FOUR!" The heel returns to the ground now, too.

"Ready! FIVE!" The right heel pops up. "Ready! SIX!" Now the right leg is up. "Ready! SEVEN!" Right toe down. "Ready! EIGHT!" Right heel down. "OH YAAAAAH!" yelled the band members. That's learning to *Drive It!* One beat at a time.

The trick is when there was a long pause between "TWO!" and "THREE!" That's what Dr. Bartner called "holding the chair" and it can be painful to the gluteus max. Who knew marching band could be so physically demanding? Practicing this move over and over and over again creates muscle memory, so the positioning of the leg becomes second nature. Put it all together into one smooth, sharp motion, and that's marching Trojan style. No slacking, though. If it gets sloppy, with toes dangling all over the place and no snap in the step, first of all—TAKE A LAP!—and prepare to drill it, because Bartner never hesitated to come back to basics. The crisp marching has to happen without thinking about it, because the band members' brains will also be engaged in playing music. Get the feet on autopilot so the lips and fingers can coordinate easily.

Getting these band guys and gals to learn to march and play music at the same time was a trick, but even more challenging was the attitude that required serious adjustment. "Practice was really like a war some days," Bartner lamented. "It was constant. Many of them wouldn't do as they were told. What bothered me was that they just didn't want to work that hard. They didn't want to put forth the effort to learn a new style. That was a problem." What was even more of an issue was that he had limited resources to make improvements. "The band was probably the least respected band in the country. Even the people at this university couldn't stand this band. There was no budget, there were no phone calls for gigs; it was like the eyesore of this campus." Sure, many of the musicians were talented and could hit the notes, but eighty men and a dozen women don't cover the field for a halftime show. Before Bartner got to USC, the previous director did what he felt he had to do. For high-profile games like UCLA or the Rose Bowl, he would hire high school and junior college kids to fill out the field. He'd pay them twenty-five dollars and a free game ticket for their time. No disrespect intended, but that was not something Bartner was willing to do. He didn't believe that filling in the ranks with outside students would help build the Trojan pride he wanted to encourage. He also knew he didn't move his family across country to fail. He knew he had to figure out something to bring this band to life.

## Trojan Pride

There had to be a way to instill pride and spirit and enthusiasm in the ranks. "People ask me about my vision," Bartner recalled. "There was no vision. I was just trying to survive." Then something occurred to Dr. Bartner: Let the kids run it. Give the students opportunities to make decisions. Help them be responsible for one another, lead one another. Listen to their input and implement it. If this band was going to survive, let alone thrive, it needed student involvement and some new Trojan traditions!

One day, Dr. Bartner was at the University Commons dining hall, in line to get some lunch, and suddenly, he felt a hand grip his neck, like a vice, like he was being elevated off the ground. And from behind, he heard a gravelly voice. "Bartner! I'm gonna teach you how to run a band. I'm gonna teach you how to *train* a band. You come out to my practice and you watch me train my defensive linemen." The death-grip on his neck was from none other than Trojan Defensive Line Coach, Marv Goux (pronounced Goo.) Coach Goux was known for his spirited and rather colorful motivational talks in the locker room and on the practice field. That's putting it nicely—the guy liked to yell and scream and cuss. Football players both feared and revered him—simply because he knew what he was talking about. Goux had been a star player himself as a starter in 1952, 1954, and 1955—even elected team captain his senior year. He was on the injured list in 1953, after he intercepted the ball and took a hard hit to the hip and back at the 1952 Notre Dame game. That hit not only put him out for the next season, but it also ended his dreams of being a professional player. But for the love of the game, he became a coach instead, landing a spot at USC only one season after graduating with a degree in physical education. Goux had been there with Head Coach John McKay when USC won the Rose Bowl in 1970, the year that first attracted Bartner's attention to the University of Southern California. "Following Goux's orders, I went out to watch the team practice, and I observed him. He taught me how to be a Trojan, what it meant to put on the cardinal and gold. He had an aura about him. He was the epitome of being a Trojan, and I adopted that philosophy." Now, there were two Trojan leaders looking for a way to ignite the Trojan spirit in a band where there wasn't really a spark—until something spontaneous occurred after practice one Friday afternoon.

It happened by accident. The band and the football team each have their own practice fields just across McClintock Avenue from each other in the middle of campus. The team drills on Howard Field and the band on Cromwell Field. The football players had finished for the day, and Goux accompanied them to where the band was practicing. They had to pass by there anyway on the walk to the basement locker rooms. That's where they held rallies since Bartner started in 1970. In those days, about 150 players, musicians, and coaches crammed into tight spaces and low ceilings so that Coach Goux could shout some motivation and the band could play the fight songs in a show of unity before the next day's home game. It was LOUD in that basement, and Goux got so fired up that sometimes he'd knock out a light on the low ceiling or yank a locker door off in his unbridled enthusiasm. On this particular Friday, though, they'd moved things outdoors, and the end zone of the band practice field was awash with cardinal and gold football jerseys as the band and Song Girls wrapped up rehearsal. The musicians marched across the field to play some new tunes for the team. Dr. Bartner had the band learning to play "fun songs" that could be heard on the radio and easily recognized, like "All Right Now" by Free. The band was belting it out, and out of nowhere, Coach Goux started dancing. He and a Song Girl were in the middle of the crowd, dancing away, and then some football players joined in, as did some other Song Girls and even some band members. It was a Trojan dance party—and Dr. Bartner knew something revolutionary was happening. This was big. This was building a bond. And then, several Fridays later that fall, in a similar post-practice scenario, Goux suggested that a football player head over to the ladder—the ladder that is reserved for the band director. Star player Lynn Swann climbed to the top and stood ready. The band turned to face him, and the wide receiver conducted the band playing "The Lone Ranger," a new tune at the time. The band and the team—and Dr. Bartner—all loved it!

These two separate events contributed to one big revelation.

The band and the team had officially bonded and formed a new version of the "Jock Rally." Dr. Bartner saw in that season that the band now had renewed purpose. This was the beginning of something special—a unique, symbiotic relationship that does not exist at any other college campus. The team had become part of the band and the band had become part of the team. "Coach Goux gave the band an identity. Before that, they didn't want a great band. Now that we locked the band and the team together, that synergy made a difference. He gave the band a reason to go to the games and play all the tunes. And Coach Goux helped to create 'Art Bartner, the Band Director.' He taught us all how to be Trojans."

Goux and Bartner talked about some guidelines: Everyone on the team has a responsibility. Define those responsibilities. Hold them accountable. Drill the fundamentals at every practice. Praise the good. Correct the mistakes. Give them motivational speeches. Connect on their level. Be the Coach! Be intense. Yell and scream if you have to. And, let them have fun. Dr. Bartner took that advice to heart and is forever grateful to Goux for his mentorship.

## Developing Leaders

Dr. Bartner knew that whatever Goux knew was true because the USC football team was tight. Those guys all had each other's backs, literally, on the field and off the field, win or lose. "It has to do with the heart," Bartner reflected on Goux's dedication to Trojan Spirit. "We gotta bleed cardinal and gold. Be loyal and trustworthy." They took care of each other, no matter what. It was a family, a Trojan family—and that's what Dr. Bartner wanted for the band. His burning desire was for a bigger, better band. To accomplish that, he'd have to develop a structure to support the growth he wanted. Dr. Bartner organized student leadership levels, each with increasing responsibility. It was a system he had learned from Bill Moffit at Michigan State University when he was still teaching high school band. Freshmen first-year students were rookies, still figuring out campus life and adjusting to being on their own, so their primary responsibility was to simply to learn the ropes, the rules, and respect the upperclassmen—and Dr. Bartner, of course. Sophomores were in between as old members, no longer lowly freshmen, but still not experienced enough to take on a leadership role. Juniors and seniors, however, had the opportunity to become squad leaders. Each squad had four members, so the leader would assist the other three members in learning their music and their place on the field for halftime shows, as well as watch their backs off the field. Senior musicians obviously had the most experience and more developed skills, so they could be voted section leader. Yes, that meant just like the football team voted for their captain, section members held a secret ballot to select who they wanted to be their leader. If a particular instrument group ever managed to have more than twenty members, it may get two seniors to co-lead the section. Having this structure created a chain of command and took some pressure off Dr. Bartner. Band members reported to squad leaders who reported to section leaders who then reported to him. That way it wasn't a dictatorship. Dr. Bartner hoped that developing students in this manner would give them ownership and pride in their band, the same way the football team supported its own.

The first few years of implementing this hierarchy were complicated, though, because this kind of Trojan Spirit was still new, even to the leaders. It took a while to weed out the ones who didn't really want to be there. "You gotta want it," Dr. Bartner said. "It's a commitment. We spend about twenty hours a week together, learning music, practicing the halftime and pregame shows and then all day performing for the game. It's a lot of work. And if you don't want to be here, it's obvious, and those kids can make it miserable for the ones who do want to be here." And there were a lot of reasons to want to be part of the band, such as getting to meet famous musicians like Henry Mancini.

"Once in a while, you get a lucky break," said Dr. Bartner about an invitation to meet with composer, arranger, piccolo and piano player, Henry Mancini. The meeting was arranged in a simple phone call from Mancini's personal assistant to the band office out of the blue—and the timing couldn't have been better. Dr. Bartner had given his one teaching assistant (a.k.a. "T.A.") an opportunity to create a halftime show for the upcoming Notre Dame game. The show was around the corner, and the T.A. only had one chart done—ONE! When Dr. Bartner found out the show was nowhere near ready, he started to panic, and then he got the message to meet in Mancini's office. Sitting in the cigar-smoke-filled room, Art and Henry talked about collaborating for an upcoming television show. The composer had a huge reputation in Hollywood, having written the theme for *Peter Gunn* and *Pink Panther*, to name a few. "Here's this genius guy you look up to, and I'm sitting in his office, the first celebrity that I've ever met. And he reached out to me because he wanted our music to be part of his show. I JUMPED at that opportunity!" Together, they decided that Mancini would record the Trojan Marching Band during halftime and put that performance on an episode of *Monsanto Presents Mancini*. The composer's crew endured the pouring rain at the USC-Notre Dame football game in November

1970 to film Mancini conducting the band as it played "Peter Gunn" at halftime, along with some of Mancini's other hits, including "Baby Elephant Walk" and "The March of the Cue Balls." "It turned out great," Dr. Bartner remembered. "Except for the weather. It rained from beginning to end. And since the field was sand based, it was like a lake out there. But it was still a great halftime show. Mancini conducted his heart out. I was amazed by the way he handled the rain—it didn't affect his performance at all. He smiled as he conducted, even during the downpour." The episode aired in spring of 1971—and that was the beginning of the vision of the TMB as Hollywood's Band!

While the opportunity to have Henry Mancini conduct them on the football field may have been lost on most band members, a handful of guys "got it" and began to see the potential for the TMB. Guys like Ken Dye. He had a fun thought, masterminded with the rest of the core group of leaders: let's have the whole band travel to South Bend, Indiana for the next Notre Dame game. Now there's an idea. Dr. Bartner considered the logistics of getting ninety-six students, many of them undisciplined, on a plane to fly halfway across the country, with their instruments, including drums and tubas. Plus, he'd have to figure out where to stay, how to get around from Chicago to South Bend, where to rehearse. Great idea. But it would be fun. And it would get the kids involved and give them something to look forward to. So, he agreed to let Ken Dye take on the role of band manager and help organize the trip. Dr. Bartner connected him with the university's travel agent, Bob Manners, to make the arrangements. Ken was in the band the year B.B.—Before Bartner. As a physics major, he played trombone in the band just for something to do. He recalled that he saw what the band was like before Bartner arrived, and it wasn't great, but he was eager to help make it better. He even changed his major to Music Education. Dr. Bartner was delighted that Dye had the value system that he was looking for to help change the culture of the band. Dye bought in, and if he thought going to Notre Dame would get more kids to buy in, then Dr. Bartner was all for it. Now all they had to do was figure out how to pay for it.

## High Note: Be Disciplined

Dr. Bartner felt pulled in several directions trying to build this band. Making progress in a chaotic atmosphere is not just challenging, it can be outright difficult. Creating stability from a frenetic environment requires bringing new order to what's out of order, and that means breaking the complex down to the basics. The structure of an organization is only as strong as its foundation. Inviting the band to be co-ed, reorganizing the scholarship system, and training the *Drive It!* marching style count by count was a good start for Dr. Bartner, as was the discipline training and encouragement from Coach Goux. ***Driving it toward further sustainable growth means instilling foundational principles—and the discipline to follow them—into every level of the organization.*** Develop a leadership model in which each member has personal involvement, as well as responsibility and accountability for themselves and to each other. When expectations were not met, Dr. Bartner delivered consequences, like taking a lap—discipline with a purpose that was actually fun! When everyone is driving it toward the same goal with purpose, passion, and perseverance, growth happens naturally. *Be disciplined.*

# 4

# FINDING FUNDING

*Dr. Bartner shares his appreciation with lifelong TMB supporter Ken Cotler at an annual "Up the Irish" fundraiser, 1986.*
Courtesy: Barbara Bartner

# CHAPTER FOUR

## FINDING FUNDING

A one-man-band—that's what it felt like to Dr. Bartner those first couple years. He had a few fairly dedicated student helpers and one teaching assistant in the band office, but they could only do so much, and Art still held the ultimate responsibility for coordinating and organizing everything—and paying for everything. The budget from the university did not go very far. A total of $15,000 per year was designated for entertainment at football games: $5,000 for the new Song Girls; $5,000 for the white horse mascot, Traveler; and $5,000 for the Trojan Marching Band. The Band Grant scholarships were managed separately, thank goodness. But, as Bartner wanted the band to grow, so his budget must grow, too—especially if he was going to take the full band to the Notre Dame game. He'd have to put that idea on pause for a bit while he developed a new skill that was obviously a necessity in the college band industry: fundraising. He'd have to learn quick because there were a lot of big expenses on the horizon.

### Outfitting the Band

The Trojan Marching Band was in desperate need of new uniforms. That was one of the first things Bartner wanted to transition. Besides being clunky and uncomfortable, the gold-ish plastic "shield" that the bandsmen donned restricted their ability to perform. The shields literally constricted the musicians' breathing, so they simply couldn't take a deep enough breath to play their instruments as well as the could without the shield. Plus, they were old and worn, and the capes and pants lacked any charisma they may have had when they were new twenty-some-odd years ago. The hard-plastic, painted-plume helmets had seen better days as well. Oh, and the rain that poured on them during the Mancini halftime show basically trashed the uniforms anyway, which may or may not have been on purpose (although, who can predict the weather!). The outfits would definitely have to be replaced before the next season, so Dr. Bartner initiated "The Trojan Helmet Club." Anyone who joined the club with a contribution of five hundred dollars or more would receive a piece of history: an inscribed Trojan helmet and a copy of the latest recording of the USC fight songs. Their gift would support the band in acquiring new performance wear and headgear. To prove the value of the donation, the composer of the USC Fight Song was the first to join and contribute to The Trojan Helmet Club. The School of Dentistry student, Dr. Milo Sweet, wrote "Fight On!" for a student spirit contest in 1922, and it has been the official inspirational tune for the Trojans ever since. Dr. Bartner was very grateful for the dozens of contributions that followed Dr. Sweet's, because the band's bank account started to grow, but it still had a long way to go.

The old uniforms had to suffice when the Trojan Marching Band got invited to perform at Disneyland, as part of the Lincoln and Washington birthday ceremony in Town Square called "I Am an American." It was the first time that Dr. Bartner's band was asked to march down Main Street, but it certainly would not be the last. In fact, Dr. Bartner was just learning that Disneyland and the University of Southern California had a very long history together, and he was about to experience the benefits of it. After serving in World War II, a young man named Tommy Walker wore two helmets at USC—one for the band and one for the football team—although neither resembled the type of headgear associated with USC in the 1970s. Walker was both the drum major and a placekicker, and he'd peel off his band outfit and faux fur busby so he could run down to the field and kick extra points. He was a Trojan to the core, and thus became affectionately known as "Tommy Trojan." When he graduated in 1948, he held tight to his Trojan Spirit and became the new USC band director, a post he held until an incredible opportunity came up in 1955. That's when Tommy Walker became the very first Entertainment Director for the brand-new Disneyland. After nearly a dozen successful years bringing creative innovations to the theme park, he departed the Magic Kingdom to create his own production company. His resignation made room for another 'SC alum to take the helm of Disney Entertainment: Robert (Bob) Jani (pronounced yaw-nee). Little did Dr. Bartner know what influence Jani would have in his life in a couple more years.

Bob Jani was not entirely new to Disney. In fact, like Walker, he was there for the beginning of it in 1955. He was twenty-one, fresh out of college, when he became the head of Guest Relations at Disneyland, a position he kept for two years. He spent some time as Entertainment Director with the U.S. Army before returning to USC to be the Director of Special Events—fitting since his bachelor's degree was in Stage Productions and Design. One of the only things Dr. Bartner knew about USC when he interviewed was that the Trojans had a real white horse on the football field. Now he knew where that mascot came from: Bob Jani approved the idea! A group of USC students led by Ed Tannenbaum had watched the striking stallion and rider during the 1961 Rose Parade and thought they would be a perfect addition to the pageantry of the Trojan Spirit. They took the idea to Jani, who agreed, and indeed, Traveler has been on the field for USC home games at the Coliseum ever since. Jani had an instinct for showmanship and performance, and he was about to help Dr. Bartner take the Trojan Marching Band's image to another level.

Now familiar with the connection between Disney and USC, Dr. Bartner took a risk. He had nothing to lose, so he got on the phone and called Bob Jani's office at Disney to ask him, "Would Disney design a new uniform for the Trojan Marching Band?" Sometimes it's who you know, and Jani's office connected Bartner with Disney's head costume designer, Jack Muhs. Muhs was known for his recent work with costumes on the hit show, *Wild, Wild West*. Within a matter of months, Muhs had developed a new look for the Trojan Marching Band, complete with gold "moon boots." Gone were the plastic gold shields. The cardinal cape was a bit longer, and a bold, gold, Greek key design outlined the border of the tunic and the length of the arms. Dr. Bartner believed this was a uniform the TMB members would be proud to wear—even if they still had to wear the twenty-year-old helmets. Bartner wanted to order the outfits, but it was simply not in the budget. The Trojan Helmet Club hadn't grown enough yet to cover the cost. He was a proud man, so he didn't want to ask for help, but Dr. Bartner knew must, because he still had a lot to learn about the fine art and finesse of fundraising. He would have to ask the dean—the man who hired Bartner after that fateful conversation with William D. Revelli. As more luck would have it, Dean Grant Beglarian agreed with the need and made it work. He went out and found a donor for these uniforms. Dr. Bartner still doesn't know how he did it or who it came from, and he doesn't even remember the cost. All he knows is those new uniforms were the beginning of a mutually rewarding relationship between USC's Dr. Bartner and the wonderful world of Disney.

## Branding the Band

Dr. Bartner was hoping that along with this new look for the band would come a new attitude in the band. He was weary of the daily battles. He spent many hours with his core group of guys, listening to them, getting their suggestions on how to make this ensemble better. "It was important for me to get student input. That's an important part of my philosophy as a band director." Maybe with student input, along with Marv Goux's motivation and Bob Jani's innovation, the Trojan Marching Band could become something fabulous. But he still had the little problem of having very little funding. It was time to brand this band with something money can't buy: Trojan Spirit. He set out to lay out what it means to be a "Trojan." The moniker came from a time when the university was struggling to stand out, academically or athletically, in the early 1900s. Then-president Dr. George Bovard asked a *Los Angeles Times* sports reporter to select a nickname that was befitting the college. That reporter, Owen Bird, said he had repeatedly noted the fighting spirit of USC athletes, always giving all they had and never wearying to do so, and he could think of nothing more symbolic than a Trojan.[1] The name has stuck since 1912. The statue at the center of campus, known as "Tommy Trojan," (unrelated to Tommy Walker, by the way) was dedicated on the university's semicentennial in 1930. It has an inscription of five words on the granite pedestal: Faithful. Scholarly. Skillful. Courageous. Ambitious. While, yes, those words ring true, Dr. Bartner felt there was even more to it than that. He believed there to be a persona, a mystique, a dramatic flair that epitomizes the Trojan Spirit. And THAT is what he wanted to draw out of his musicians and give this band a reputation unlike any other in the nation. Maybe then the funds would follow.

It starts with music. The fight songs. "Fight On!" is one of the most meaningful, compelling tunes on any college campus. Legend has it that Milo Sweet's composition was blared from the deck of a transport ship carrying American soldiers to a beach in the Aleutians Campaign of World War II. It is said the troops let out a roar and captured the island. That bit of history lends credence to why "Fight On!" is such a powerful mantra. Trojans instantly know each other when they say "Fight On!" and hold up two fingers, index and middle, facing out, in the form of a "V" for Victory. Trojans memorize and internalize the words about fighting on to victory.

Dr. Bartner wanted to instill in this band that Fight On! mentality. "It's about effort, never quitting, giving it your all until the whistle blows. It's an attitude," he said. "We're aggressive, physical, always yelling, always playing, always involved in every play on the field. We are part of the team. This is who we are. And it all goes back to the fight song. Fight ON!" That's why he has his band play the first chorus of "Fight On!" for every first down during a football game and all three choruses for every touchdown—contributing to the incessant drive, emotional stamina, and physical strength required to win.

The Trojan attitude is something that Dr. Bartner personally had to embody as he ran the whole show, because it was nearly overwhelming at times. He was arranging the music, writing the drills, paying the bills, managing and mentoring students, and still trying to spend quality time with his young family. So, he thought about what component he could delegate (that wouldn't cost him an arm and a leg, because: budget!), and it was the music arranging he could use the most help with. He really enjoyed putting notes down on paper for each instrument to bring all the different sounds together to make a song come to life, but it was time-consuming. "I realized there were other talented guys out there who could get the job done a lot faster and better than I could," Bartner said. "It was just too much. There weren't enough hours in the day to do everything at a high level." And high level was important to him. He had used some pieces that a man named Marvin Branson at Long Beach State had arranged, but he wanted someone more permanent. He had heard about a guy named Tony Fox at Santa Monica City College, so he went looking for him.

Tony Fox agreed to do some charts exclusively for the USC band on a trial basis at a very affordable rate—a key component in Dr. Bartner's book. As part of Art's effort to bring more contemporary, popular tunes to the band, the first chart Fox arranged was "Make Me Smile" by Chicago, and it did make people smile, as did several other pop culture tunes he arranged, based on student suggestions for songs they wanted to play. Dr. Bartner was all for playing tunes that the band members wanted to perform! Perhaps the greatest contribution Fox made to the band early on was an arrangement that would become the preamble to another Trojan fight song. The driving, pulsing rhythm of "Tribute to Troy" was composed Dr. Bartner's predecessor, Ronald Broadwell. Fox's ten-bar opening to that tune became known as "Fanfare." "It's slow and dignified—and reeks of Ben Hur. It captures the mood and atmosphere for the beginning of a show." Dr. Bartner used those powerful notes as a means to establish the proud presence of the band at the beginning of a field show he created to be performed before home football games. This pregame concept was the outcome of one of the brainstorming sessions Dr. Bartner had with his core group of students. They also came up with a new nickname for the band: "The Spirit of Troy." It was Dr. Bartner's intention that every opponent the USC Trojan football team would face from then on would come to dread the sound of "Tribute to Troy." The musicians decided they would play it over and over and over again during football games, every time the Trojans made a play on defense. The sound is something the USC team and fans would come to love, and other teams would come to hate. This kind of branding has no price tag and is more valuable than having a big budget.

## Making Connections

Even with Dr. Bartner and the band's commitment to play the fight songs, the USC football team was in a bit of a slump for a couple of years, going 6-4-1 the first two seasons of Art's Trojan career. He felt the conference-losing, poor record was probably a blessing in disguise, because although it had new uniforms, the Spirit of Troy still was not the band Dr. Bartner wanted it to be. He did not yet believe it was fit to perform on a national scale. But in 1972, there was an about-face, both for the Trojan football team and the Trojan Marching Band. This shift would take the band one step closer to the fame that was its destiny and would also help in the fundraising department. It allowed for opportunities for USC alumni to pick up the phone, call the band office, and offer: "Hey, Dr. Bartner. I want to help you raise money for the band." That's exactly what a gentleman named Ken Cotler did in the fall of 1973. He was an avid Trojan fan and he saw potential not only in the band, but also in Dr. Bartner. "He told me that someday, I would be the face of the Trojan Marching Band," Bartner remembered. "I was 32, maybe 33 years old then, and my band was still pretty bad and hadn't gotten any major recognition yet, so I had a hard time believing him." Ken said he wanted to help the whole ensemble get to the Midwest for the Notre Dame game in 1973, since uniforms and helmets had taken financial priority in 1971. (The rivalry game alternates home fields every other year.) Ken knew the perfect time and place to host a rally. #1 ranked USC was scheduled to play #8 University of Oklahoma on September 29. It was a huge matchup because Oklahoma had finished #2 behind USC in the Trojan's National Championship season of 1972. (More details about that season coming momentarily.) So, Cotler offered to host a fundraising rally Friday night before the game. Cotler owned a clothing store and was the president of the retail association for Arco Plaza in downtown Los Angeles, so it would be a great location to hold a ton of people. Arco Plaza had opened the year before as the tallest twin towers in the world. (New York's World Trade Center towers were completed three years later.) So, Dr. Bartner and the Trojan Marching Band performed in the shadow of the skyscrapers, simultaneously shining a spotlight on the need for funds to get the full band to Chicago. Some two thousand people showed up the night before the Oklahoma game for what was the first football rally in downtown Los Angeles in more than four decades. Turns out, fundraising can be fun! Cotler also held a private party at his home—affectionately called "Up the Irish"—in which he invited fellow Trojan fans to come for appetizers and drinks and encouraged them to make contributions to the cause. The band attended to perform a few popular tunes and the fight songs, and thus began a lifelong mentoring relationship between Cotler and Dr. Bartner and the Spirit of Troy.

This kind of fundraising was made possible after the USC Trojan football team won the National Championship in 1972. Dr. Bartner felt like the band and the team were in sync, feeding off each other's intense energy. This was more like it! The Spirit of Troy looked sharp on the field with—finally!—brand-new helmets to complement its new uniforms and it was sounding just as sharp—well, they were in tune—as they performed in the sold-out football stadium. With the Los Angeles Memorial Coliseum holding some ninety thousand people, it was a very visible venue for other artists who loved performing. While Henry Mancini may have been the first Hollywood celebrity to take the field with the band when he taped the halftime show at the 1970 Notre Dame game, he definitely would not be the last. Dr. Bartner wanted another big shot for the 1972 Notre Dame game, so he reached out to a world-renowned drummer. Famous jazz musician, Louie Bellson, agreed to guest star during halftime as part of Dr. Bartner's "Salute to Big Band Drummers." The drummer had his *Conversations: A Drum Spectacular* album recently released with Buddy Rich and Kenny Clare. Besides playing with the Duke Ellington band for several years, Bellson was also the musical director for his wife's television program, ABC's *The Pearl Bailey Show.* Bellson is credited with pioneering the double-bass-drum setup when he was only fifteen years old, and that's what he showed off when he played "Carnaby Street" with the Spirit of Troy. Bartner, Bellson, and the band rocked the halftime show, and the Trojan football team dominated the game. The Trojans had gone undefeated all season with Coach John McKay at the helm, outscoring their opponents 425 to 117 throughout the season. That included beating the Irish 45-23 at the Coliseum. That meant #1-ranked USC would be going to the Rose Bowl on New Year's Day 1973. That meant that Bartner and the band would be back on campus right after Christmas to prepare for the five-and-a-half-mile parade and to learn a brand-new field show. That also meant a lot of work to do in a short amount of time, and Dr. Bartner couldn't believe who was calling him to collaborate on the nationally televised Rose Bowl halftime show.

## High Note: Be Collaborative

With the first flicker of fame igniting from his Mancini halftime show and his first Rose Bowl on the horizon, Dr. Bartner knew there was huge potential for these students, these musicians, this program—but a one-man band can only do so much. As the vision grows, so must the commitment, the support, the discipline, and the organization of resources. Hiring Tony Fox as a music arranger for the band, requesting Bob Jani's Disney costume designer to create new uniforms and then enlisting Grant Beglarian's help to pay for them, and learning how to raise funds with Ken Cotler were vital to solidifying the foundation of the band. ***Collaboration with others who offer experience and expertise beyond your own is key to driving it toward sustainable growth and success.*** Be willing to ask for help, be willing to receive it, and be willing to give it. It takes a team persevering together and trusting one another to drive it toward the common goal successfully. *Be collaborative.*

# 5

# SCORING BIG TIME

*The band members' view from on board a bus as police escort the Trojan Marching Band through fan traffic to perform at the Rose Bowl in Pasadena, California.* Courtesy: Tim Seno

# CHAPTER FIVE

## CLIMBING THE LADDER

Dr. Bartner had a month to get his act together—that is, thirty days to coordinate everything his band would need to perform the biggest show of his budding career. After beating the Irish on December 2, the USC Trojans secured their spot in the nation's most celebrated postseason game: The Rose Bowl, traditionally held on January 1 at the Rose Bowl stadium in Pasadena, California. The classic game wasn't new to the 'SC football team, but it would be Dr. Bartner's first appearance there as band director. He felt the Spirit of Troy could actually be ready, since they had new uniforms, new helmets, and a new sense of purpose as they were supporting a winning team. Bartner had started toying with an outline for a new field show, because with every "W" the Trojans recorded, it looked more and more like they would be going to a bowl game of some sort. "I'm sure that your music helped to put the Trojans in the Rose Bowl, believe it or not," said "Fight On" composer, Dr. Milo Sweet in a written note to Dr. Bartner. [1]Art had to agree that the synergy between the band and the team caused an incredible energy at all the matchups. Even the band members had a sixth sense at the beginning of band camp that something grand was going to happen that year. The Rose Bowl was both the culmination of a tremendous season and the commencement of a new era for the Trojan Marching Band. The proof came when Dr. Bartner got another phone call that would officially launch Hollywood's Band into the national spotlight.

## Celebrity Status

USC first-semester classes ended mid-December, so the band members went home for the holidays with the mandate that they return the day after Christmas. They would have less than a week to learn a parade lineup and new music and field maneuvers for a fresh halftime show. That meant Dr. Bartner basically worked through the holidays to create the new performance charts. Fortunately, he had some help from a man named Henry "Hank" Ehrlich who called Art after the bowl game positions were announced. Mr. Ehrlich was familiar with the Trojan Marching Band field shows featuring Henry Mancini and Louie Bellson, and he had an idea for another idyllic lyrical performance. Ehrlich was the public relations director for Paramount Studios, which had just released a movie called *Lady Sings the Blues.* The motion picture tells the life story of Billie Holiday, a beautiful young jazz singer popular in the 1940s whose life ended too early after battling bad relationships, alcohol, and drug abuse. The star of the movie was none other than Diana Ross. No longer with the Supremes, Diana Ross was out to make a move from music icon to movie star, and this film was her break-out role. Even though some critics were captious of her performance on the big screen, she was in the running for an Academy Award nomination for Best Actress. Ehrlich had been showing off Ross and the movie on magazines and red carpets everywhere, and what better opportunity could there be than a hundred thousand people at a live venue, plus another couple million on live television. So, Ehrlich wanted to collaborate with Dr. Bartner on a performance.

The gentlemen agreed to meet at Scandia on Sunset Boulevard—the hottest of classy hotspots for Hollywood stars in the sixties and early seventies. Famous actors, actresses, producers, and directors could be seen hopping out of dark-windowed limousines as they made their way to a reserved table at the Scandinavian restaurant so they could cut a deal for their next film, or just relax out of the limelight. Frank Sinatra had his own office upstairs, complete with a personal shower. James Garner was a Sunday brunch regular while filming *The Rockford Files*. Natalie Wood, Warren Beatty, Liza Minelli, and others were frequent guests at Scandia. So, here was Dr. Arthur C. Bartner, a thirty-two-year-old marching band director who grew up in New Jersey, having lunch with a big-time Hollywood movie house public relations director, talking about a college football game. "Ehrlich is a key guy in my life. He and I became very good friends. He was a guy who made things happen, and I wanted to make things happen, so we got along great. We had the same goals. Hank became the conduit between me and all sorts of show business opportunities that would benefit his movies, the Trojan Marching Band, and all these students with once-in-a-lifetime opportunities over the years." Having Diana Ross sing a song accompanied by the Trojan Marching Band at the Rose Bowl halftime show was just the beginning.

Before the performance, though, came rehearsal. The band didn't have a lot of time to learn the music, but they were prepared when the starlet came to campus on the Saturday morning before New Year's Day. Dr. Bartner said she was literally blown away, as she startled back and gasped the first time she heard the band play the arrangement of the song selected from her movie. He remembers her saying, "I never heard anything so loud," and she was amazed at how booming this performance was going to be, and she liked it, as did her music director, and so the show would go on! During one of the breaks in rehearsal, Dr. Bartner wanted to get a photograph for posterity, especially since his children came to campus with him that day. He realized Steven and Debbie really had no idea who Diana Ross was, but they would someday and would then appreciate the picture. Ms. Ross left campus, the band finished practice, and Dr. Bartner only had another day to wait before the Spirit of Troy would be part of a historic day broadcast on national television.

## Coming Up Roses

All work and no play makes for a grumpy bunch of kids, especially since they were technically on vacation from school, so Dr. Bartner made sure to include some fun excursions for the band during Rose Bowl week. In fact, one perk of being invited to the Rose Bowl is that the football teams and the marching bands also get invited to Disneyland! The football players and coaches get to take a break from practice for a day to do photo-ops outside Sleeping Beauty Castle and then Disney VIP hosts take the team around the park. A few days later, the band gets to perform a parade down Main Street and a mini concert in Town Square. "To this day, there is no greater thrill for me than to march down Main Street," said Dr. Bartner. "There's something about getting all these guests excited about music and entertainment. I just love that kind of thing. And the kids never get tired of it either, especially since they get the run of the park after their performance." While the band kids cruised "It's a Small World" and conquered the "Matterhorn," Dr. Bartner was simply focused on walking the route and rocking the house on New Year's Day.

Step-off for the Tournament of Roses Parade is 8 a.m. Pacific

Standard Time. That's when the pace car starts rolling down Colorado Boulevard for the five-and-a-half-mile route. All the bands, floats, and equestrian teams have to be lined up a couple hours before that, so doing the math, that's a really early call-time for the band members—especially after New Year's Eve celebrations! Dr. Bartner did everything he could to make sure all one hundred and thirty-five kids had their uniforms, helmets, moon boots, instruments and/or Silks ready to go to board a bus to Pasadena. He would feed them breakfast at 4:30 a.m., which was important not only for their nutrition and energy, but it was also a secret way to find out who had overslept! It's about a thirty-minute bus ride from campus through downtown Los Angeles, over the hill by Dodger Stadium, through the tunnels, then down and around the curvy 110 freeway to arrive at their staging area off of Orange Grove Boulevard. Once they found their spots, it was a lot of hurry-up-and-wait until the parade got moving down the road. "All I remember is, it's COLD!" said Dr. Bartner. "It's always cold because the sun is not up yet. But waiting for our turn is a good way to get warmed up and check the alignment." Each entry would fall in line at its appointed time and move about 2.5 miles per hour. It would take a little over two hours to go the distance. The Spirit of Troy, the University of Southern California Trojan Marching Band, under the direction of Dr. Arthur C. Bartner, had helmets on, ready to march his first Rose Parade. "I get excited every time, because it's SHOWTIME!"

Dr. Bartner could have the band rehearse marching while playing the fight song a hundred times, but there's no way to sufficiently practice "The Turn." Anyone who has ever watched the Rose Parade on television has seen the forty-five-degree right hand corner from Orange Grove Boulevard onto Colorado Boulevard. It is something to navigate a giant multi-story, extra-long float gracefully around the bend. It's another thing entirely to get the ranks of a marching band to stay perfectly aligned the whole time, especially while driving it and playing "Fight On!" nonstop. Once they straightened, the TMB players were in front of the grandstands and the television cameras, playing and marching full-out, with a proud Dr. Bartner walking alongside. Fifteen Silks with cardinal and gold flags led the way, followed by about a dozen rows of ten musicians. A few entries ahead of the band was a red-rose, garland-covered white convertible carrying the First Lady of the United States, Pat Nixon, who served as the Guest of Honor for the 84th Annual Tournament of Roses. Ms. Nixon was an 'SC alum and during an interview for the television broadcast, she shared her delight to be in the parade supporting USC before getting to watch the Trojans play in the game. The Grand Marshall of the 1973 parade was another 'SC alum—"The Duke," otherwise known as John Wayne, but his name was Marion Morrison when he was an offensive tackle on Howard Jones' Trojan team in the mid-1920s. His football career ended early after breaking his collarbone, not on the football field, but in the ocean from a surfing accident. A few band members remember seeing the famous Hollywood star in his car before the parade began.

Tens of thousands of fans lined the parade route, many of them literally having slept on the curb, enduring overnight temperatures in the low fifties to keep their front row spot and get the best view of the floats, bands, and horses. Dr. Bartner was proud of the TMB's performance, even with the chilly Santa Ana windy weather, 60°F and 20 mph for most of the route, with gusts of 30 to 50 mph. "The best thing is when a float stalls and the parade stops moving, because then we can break into an impromptu concert," said Dr. Bartner. "The band breaks rank, and the players get to run to both sides of the street and really perform and interact with the crowd. Then, when the parade starts moving again, I blow the whistle and like magic, the band is back in line, and we take off down the street. It's a great piece of showbiz." The first half of the parade would move fairly quickly, but the second half felt like it would drag, as the musicians' chops started to get tired. Even so, they kept driving it! Dr. Bartner and the band could hardly wait to turn the second big corner of the parade and head toward the park, where waiting for them was food, drink, and a spot on the grass with their name on it. The band had about an hour break after the parade to rest and eat before heading to the stadium for the game. All the other ensembles were in the park as well, including the opposing team's marching band. "We had a mini 'battle of the bands' in the park. Even with tired, sore lips, we went back and forth playing tunes," Bartner recalled. "Then the bands started singing songs back and forth. We sang our fight song, they sang theirs. That's when I stopped it. Some of the lyrics were changed and they got a little carried away. Besides, it was time to board the buses." Bartner thought it was pretty cool that the buses carrying the bands for the teams competing on the Rose Bowl would get a police escort through the traffic to the arena. Taking their seats where they would stand in the endzone bleachers, band members were awestruck at the size of the audience. The 1973 Rose Bowl set an all-time attendance record that still holds nearly five decades later: 106,869 people filled the stands to watch the USC Trojans play the Ohio State Buckeyes. As an athlete himself, the significance of this matchup was not lost on Dr. Bartner, and he knew he had to keep the band blaring all four quarters.

The NCAA Football National Championship was on the line. USC was undefeated and ranked #1, as it had been since the second game of the season. Ohio State was ranked #3, with a season record of nine wins and two losses. Oklahoma was ranked #2 and had already beat Penn State in the Sugar Bowl the night before, finishing their season 11-1. The outcome of this Rose Bowl would determine the final rankings of the season and who would officially be national champs. As much as Dr. Bartner wanted the football team to prevail, he also wanted the Spirit of Troy to represent the University of Southern California well on the field. Ohio State was one of the best bands in the country, and he wanted to make a good showing in front of them. Contractually, both bands got to do a short performance before the game and at halftime, too. Bartner remembered that Ohio got the biggest applause at pregame because they performed their traditional "Script Ohio"—with a tuba player running out to "dot the i." But Bartner knew he had an applause-guaranteed, show-stealing secret weapon coming up for his Rose Bowl half-time show.

USC and Ohio went into the locker rooms for halftime tied at 7-7, not exactly where the Trojans wanted to be, especially since the quarterback was nearly sacked on the last play of the half before he threw the ball to a receiver who fumbled it. It wasn't looking good, but Coaches John McKay and Marv Goux were known for their ability to pump up the players for the second half. While the team regrouped, the Ohio State Marching band did their thing on the field, and the TMB lined up to take the field. Dr. Bartner believed halftime belonged to the Spirit of Troy.

## Going for the Win

Marching out in a giant chevron, the ranks then split into four circles that expanded and contracted to the beat of "Listen to the Music" by the Doobie Brothers. The circles melted into squares that intersected and created a moving rectangle before halting in concert formation. "One of the most important parts of any song is the lyrics," said the stadium announcer, who also could be heard on the live television broadcast. "Many of today's popular tunes carry social messages through their lyrics. For an example, you only need to tune into your radio and listen to Chicago's latest rock hit, 'Dialogue.'" The Trojan Marching Band played the rock chart to feature the eight Song Girls, fifteen Silks and pair of baton twirlers. Then came a Trojan dance routine. "In the visual medium of television, music both creates and heightens emotions to enhance what you see. Sit back, relax, and listen while the Trojan Marching Band dances to Isaac Hayes' 'Theme from Shaft.'" With the band playing and jiving, everyone in the stadium was distracted from noticing that a helicopter had flown into a clearing in the field near the stadium to make a special delivery. Then finally, the moment everyone, especially Dr. Bartner, had been waiting for. The band had formed a large concert set covering the field from the thirty to the thirty, and the announcer made the introduction: "Music and movies go hand in hand. Many movies have been based on the lives of famous musical personalities. The hottest movie in America today is *Lady Sings the Blues,* based on the life of jazz singer, Billie Holiday. And now to sing 'Love is Here to Stay' from that movie, the Trojan Marching Band proudly presents its star, Miss Diana Ross."[2]

A vision in white, with an airy, bright-green mink fur wrap, stepped out to the hashmark on the fifty-yard line, and with a big smile, Diana Ross grooved and sang about everlasting love being forever and a day. The crowd went wild. Millions of people across the country watched on live television as Dr. Bartner conducted the band with a shining celebrity taking center stage. "She was stunning!" said Dr. Bartner. "She definitely looked like a movie star!" This wasn't a typical college football game show—it was big time entertainment. The TV camera even cut away to a cheering First Lady Pat Nixon, who was indeed in the stands rooting for the Trojans. She, along with one hundred and six thousand others, applauded as Diana Ross hit the final vibrato that love was there to staaaaaaaaaaaay right as the football teams returned to the sidelines. Dr. Bartner blew the whistle commanding the band to quickly high step it off the field, and then he climbed down his ladder, feeling triumphant. "I felt like we as a band had finally gained the respect of football fans across the country. I felt like we had hit a home run!" Now if only the football team would carry that momentum forward and win this game!

The Trojan Marching Band only got to play all three choruses of "Fight On!" once in the first half, because there had only been one Trojan touchdown. But whatever McKay and Goux said in the locker room must have worked, because the 'SC players came out fighting on—and the band was there with the fight songs to help them drive it down the field! Within the first three minutes of the second half, the Trojans had another touchdown. The band began to play and never stopped. An Ohio State field goal was answered by two more Trojan touchdowns in the third quarter, then two more in the fourth, and USC was ahead by 32. One last Ohio State TD couldn't save the Buckeyes, and the Trojans went on to win the game, 42-17. USC set another Rose

Bowl record that day, with the most points in a half, resulting in one of the highest scoring Rose Bowl games in history. Dr. Bartner and the Trojan Marching Band were proud to be part of this momentous day. With a perfect 12-0 record, the 1972 USC Trojan football squad became the first team to ever receive a unanimous #1 vote in all the polls to become National Champions. Sports commentator, Keith Jackson, would later call the 1972 Trojans the greatest football team he ever saw.[3] Dr. Bartner was feeling like a champ, too, having pulled off the biggest half-time show of his career. This 1973 Rose Bowl performance was just the first note of what would become the long, beautiful—and sometimes quite challenging—concerto that is Dr. Arthur C. Bartner's life as he fulfilled many dreams leading the members of Hollywood's Band.

## High Note: Be Prepared

With new uniforms, an improving attitude in the ranks, and a growing sense of purpose in supporting a winning team, Dr. Bartner felt this band might actually be ready to turn a corner and become the great program he believed it could be. It appeared others were beginning to notice that possibility as well. Hank Ehrlich's support and collaboration to create a star-studded halftime show at the Rose Bowl was an amazing opportunity, and if Dr. Bartner wanted to capitalize on it, he knew he and the band had to be prepared. That meant paying attention to the details—every note, every horn angle, every line on the field, and every chair-step in parade ranks. ***The level of success you achieve is directly related to the amount of drive you put in, because how you practice is how you perform.*** Sloppy practice leads to a sloppy performance, and that is not something Dr. Bartner allowed. It goes back to passion and discipline—the band's growing *Drive It!* tradition. The commitment to work together and practice their music and marching for the parade and the show with energy and enthusiasm led to a home run with the Diana Ross halftime performance. Success comes when perseverance, preparation, and opportunity unite. *Be prepared.*

# HALFTIME

## EXCELLENCE

Courtesy: Ling Luo

# 6

# SHINING REPUTATION

*Fleetwood Mac and the Trojan Marching Band, aka Hollywood's Band, at Dodger Stadium for the making of "Tusk," 1979.* Courtesy: Scott Steele

# CHAPTER SIX

## SHINING REPUTATION

The national exposure from its halftime performance in the Rose Bowl on the first day of 1973 definitely put the Trojan Marching Band on the map. Now it had something to live up to, and it was a tall order for a still-rookie-director and his growing ensemble. The "home run," as he called it, with Diana Ross helped in the recruiting department, and while that was great for doing more with the field shows, it also meant more logistics and higher costs for travel. Putting them on buses for an eight-hour ride to the Bay Area for a Cal or Stanford game was one thing. Getting them and all their equipment halfway across country was another. Wherever they would go, Dr. Bartner knew that song choices and appearances going forward must be considered carefully in order to build on the reputation the Trojan Band was beginning to establish with more and more Hollywood connections. Once the celebrities started calling, they never stopped.

### Surprising the Gold-and-Blue

Coming off its 1972 National Championship season, the Trojan football team was favored for a repeat in '73, and now the team actually had a decent band to support it. Playing the fight songs in the stands, the Spirit of Troy helped the team drive it down the field for another undefeated season, at least leading up to the big rivalry game. Thanks to the suggestion by the band's student leadership group, including Ken Dye, and with the help of the fundraising efforts of his mentor and friend, Ken Cotler, Dr.

Bartner was taking the whole band for the annual matchup against Notre Dame. The Gold-and-Blue and the Cardinal-and-Gold have long held a huge rivalry, and the Trojan team wanted the band's backup! This trip to South Bend, Indiana was the first for the full band since 1927. The ABC network televised the game live, and during the announcer's opening comments, he mentioned that it was Notre Dame's Homecoming, all while the Trojan Marching Band played USC's fight songs behind him. Later, as the halftime show began, the commentator remarked on the effort it took to get the band to South Bend. "They put on various rock song music festivals, like yesterday in Chicago at Civic Center Plaza, and the opening of various stores in California, to raise the twenty-five thousand dollars to make this trip. So, to The Trojan Helmet Club—the band support group—and other organizations, we salute them for having that much interest in their university and the football team."[1] What he did not mention was the shockwaves from the tunes the band performed, accompanied by the USC Song Girls in their form-fitting cheerleading outfits. Dr. Bartner recalled that the conservative university audience was in total shock to watch the women dance while the band played the hard rock song "Frankenstein" by Edgar Winter Group. Assistant Director Tony Fox had expertly arranged the rock chart and the band loved to play it. The three-minute standing ovation that followed the performance surprised the musicians and solidified that this band could play anything!

Unfortunately, having all one hundred and seventy-five members of the band on the sidelines could not help the Trojans get the win this time. With five thousand USC fans out of sixty thousand watching in the Notre Dame stadium, the Fighting Irish ended USC's twenty-three game-winning streak and along with it, their hopes for a back-to-back national championship. Even so, the band never gave up on the team, and it never will. Decades later, the full band continues to travel to South Bend every other fall to fuel the rivalry. Ironically, the leader of the student group that suggested the band go to Notre Dame in 1973, trombone player Ken Dye, became the band director for the Irish Marching Band in 1997. Dr. Bartner and Dr. Dye collaborated on multiple projects through the decades and remain friends to this day.

## Diamond in the Rough

If this band was going to keep going places, Dr. Bartner had to keep the big names coming to campus. And so, he did. Art's friend in the movie industry, Hank Ehrlich, called to offer another star performer, this time for the USC-UCLA crosstown rivalry game. One Tuesday afternoon music rehearsal in November 1973, the band members warmed up while waiting for their band director to arrive. Bartner came to Cromwell Field with a guest, none other than Neil Diamond. Cheers erupted as the multi-gold-album, award-winning artist waved at the students and stood ready to listen to the band play one of his compositions from Paramount's newly released film, *Jonathan Livingston Seagull.* "Dear Father" poured across the field. Diamond called the performance fantastic. The song had only been publicly released a month earlier, and the movie had only been out for three weeks—and the Trojan Band was already capitalizing on its popularity.

Neil Diamond considered himself more of a composer than a conductor, though, so instead of taking the ladder at the halftime show four days later, he stood smiling in the rough grass on the sideline while his tune was crooned into the stands before the sold-out Coliseum crowd. The spinning swirl of heat from the twirlers' fire batons added to the glow on the field. Covering the rivalry game live on ABC College Football, Keith Jackson announced, "A gentleman who is being featured here at halftime is a man who has given us an enormous amount of entertainment, and who is, I'm sure, going to give us much more in the years to come. As the USC Trojan Band is saluting, along with the card section, the music of Neil Diamond."[2] With his shoulder-length dark hair contrasting his white jacket and bell-bottom pants, the music legend applauded the concert formation, until Dr. Bartner stepped down from conducting to walk over and shake his hand and thank him for coming. Diamond's movie soundtrack album won a Grammy in 1974 for Best Original Score Written for a Motion Picture or Television Special—and actually made more money than the film itself, selling two million copies in the U.S. With Ehrlich's help, it was looking like Bartner sure knew how to pick 'em as he worked to polish the band's growing Hollywood reputation.

## Rose Bowl Golden Years

It's hard to tell whether it was the band supporting the team's excellence or the team helping the band's rise to prominence. Either way, regular appearances in the nation's biggest bowl game contributed to the celebrity status of both. The USC Trojan football team played in the Rose Bowl ten times in thirteen years —basically dominating the arena in the seventies. That was fortuitous timing for a new band director trying to make a name for himself and his program. Because, where the team plays, the band performs. And in those days, the television broadcast would actually show most, if not all, of the halftime performance, which provided an incredible opportunity for Dr. Bartner and the Trojan Marching Band to build its reputation—especially in three back-to-back Rose Bowls, all against Ohio State.

The 1973 Rose Bowl was Dr. Bartner's first bowl game appearance, and Diana Ross stole the show. Even with the 1973 loss to Notre Dame in South Bend, the USC Trojans still earned a berth in the 1974 Rose Bowl, and Dr. Bartner wanted to come up with something grand for the shows. For pregame, the Trojan Marching Band featured up-and-coming Broadway singer and television star, John Davidson, singing the National Anthem. For halftime, Dr. Bartner was thrilled to have the popular funk band "Tower of Power" guest star with the Trojan Marching Band. They performed their top-20 hit called "So Very Hard to Go," but unfortunately, it was a bit of miss with the audience and with the Los Angeles Times newspaper coverage. Bartner was disappointed that the crowd didn't love the show as much as he did, and that the team lost the game! But both the team and the band got another chance with the Rose Bowl in 1975. The Trojans beat Ohio State in a close game, 18-17. And the band had a hit halftime performance titled "Make Your Own Kind of Music," featuring the music of jazz trumpet legend Maynard Ferguson as well as the Sly and the Family Stone tune "Dance to the Music." It went over much better with the crowds, and in fact, the TMB still plays that tune nearly five decades later!

For the 1977 Rose Bowl, the Trojans beat Dr. Bartner's alma mater, the Wolverines of University of Michigan. On the field at halftime, Bartner showed off his pride for his new hometown with the theme "Los Angeles: Capital of the World." The band played "California Dreamin'" by The Mamas and the Papas, as well as Donna Summer's "MacArthur Park." The performance was so well received that both the band and the team received an award from the city of Los Angeles. Mayor Tom Bradley, who had been elected in 1973 as the first black mayor of L.A., invited the USC Trojan musicians and band director and football players and coaches for a ceremony where he honored them for honoring the city. "It was a big banquet. Coach John Robinson was there because the team got an award for winning the bowl game. And the Trojan Marching Band got an award for promoting the city of Los Angeles. It was pretty cool!" And, by the way, it wouldn't be the last time Dr. Bartner and the TMB were invited to city hall.

USC beat University of Michigan again in 1979's Rose Bowl, where the band played John William's iconic score from *Superman*. That's also the year Dr. Bartner introduced the band playing "Animal House" from the movie soundtrack, which is another tune that still lives on in TMB tradition today. Fans love that song because in the middle of it, every band member—including the tubas—lay on their backs and kick their feet in the air for a hilarious display of solidarity. And when the rest of the band gets up, the tubas don't. For all the incredible success and collaboration happening with Hollywood throughout the seventies, Dr. Bartner and the Trojan Marching Band hadn't seen anything yet.

## In Full Color

In the early seventies, Dr. Bartner was finding his footing as a transplant from the Midwest to the West Coast. The regions had distinctly different philosophies and styles, and he quickly discovered that what worked in Michigan certainly did not fly in Southern California. So, the band director took advantage of USC's location and found his own niche. Less than a decade into his Trojan career, Bartner had a firm foundation in the celebrity community—and the band was growing into its nickname "Hollywood's Band." The moniker was reinforced by the ensemble's first motion picture appearance in MGM's *That's Entertainment II* in 1975. The movie about the history of movies was hosted by Fred Astaire and Gene Kelly and featured clips of films starring some of the biggest names in Hollywood, like Judy Garland, Clark Gable, Doris Day, and Mickey Rooney, to name a few. The TMB's part, if one could call it that, was relatively small—simply a sped-up video of them marching on the field to form the word "AND" as part of the opening credits—but still, the band was in a movie alongside Hollywood bigwigs.

The increasing visibility of Hollywood's Band led to another opportunity with a performance at the 1976 Hollywood premier of *King Kong*. Someone else at that event was very impressed with the Trojan Marching Band: Bonnie Churchill. She had a nationally syndicated newspaper column with stories about Hollywood's biggest stars, as well as a nationally syndicated radio show in which she interviewed celebrities. "She interviewed me for an hour," Dr. Bartner recalled. "And it was heard all over the country. I'm not even sure how many people heard me talking about the band. It was a pretty big deal." Churchill also introduced Dr. Bartner to a California impressionist artist she knew named Robert Jensen. Later that year, Jensen painted a portrait of the USC band during an event at the convention center, and he never stopped painting Bartner and the band. That simple introduction led to a series of paintings of the Spirit of Troy and a lifelong friendship for Dr. Bartner.

Bartner and the TMB were now regularly asked to perform at other events around Los Angeles where famous faces were appearing, including stars like Sammy Davis Jr. and John Wayne at Super Bowl XI in 1977. The Trojan Marching Band was part of the promotion for the game with a show called *Super Night at the Super Bowl*. "We went out to John Wayne's house in Naples, California and we filmed this promo with John Wayne. We got to meet this legendary former USC-football-player-turned-Hollywood-star," said Dr. Bartner. "We took a picture, but I wasn't in it. Who wants the band director in the picture? And the band kids also got a picture with Sammy Davis, Jr., who came out of the production tent. He came over and talked to the band. Don Rickles was there, too. It was a great night for the band." Later in 1977, Hollywood's Band performed at the ABC Entertainment Center where Muhammad Ali was premiering his movie, *The Greatest*.

What really landed the band in the forefront were the multiple television appearances, including shows like the *Dinah! Christmas Special* with Rock Hudson in 1974. Dinah had invited Dr. Bartner to sit on the interview sofa, right next to Rock Hudson. Dr. Bartner can't remember what she asked him on the show, but he does remember the band played several Christmas carols while Rock Hudson acted as drum major. Then, in 1975, members of the band got to wear tuxedos and play seventy-five of "the one hundred guys" in the hit TV show, *Mitzi and a Hundred Guys*. That was a special invitation because Dr. Bartner's children, Steven and Debbie, were allowed to attend the taping of the show. It's one of his favorite photos with his kids. To top it all off, in 1976, Dr. Bartner was called to have the band be part of the finale for the *48th Annual Academy Awards*. Elizabeth Taylor and Gene Kelly introduced the Trojan Marching Band onto the stage at the Dorothy Chandler Pavilion. "There were tubas on stage, drummers in the pit, the rest of the band in the aisles and balconies," Bartner reminisced. "We played 'America the Beautiful'—and it was amazing and momentous." Hank Ehrlich had introduced Dr. Bartner to composer John Williams, who was the music director for that year's Oscars, and another Hollywood connection was born. The mystique and magic of the marching band sound was getting plenty of attention, and it caught the ear of a hot rock band in the summer of 1979.

## Going Platinum

It was near the end of the school year, a Thursday afternoon in late May. The band members were waiting for Dr. Bartner to arrive for rehearsal. (They knew to be there early and ready to go before the band director arrived.) Dr. Bartner walked up and casually introduced Mick Fleetwood, of Fleetwood Mac, to the hidden jaw drops of the band members. The rock band was riding the wave of success for its second album, *Rumours,* and was in the throes of making a new album with a new sound—and Mick wanted Hollywood's Band to help. He loved the big brass sound of the Trojan Marching Band. Fleetwood Mac had been on tour in Europe, and Mick was trying to sleep after a late night of performing when suddenly a loud noise woke him up. It was a brass band marching by his hotel room window. As Bartner shared how Mick told him the story, Fleetwood said he was obviously a bit upset by the interruption to his slumber, but he decided he liked that sound and thought, *Maybe on my next album.* And the seed was planted. He returned to the States after the tour ended, and promptly called the office of the Trojan Marching Band. Dr. Bartner, however, was not in the office when the call came in. His assistant director, Tony Fox, happened to take the call, in which Mick Fleetwood said he was looking for a big brass band to be on their next album. Fox immediately called

Bartner. Bartner immediately called back Mick and said, "You can count on us. What's the next step?" That next step was for Dr. Bartner, Tony Fox, Mick Fleetwood, and Lindsey Buckingham to meet and figure out the music. So, in Studio B in Santa Monica, California, Buckingham played a tape of their new song so Fox could chart the tune in a way that the TMB members could play it—including an incredible drum solo midway through the song. Fox crafted the arrangement, and it was time to take it to the band to practice. When Mick Fleetwood came to campus that day in May, after ten minutes of meeting, greeting, and handshaking, the rock star handed out sheet music to the college musicians and Hollywood's Band belted out the notes to "Tusk"—and that was the first time the USC band version of the song was ever played or heard by anyone, ever.

By 1979, Dr. Bartner had grown the band to about two hundred fifty musicians, but because school was out of session, more than half missed the gig as they were already back home or working their summer jobs. Still, one hundred twenty Trojans were transported from campus to nearby Dodger Stadium to record the record and make what would become one of the first-ever "music videos." As they stepped off the bus into the hot and muggy stadium, the young men and women each signed a release and were paid one dollar for their time and talent. Then rehearsal began.

Saxophone players filled a dugout, trombones took one side of the outfield, and trumpets took the other. Dressed in a blue Dodgers t-shirt and signature floppy white hat, Mick Fleetwood took the infield and used a snare drummer's instrument to demonstrate the beat with percussionists. After getting a feel for the music, the whole group pulled together around the bases, with Dr. Bartner on a ladder facing second base. The drum major got to hold up the sheet music, arms high over his head, and turn the pages for Dr. Bartner to direct the rehearsal. Behind them, Mick kept his eyes closed, with his hands pressing his earphones tight, listening and stomping to the beat. Tall microphone stands stood in the dirt while the musicians were at attention in the grass at the rim of the infield. The first few run-throughs were slow and a bit off rhythm.

"I love what they're doing. I really love what they're doing, but the timing is a little bit off," said Christine McVie from inside the mobile sound engineering booth.

"They're working on that right now. They just have to get used to following him and really feeling that pulsation," said Trojan Band Music Arranger, Tony Fox. Then over radio to Dr. Bartner, Fox said, "The reason they want to do that first half over again is because where the tubas come in, the band has a tendency to rush it just a tad, in that last take."

"BAND!" Bartner shouts. "Don't rush where the tubas come in. BUH! Buh-Buh-Buh..."[3]

The band eventually got through the tune to meet Fleetwood Mac's approval. The challenge was to get a recording in which the Trojan Marching Band players matched up perfectly with the sounds on the tape that the rock stars had previously recorded, but it finally worked. Dr. Bartner and the TMB had no idea if it would be a hit tune or not. They were simply playing music and having a good time.

That rhythm started out years before this recording extravaganza as "just a riff" that Fleetwood Mac would use to warm up in the studio. At least, that's what Mick shared with some band members during a break. The musicians got to eat lunch before getting into their uniforms to put on a show for the cameras. Buffet tables covered the entire baseline from home plate to first, covered with fresh fruit, sandwiches, chips, soda, and for those of age, cases of Heineken beer. One band member recalled thinking, *So, this is the way Hollywood does it!* After the meal, the musicians returned to the parking lot to change in the buses that doubled as dressing rooms.

"Who are we to deserve the USC band to play for us, you know?" Stevie Nicks questioned with Christine McVie as they walked past the devoured trays of food.

"Oh Stevie, don't be so humble," Christine said.

"Well, no, but I mean, really. That's a lot of people playing that song."[4]

Then it was time for "helmets on!" Cameramen, their grips, and audio crews strolled through the crowd of musicians clad in cardinal and gold capes and boots. In his standard red coat and dark slacks, Dr. Bartner led the band from the parking lot to the entrance of Dodger Stadium for what would become one of the greatest events in Trojan Marching Band history.

Mick Fleetwood, Lindsey Buckingham, Stevie Nicks, Christine McVie, and a cardboard cutout of John McVie (who was out of the country that day) grabbed seats in the stands to await the grand moment. Led by the gold chest-plated drum major holding his sword high and flag twirlers with cardinal and gold banners blowing in the wind, the Trojans marched their way around the entire stadium. Horns swinging, the line of Trojans more than covered the bases, and Fleetwood Mac had their big brass sound for their new hit song, "Tusk"—the title track for their new album. "This is the hottest thing that's happened to 'SC's band," Dr. Bartner said.

Mick Fleetwood had a camera crew capture the whole magical, hot-and-sweaty day on film for use in the music videos to air on the brand-new channel, *MTV: Music Television* when it launched in 1981. This brand-new medium caught on, and people around the nation were listening and watching the USC Trojan Marching Band drive it around Dodger Stadium—adding to the celebrity status of what was now, for sure, Hollywood's Band. The city of Los Angeles was hearing "Tusk" on radio stations continuously. In fact, the school newspaper *Daily Trojan* reported on September 18, 1979 that a KLOS radio spokesman said the song was "totally hot" and they couldn't schedule it in rotation often enough to meet audience demand.

At the end of the recording and filming day, Dr. Bartner presented the Fleetwood Mac stars each their own commemorative Trojan helmet and made them honorary Trojan Band members. Many TMB members gave FM members hugs in gratitude for an incredible experience. Stevie Nicks grabbed a baton and strutted her stuff, twirling like a pro to the applause and cheers of her bandmates and the Trojan ensemble. Fleetwood Mac later made a generous donation to the Trojan Band fund to help finance the next trip to Notre Dame and to also kick off the effort to raise money for new band uniforms, since the Disney-designed outfits were nearly ten years old already!

The Trojan Marching Band retired the decade-old uniforms and debuted those new ones a year later at the USC Homecoming game at the Coliseum in 1980. The halftime show starred Mick Fleetwood playing bass drum, Stevie Nicks twirling baton, and Lindsey Buckingham conducting the band's performance of "Tusk" in front of a screaming crowd. The group presented Dr. Bartner with the Platinum Album for *Tusk* which had sold over a million copies by that point. "I didn't have any clue just how big 'Tusk' was going to be," said Dr. Bartner. "I thought we were just going out to record this number and make a video. Then, I was driving to school one day that fall, and I heard it on the radio. The announcer said, 'Now from Fleetwood Mac, here is 'Tusk'—featuring the Trojan Marching Band.' And I was in shock. I had NO idea how big this was going to be from that moment on."

Fleetwood Mac went on tour with the album, including a series of concerts at the Los Angeles Forum where, of course, the TMB accompanied them. Fleetwood Mac played on a stage with a curtain behind them, and when it was time to play "Tusk," the curtain opened to reveal the Trojan Marching Band, big brass blaring, and the audience went wild! "At The Forum, we became rock stars!" said Dr. Bartner. "We were even invited to a private party when the album came out. Only people involved in the production of *Tusk* were invited: producers, sound guys, film guys, and the Trojan Marching Band. We traded tunes with Fleetwood Mac. They'd play a tune, then we'd play a tune. No other college band in the country can say they've had a battle of the bands with Fleetwood Mac!" (Fleetwood Mac re-released the song in 1997, again with the musical assistance from the Trojan Marching Band—and it went quadruple platinum.) No matter where they perform it or how old the song gets, it never gets old! "Tusk" is still THE most requested rock chart that the TMB plays at every game and gig. At the conclusion of the seventies, there was no question that the Spirit of Troy, The University of Southern California Trojan Marching Band, was indeed, Hollywood's Band.

## High Note: Be Visible

Dr. Bartner's perseverance was paying off! He decided he was going to make something out of next-to-nothing with this band, even if it required asking for support. He welcomed engagement with band members, which strengthened the foundation of the organization and united them with a passionate purpose to support the team. The band was experiencing how their discipline and commitment to *Drive It!* during practice led to successful performances, which invited even greater opportunities. When Fleetwood Mac called on the band to collaborate with them on "Tusk," Hollywood's Band drove it to another whole level of visibility. ***Being visible contributes to a desire to perform at a higher level of excellence, which attracts even more success.*** A shining reputation is built gradually, one performance at a time, but it can be tarnished overnight. That's why a commitment to excellence includes discipline, responsibility, accountability, and knowing the choices you make are being watched. *Be visible.*

# 7

# PIVOT POINTS

*Barbara Bartner joined her husband on a trip with the Trojan Marching Band, 1973.* Courtesy: Jeannine Zakaryan

# CHAPTER SEVEN

## PIVOT POINTS

No other college marching band in the country has one platinum album to its credit, let alone two. In fact, the Trojan Marching Band has a lot of things that no other university ensemble has—and that's what Dr. Bartner wanted. The unique sound and style of the Spirit of Troy has set it apart and allowed for a lifetime of once-in-a-lifetime opportunities for Dr. Bartner and the band. The chance to play music on live television, appear in major motion pictures, and perform with and for world-famous personalities—the momentum of so many momentous moments kept building the reputation of Hollywood's Band. Alas, to Dr. Bartner's dismay, even with the progress made through his first decade on campus, some band members still just didn't get it. These young men and women had so many opportunities before them, and for some reason, a handful of students didn't seem to want to get their act together. "The greatest fear for any band director or teacher is that you lose control," he said.[1] He either had to regain control or throw in the towel—neither of which would be easy. The time would soon come when Dr. Bartner must decide if he could take the bad with the good and keep this band intact. It was time to pivot.

### Welcome to Disneyland

Back before "Tusk" took the TMB's reputation to new heights, Dr. Bartner had a captivating opportunity come up. While he was disappointed that the crowd at the 1974 Rose Bowl didn't love the "Tower of Power" halftime show as much as he and the band students did, that season would still prove to be transformational for the band director's career. As is customary every time the band gets to go to the Rose Bowl, they also get to go to Disneyland during the week between Christmas and New Year's. This time, after the band marched down Main Street, they halted in front of Sleeping Beauty Castle to perform a concert. Dr. Bartner looked at this gig as an opportunity for the kids to play some great jazz tunes. One of his favorites was "Channel One Suite" by Buddy Rich. It had a great drum feature midway through that Dr. Bartner really enjoyed. He didn't realize it then, but Dr. Bartner had a secret observer during that performance: Bob Jani. Besides perhaps wanting to see the new uniforms his costume designer had put together for the band, Jani had another purpose for unobtrusively checking out the show. It would be a few months before Dr. Bartner found out why the Disney Entertainment Director (who later became vice president) made the time to watch the new Spirit of Troy band director do his thing.

Dr. Bartner had no idea that during that concert, Jani was taking note of his energy, enthusiasm, and love of music—and how he got the kids and audience involved, too. So, when Dr. Bartner got a call from Disneyland's Music Director in the middle of 1974, he was shocked. Jim Christensen wrote soundtracks for Jani's innovation of the "Main Street Electrical Parade" and many other famous, long-standing Disney productions. He was also in charge of the All-American College Band, a summer program for the best of the best of college musicians. He explained to Dr. Bartner that there were two groups, one at Disneyland in Anaheim and the other at Disney World in Orlando, Florida. He also shared that Bob Jani had covertly watched Dr. Bartner's recent show at Disneyland's castle, and he was impressed. Christensen told Dr. Bartner that the current director of the Orlando band was departing, and he asked if Bartner would consider taking over in the summer of 1974. It would mean a lot of traveling and spending much of the summer in Orlando, but "How can you say no to an opportunity like that?! We're talking about Disney! I could see how it could be a great learning experience for me working with show business professionals, and it could only benefit the USC band, too. So, I said yes, I'll take the job." Thus began another whole chapter in Dr. Bartner's life, adding the World of Disney to his Spirit of Troy—all contributing to the growing fame of Hollywood's Band.

## Conflicting Demands

The truth is, though, Dr. Bartner had a lot on his plate. The bigger, better, and more recognized the TMB became, the more work there was to do, which was great, but it could be very stressful and distressing at times. Fortunately, he had his wife and kids to go home to every night, even if many of those nights were quite late. "It's pretty hard to 'make a playdate' with me. I'd wind up canceling much of the time because the band became my social life. But my wife was able to build her own friendships and social life and I'm grateful for that. She's made lifelong friends." Several other young families with small children moved into the same apartment complex at about the same time the Bartner family had, so Art's kids had friends the same age. That meant his wife also had girlfriends with mutual interests. Even though they spent a lot of time apart, Barbara and Art were the best of friends. She would call him "Artie" or "Mr.

Mellow" at home. He would simply call her Barbara. "Her personality is such that there are no nicknames for her!" She always was and continues to be very protective of her husband, watching out for his health when he would work so much, and never speaking a negative word about him or anything he or the band has ever done. And Artie takes care of her as well.

That's because Barbara, Steven, and Debbie were his rocks. He was very devoted to them, and he wanted to spend as much time with them as he possibly could. Their apartment in Redondo Beach was just down the street from the kids' elementary school, where Barbara worked as a teaching assistant. She could walk the kids to school. Dr. Bartner spent plenty of time at the elementary school, too, because even with everything going on at USC, he was also the fourth-grade trumpet teacher. His son Steven had taken an interest in music, and Art wanted to make sure he had the best foundation with the instrument. Dr. Bartner spoke with the principal and music teacher at the school, and they agreed to let the USC band director volunteer his time to instruct the half-dozen or so trumpet players. Dr. Bartner appreciated being able to give lessons the way he had received when he was a kid. Like father, like son, Steven also loved to shoot hoops, so Dr. Bartner coached the youth basketball team, too! One year, his son's team even won the league championship. But, as Steven grew, through fifth, sixth, and seventh grades, his talents advanced beyond his father's coaching abilities. Art felt perhaps he was becoming too demanding, maybe yelling too much, and realized his son's high school teachers and coaches could do a better job. As much as it hurt his heart, he gave it up—both trumpet teaching and basketball coaching. Besides, Dr. Bartner had ever-increasing demands on his time with not only Hollywood's Band, but now his new position with the Disney Band as well.

Dr. Bartner found himself jet-setting across the country as the new director of the All-American College Band for Disney World in Orlando. As Disney's Director of Entertainment, Jani developed the Anaheim AACB in 1971 as an opportunity for young musicians to learn the art of showmanship and entertainment. College kids around the nation could audition for one of twenty coveted spots where they would get to learn from the best of the best, get paid to perform at Disneyland, and learn first-hand from famous people in the industry. It was also a great training and recruiting ground for Disney to find musicians for its many musical shows. With the success of the Anaheim program, Jani started the Orlando AACB in 1972. When its director departed after only two seasons, Jani needed a replacement, and he knew Dr. Bartner was the perfect fit. To audition musicians, Dr. Bartner flew to New York City one day and Chicago the next. Another of the four or five spring weekends, he would go to Orlando or Dallas, or another music hub city. He and another adjudicator used their expertise to audition fifty to seventy-five musicians in a weekend, with Dr. Bartner evaluating brass and his partner judging percussion and saxophone. They were not only looking for students who could play music, but for those who also had an outgoing personality and presence to perform and entertain thousands of people at the amusement park during the eleven-week program. Dr. Bartner spent the summer of 1974 in Orlando, and so did his family. He was able to bring Barbara, Steven, and Debbie with him, which was awesome because they got the run of the park! After three summers in the Sunshine State, Dr. Bartner got to take over the assignment in the Golden State, as he became the resident director for the Anaheim AACB program beginning in 1977—a commitment that lasted for twenty-eight years. It was much better to go home to his own bed each night after a long and loud day of music and crowds. He loved it, though! The twenty-piece ensemble consisted of kids who not only desired to be there, but even had to audition to be there. They wanted to learn and perform, not give Dr. Bartner a hard time.

## Taking Charge

With the smaller band at Disneyland, Dr. Bartner could be calm, cool, and collected and still be in charge. But the bigger, louder, (sometimes more unruly) Trojan Marching Band required a different approach. Bartner had learned that lesson when he first came to campus. Football coach Marv Goux sat down with Art and said, "Listen, what this band needs is discipline. You gotta be the coach!" Add that philosophy to his personal college experience marching under the Godfather of Collegiate Bands, William D. Revelli, and Dr. Bartner's pedantic, pedagogue persona was born. Revelli once accused Bartner of not being devoted enough to be a college band director, but that couldn't be further from the truth. As he matured, Bartner became very serious, an exacting perfectionist and frequent tyrant, much like Revelli, just more tolerant. "I respected him, but Revelli is the only guy, if I ever saw him coming, I would have crossed the street to avoid bumping into him," Bartner said. "I'm tough and demanding, but I don't intentionally belittle people like Revelli did. I didn't like that he'd call people out in front of the whole group. He developed a fear factor, which I don't do. I try not to lose my sense of humor. That being said, I am pretty intense." When band members pulled a stupid stunt of some sort while on the field, or if they were being lazy or flat-out disrespectful, Bartner was known to get red-faced angry with "veins popping in his neck," as students would describe it. But he also made an effort to temper his temper with a sense of humor as best he could, to lighten the mood if needed. Bartner created his personality out of necessity. In the beginning, he was only a few years older than many of the "kids" in his band, so he had to do something to take command, especially because some of them were ridiculously rambunctious. They were college kids out on their own for the first time, out of their parents' watchful eyes, experimenting, testing the waters, pushing the envelope, every cliche imaginable. He had to do something to get their attention and bring discipline into the band. "I'll be the coach. I'll run this band like a football team. I'll wear these kids out, so they're too tired to act out." And that's how "Torture Drills" came about.

At the start of every rehearsal, Dr. Bartner called the band to attention, and the first thing they'd do was a Torture Drill. That name may sound awful, but it's simple really. It made for a great warm-up. It is marching in place full-out to all three choruses of "Fight On!" It's a short tune. When played at the correct tempo, it's less than sixty seconds. But that single minute would make a big difference in the spirit of the band at any given moment. Any time the band would start to lose focus, Bartner could yell "TORTURE DRILLLLLLLL!" from his ladder on the sideline. "BAND, TEN-HUT! Tweeee-EET. Tweet-tweet-tweet-tweet-UP!" Instruments would snap up and start swinging, and as they marched and played, it got their blood pumping and heart beating, building passion and unity in the ranks. It also had the added benefit of helping to build their "band chops" and perfect their ability to march and play at the same time. The Torture Drill became a tradition that students loved to hate, something they both dreaded and anticipated at the same time. Tuba players understandably found the drill to be more of a challenge and learned how to look like they were driving it, even though they weren't. Bartner knew it all along and cut them some slack because those instruments are heavy. Other sections would intentionally play wrong notes or extra notes, which more than irritated Dr. Bartner, but it was meant to be goofy and build camaraderie, so sometimes he let it slide, but only during practice—never during performance! It didn't matter if it was a 7 a.m. game day call-time, everyone would drive it during that minute-long drill. Even after band members had played tune after tune on their feet in the stands for the entire game and marched from the Coliseum back to campus, the last thing they would do before being dismissed was One. Last. Torture. Drill. The band marched the fight song with every last ounce of energy, drawing from an internal source, a hidden reserve, to power through with passion 'til the very end. This was the pride and spirit Dr. Bartner wanted to instill in every member of his band—and it worked. Most of the time.

Sometimes, though, there were certain individuals who just had an attitude. Dr. Bartner would never name names because those kids knew who they were anyway. As much of an annoyance as they could be, he still cared about them, even if he had a funny way of showing it. It wasn't about embarrassment; it was about accountability and responsibility. Bartner wanted this band to be the best band in the country, and if anyone slacked off or showed up late, if they were disruptive or disrespectful, they would pay the price. He would bark at them to "TAKE A LAP!" That meant breaking rank to run around the entire band and get back in their spot to pick up where they left off. It wasn't long before running laps became another tradition, one that after a while, some band members would do on their own, even without Dr. Bartner giving the order. If Bartner called out a trombone for playing out of tune, that guy or gal would start running, and sometimes the players next to them would run, too, in solidarity. If Bartner yelled at "Joe" to take a lap for miserable marching, anyone else who had Joe in their name would also run. The only interruption Dr. Bartner would permit was if it involved the football team. When the band was rehearsing on Cromwell Field, and the team finished practice on Howard Field, the first person to notice the players walking back to their locker rooms yelled, "TEAM! TEAM!" That's when the band would drop whatever it was doing and Dr. Bartner would count "1, 2, 3"—and the band thundered "Tribute to Troy" with fingers raised in the victory sign, pulsing to the beat. This routine outside of Heritage Hall, which houses all the Trojan sports history and honors, further solidified the relationship between the band and the team. Eventually, the laps and torture drills that started out as discipline actually became fun—and that's something else Dr. Bartner wanted. "If it's not fun, why are you here?" he said. "It takes commitment to be in this band, a lot of hard work, and we spend a lot of time together. It's gotta be something a kid wants to do and have fun doing it. If not, they should find something else to do."

## Decision Time

What Dr. Bartner thought was fun and what the band members defined as fun could sometimes be two entirely different things. Profanity seemed to be part of the cultural vernacular all across campus, much to Dr. Bartner's chagrin. The pranks and rituals that were done behind Bartner's back may have been "kids being kids" and out of the band director's control, but when inappropriate behavior had the potential to reflect badly on the band or the university, that's when it became an issue and Dr. Bartner had to make a decision. The Trojan Marching Band was called on more and more often to perform at events around the city, and Dr. Bartner believed it should be considered an honor and privilege to be part of the ten-piece, twenty-piece, or whatever-sized-piece band assembled for that purpose. He expected all students to represent the university and the band with the utmost respect and pride, and if they didn't, they'd be disciplined through the Office of Student Affairs. Even still, some kids just didn't get it. "I thought, 'I built this monster. Maybe I'm not mature enough to run it the way it should be.'" The combination of general disregard from some students, with the lack of financial support or sufficient staffing from the university, and the inner turmoil of being pulled in so many directions caused the most uncertainty Dr. Bartner had ever felt during his time at USC. He seriously considered turning in his resignation. His assistant director and music arranger, Tony Fox, described Dr. Bartner as depressed during this period. Fox said, "Art felt, 'Hell, either they're going to fire me or I'm going to turn this program around.'" Bartner met with James Appleton, then-Vice President of Student Affairs, to discuss the situation. Appleton would not accept his resignation. In fact, he talked Dr. Bartner out of it. "He wanted the band to always represent the highest standards and quality," Appleton said. "When the band didn't meet those standards, it was as if his own kids let him down." If he stayed, Appleton said, the Office of Student Affairs would back him.[2]

So, rather than give up, Dr. Bartner decided to *Drive It!* and Fight On! He recommitted to his efforts to develop the Spirit of Troy into "The Greatest Marching Band in the History of the

Universe" (a.k.a. TGMBITHOTU). The band members had a decision to make, too. They could either follow the rules—and the law—or leave the band. Dr. Bartner was serious about that. Some kids may say crap about Dr. Bartner and even insult him and his intentions, to his face or behind his back. However, what many fail to realize is that everything he does, has done, and ever will do, is for the benefit of the band and the students. He dedicated his life, and in fact sacrificed a lot of it, for these kids. If some students didn't respect that, or him, that was on them. Deep down, Dr. Bartner knew he could never leave USC. Just as he was devoted to his family at home, he was committed to his Trojan family. He instinctively knew there were many more incredible experiences in store for Hollywood's Band—and for every handful of disrespectful students, there were hundreds of musicians who were ready to step up and keep up the standards, pride, and traditions of the Spirit of Troy.

## High Note: Be Transparent

For all the progress Dr. Bartner felt he had made driving it through his first decade, with the growing success and visibility of the team and the band, he still encountered challenges: from the personal, internal struggle of missing his family while he followed his passion to the professional frustrations of some students not living into the spirit of excellence he wanted to instill in the band. Dr. Bartner was providing once-in-a-lifetime performance opportunities and he was implementing Coach Goux's recommendation for disciplinary drills, but it didn't seem to be enough. ***Part of evolving to a greater level of excellence is the way you overcome challenges. Being open and honest with others allows them to support you through the difficulty and into even more success.*** Being transparent also means taking responsibility for your part in the situation and being willing to do something to change it. Rather than step down, Dr. Bartner stepped up, recognizing his shortfalls, and remembering why he decided to become a college marching band director in the first place—his students. *Be transparent.*

# 8

# PUTTING ON A SHOW

*Dr. Bartner on the ladder by the student section at the Coliseum while the marching band performs a postgame show, 2019.*
Courtesy: Ling Luo

# CHAPTER EIGHT

## PUTTING ON A SHOW

"IT'S GAME DAY! GET UP FOR IT!" is a battle cry for the Trojan Marching Band. The band has many other chants, sayings, and songs that keep the spirit flowing through the ranks and into the audience wherever the band was. Following the agreement with Student Affairs and university policy, the appropriate chants were allowed to stay, and anything derogatory was not. In fact, anyone caught uttering anything improper would get to "TAKE A LAP!" because Dr. Bartner believed this band could be arrogant and respected without any of that nonsense. The disobedience didn't go away overnight, as some were reluctant to let go of their shenanigans, but Dr. Bartner was insistent and persistent. Policing themselves and one another became the norm. Dr. Bartner looked to the leadership in the band—the section leaders and squad leaders—to set the example and maintain decorum as part of the Trojan's signature style. Hollywood's Band had much riding on its reputation, especially as visible as the ensemble was trekking to the Coliseum on Game Day on their way to putting on a show.

### Trojan Traditions

Donning full uniform, which by the late eighties included customary dark sunglasses and sweat-capturing red 'SC-logo ball caps worn backwards under the helmets, the band gathered in front of Heritage Hall a little more than two hours before kickoff. This would be the last time they could sit down until the dismissal whistle blew long after the game ended. Each section held warm-ups to get their chops ready for a long day of playing fight songs and rock charts. People in Trojan gear congregated to watch and listen. Dr. Bartner meandered from section to section making sure all was in order. When the percussion line drummed a particular cadence, that was the band's cue, and the area became a swirling kaleidoscope of cardinal and gold for about a minute, until suddenly lines clicked into form as everyone took their places. Dr. Bartner had the ensemble do one last practice run-through of that day's halftime show music, to the delight of surrounding spectators. Then, the drum major called the band to attention, and it was time to step off. It could take more than an hour to get to the Coliseum, depending on how many performance stops they made.

Cadences played by the impressive precision drumline are loud enough to part the sea of fans to make way for the band. The rule is "No one cuts through the band," and if anyone ever tried, they'd get "politely" moved aside and told in no uncertain terms to wait until the band went by. When the band stopped to perform, observers would be stuck where they were, unless they wanted to elbow their way around the swarming crowds. Dr. Bartner usually halted the band at Founders Park in appreciation of the university's top donors and in front of Bovard Auditorium near Tommy Trojan to entertain tailgaters with the fight songs, "Tusk," and maybe another tune or few, before marching on toward the Coliseum. The University of Southern California is a mostly closed campus, with only a few guarded entrances, so to get off property, the Spirit of Troy had to zig-zag across campus to get to Exposition Boulevard. Near the exit are some flag poles, one of which is delightfully dented at the base from the continuous bangs of Trojan toes. "Kicking the flagpole started out as some band guys doing it as a joke, and then the rest of the fans followed suit," said Dr. Bartner. "That's the level of influence of the Trojan Marching Band!" Los Angeles police were pre-arranged to watch for the band coming and stopped traffic to allow the ensemble to cross in one pass. Except for the tubas who go single file and belt out the deep bass beat to "Sunshine," the band must stay in its squads—no breaking ranks—as part of the demonstration of unity. To thank them for safe passage, some women in the band, unbeknownst to Dr. Bartner, gave those officers a kiss! People in their cars trying to get to parking lots waited and watched the band make its way to Exposition Park, which was always packed with thousands more tailgaters.

The Los Angeles Memorial Coliseum has been the home field for the USC Trojan football team since the stadium opened nearly a century ago—obviously well before Dr. Bartner's time. The venue was commissioned as a memorial to the veterans of World War I, and in 1968, it was rededicated to veterans of all wars. The seventy-five thousand-seat facility was finished in June of 1923, and that October, USC hosted the very first football game ever played there. The Trojans beat Pomona College, 23-7, in front of a modest crowd of 12,836 people. By the time Dr. Bartner was leading the band to the arena, the USC team would be selling out the games in the stadium that had been renovated to hold about ninety thousand fans. For his first few years, Dr. Bartner had the band make a grand entrance for the first game of the season by marching down the ninety-nine peristyle steps at the east end of the stadium. Several years later, this special arrival signified the last home game of the season instead. No matter when it happened, it was a dazzling display to see the band high step it, driving it step-by-step to the football field below.

The other entrance for the band was through the service tunnel at the other end of the field. The band marched cadences from campus to the west end of the stadium and convened in the mouth of the corridor until it was time to line up for the pregame performance. For many years, the whistle would blow, and the Trojan Marching Band would sprint and scream their way through to the field in what was affectionately called "The Tunnel Run." The rite of passage was more like a stampede akin to "Running of the Bulls," and Dr. Bartner (and university officials) feared someone would trip, fall, and/or get trampled. It didn't help that the tunnel let out beneath the stadium seating of the opposing team, so often words were exchanged, in rivalry of course, but usually unnecessarily. The potential liability became too much, so instead, Bartner directed the band to move through the tunnel stomping and shouting in orderly ranks, in a slightly more dignified and rather impressive display. The teams could hear the band, but not yet see it. "When we march out of the tunnel, it's like we are descending on the battlefield," said Dr. Bartner. "The visiting team players are the invaders who want to take over our village. Our job is to protect our home." Once warm-ups wrapped up and the opponents left the sideline, the Trojan team moved to the fifty to practice their plays, and the band moved out to play "Tribute to Troy" over and over and over, to let the team know it was here for them—one of Dr. Bartner's favorite moments before the matchup! "It's a great tradition between the team and the band. And it intimidates the opponents, too!" Trojan football players were getting their game on, and hearing the fight song would get them even more pumped up. When they could, the players acknowledged the band by holding up Fight On victory fingers. As the countdown clock clicked to twenty minutes before kickoff, the team chugged back to the locker rooms for one final pep talk, and the TMB lined up on the sidelines to perform the pregame show for those who arrived early to the stadium.

## Showtime!

Looking up at Dr. Bartner hoarsely hollering from his ladder cannot compare to staring up at ninety thousand plus wildly cheering fans in the Coliseum. Not even tons of practice can truly prepare a freshman Trojan for the immense overwhelm of taking the field for the first time. It is still awe-inspiring for band members who have already done it a dozen times or more. Following the sword-wielding drum major onto the turf after he stabs the field is a breathtaking experience—especially when the white stallion mascot, Traveler, charges around the field, too. The adrenaline rush is addictive, for the musicians on the field, and for Dr. Bartner himself. It's time to see all the practice pay off.

The Spirit of Troy announces its arrival with "Fanfare" and then takes the field playing "Tribute to Troy," one row of the bands stepping off the sideline every eight counts. "GO!-2-3-4-5-6-7-8. GO!-2-3-4-5-6-7-8." Horns blaring and drums beating, the full band drives it to fill the entire field from endzone to endzone, sideline to sideline. Then, "CHING-BOOM!" and the band plays "Fight On!" as it changes its formation several times on its way to spelling out "USC"—and then the band faces the student crowd to drive it for third chorus of the fight song. The Spirit of Troy maneuvers some more before halting in a new formation. In some years, it was a map outline of the United States, or a star, and the band played a uniquely melodic arrangement of the "National Anthem," "America the Beautiful," or another patriotic song, depending on the occasion. Then, while in concert arcs, the TMB plays a "Rock Chart," featuring performances by the Song Girls, the Silks, and the Majorette, with their swirling short skirts, swishing tall flags, and spinning steel batons, respectively. The tunes come from "the book" of about a dozen arrangements that are crowd favorites, like "In the Stone," "Frankenstein," or "Tower of Power." Usually, the band marches the transition to the next formation. Other times, when the clock is short, they play "Tusk" and do a "scatter drill"—which means the band members intentionally run around all over the place, so the field looks like a chaotic kaleidoscope, until suddenly, they all hit their mark on the same note and turn chins-up to the crowd. With every band member in their spot, spelling out "Trojans" on the field, the Spirit of Troy then drives it, half-beat steps, to the Trojan battle cry, "Conquest." Fans explode in cheers as a flash of white flies past their eyes when Traveler, the stallion mascot, gallops around the football field while the mellophones play their call: "Awoo-awooo. Awoo-awooo." Dr. Bartner, the band, and any Trojan within earshot can't help but fill with excitement and pride. That's what Dr. Bartner wants for every performance, to make an emotional impact on the audience.

## Game time!

The emotional roller coaster begins when the team takes the field. The decibels crank in the crowd as the Spirit of Troy plays "Fight On!" for the cardinal and gold offensive and defensive lines mustering on the home team sideline. Whichever way the coin toss goes, the band plays "Tribute to Troy" followed by "All

I Do is Win" and fan hands go up on cue with the Trojan victory sign. Now it's game time!

The ride continues with kickoff. From its place in the stands, the band bangs out as much noise as it can as the opposing team's kicker backs up to launch the ball down the field. Once the ball is in the air, they hold their breath until the receiver catches it and makes the return attempt, and the band responds appropriately. Dr. Bartner pays close attention, so he knows exactly what's happening in the game, coordinated carefully with a liaison for the team, Ben Chua. Every musician stands and belts out tunes orchestrated to the plays on the field. This is why the Spirit of Troy has become an integral part of the Trojan Football Team—like the twelfth man on the field. The band plays one chorus of "Fight On!" every time the team gets a first down and all three choruses when the team makes a touchdown, as indicated by the tapping of his red-ball-capped head, when Bartner commands "From the top!" Sometimes, the band has to "cut" the music quick if the Trojan team is on a fast drill, because they don't want to play over the quarterback making the next play call. Then, when the Trojan quarterback is driving it down the field and needs extra encouragement on third down, Dr. Bartner has the band play "Charge!" "Da-da-da-DUT-da-DUH!" That six-note trumpet arpeggio was part of a song written in the 1940s by none other than USC Trojan bandsman-and-football-player-combo, Tommy Walker. His widow once told *Sports Illustrated* that the musical motto was triggered by a dirty joke, but neither he nor she would ever divulge the origin, because they didn't want to "take the fun out of 'Charge.'"[1]

When the Trojans are on defense, the band blares "Tribute to Troy" with every play that holds the other team from advancing yardage, which in most games, happens A LOT. That would be why the opponents' fans sing along to "Tribute to Troy" with "Is that the only song you know? It's boring and it's slow." (Some adversaries even keep count and display the tally on a sign.) But those deep, soul-penetrating notes are the impetus of the Trojan defense, building the courage and stamina to keep the spirit alive on the field, and 'SC faithful love that it annoys the competition! "We have a tune for everything that happens on the field. That's what's so unique about what we do—until other bands across the country picked up on it. But we started it!" Dr. Bartner calls for a celebratory tune when the opponents make a turnover. That is, when the other team fumbles the ball or their quarterback throws an interception, the band breaks into a Tony Fox arrangement of "All Right Now." He will also call for one of about twenty other rock charts when the game is paused for a team or television time out.

The amazing part is that every member of the band is required to memorize every single song—no music stands or instrument clips allowed! And if the band isn't playing, it's still making noise, yelling, with their hands displaying the victory sign. The band doesn't like to be quiet, so if it's ever too still for too long, someone yells "DEAD AIR!" to get a chant started. For many years, the TMB hollered from prime seats on the student side of the field, covering the first ten or so rows of centerfield seats, but eventually, the university's economics beat out the band's harmonics, and the Spirit of Troy was moved to a new set of bleachers at the east end zone behind the goal post. Affectionately known as "the sun deck" because it's always facing the sun, the bleachers now unfortunately block the view of the ceremonial peristyle steps. While some students may have been disgruntled about the move, Dr. Bartner actually prefers the end zone, because he feels the band can be better heard throughout the stadium, especially with massive mics and speakers provided the athletic department. Additionally, in exchange for moving the seats, the athletic department committed contributions to the band's travel fund and each band member gets two game tickets for family or friends. No matter where they are in the stands or on the field, the band never lets up, it never sits down, and Dr. Bartner never leaves his ladder—except when they're taking the field to perform.

## Halftime!

The halftime shows created by Dr. Bartner are much more than simple performances. Through the decades, they've become known for being high-octane entertainment, fueled by appearances with top names in popular culture. The list of celebrities that Dr. Bartner has invited to be honored, guest conduct, or even play with the band is insane. With superstar involvement or not, it takes some four thousand hours to coordinate a season of shows because there is so much involved. First, student engagement is a priority for Dr. Bartner, so he meets with band leadership to get their input on what they think would make an entertaining performance. When the tunes are decided, the show must be charted, for the music itself and for the field. That means every move is written out count by count for every band member—which is why squad leaders are valuable. They take their copy of the chart to teach their squad what to play, where to go, and when. Assistant Director Tony Fox drafted the music arrangement for all instruments. Dr. Bartner conceptualized the field patterns and put them to paper. In the beginning of his marching band director career, Dr. Bartner wrote out everything by hand and put it through the "ditto machine." Those carbon copies on a mimeograph machine eventually made way for the photocopier, but it was decades before digital design and display were available to make the duplication process simpler. Dr. Bartner crafted a new performance for nearly every home game, so depending on the football schedule, that could be as many as six or seven stellar shows per season. Occasionally, a show was actually pieced together from parts of charts created by students in a one-unit marching band class that Dr. Bartner taught. He would have the class select songs and design a field show to accompany them, and sometimes they were good enough that he'd use them. In fact, that's where some of the most famed "rock charts" came from. Whether it was a student design or his own, Dr. Bartner believed there was nothing quite like seeing what was on paper come to life on the gridiron.

Depending on what was happening in the game, about five minutes before the clock ticked to zero for halftime, Dr. Bartner instructed the musicians to put "Helmets on!" and he dismissed them section by section down to the field. The percussion line was last to go. The drummers stayed in the stands to play cadences and keep the crowd engaged. Down-to-the-wire was not a time for the musicians to rest their chops, though, because they still jammed for the team from the sideline, encouraging the Trojans to Fight On! down to the very last second. Dr. Bartner loved when the team went to the locker room in the lead, so the band could pick up where the team left off. The band had about a minute to get in line from the time the team left the field to when the stadium announcer introduced the show. Pregame shows are full of more traditional "patterns of motion" drills, while the halftime shows are "curvilinear" drills. The difference is the shapes and designs the band makes on the field. The forms are created to coordinate with the tunes to help tell a story or develop a theme, dozens of which have included big-time music, television, or movie stars. Even on the football field, the Trojan Marching Band regularly proved that it IS Hollywood's Band.

Considering his connection with Paramount Studios' Hank Ehrlich and the development of his showmanship skills at Disneyland, the level of entertainment Dr. Bartner was able to provide for halftime shows got better and better every season. His goal was to create a crowd-pleaser performance every time, but just like the football team, "ya win some and ya lose some." One for the W column was at the first home conference game of the 1977 season, paying tribute to a new movie *Star Wars* that had been released four months prior. Silks wore stormtrooper costumes, and other members of the band portrayed Luke Skywalker, Princess Leia, Han Solo, Chewbacca, C3PO, and R2D2, and Darth Vader. True to the theatrics he was learning through his Disney exposure, Dr. Bartner included lasers that pierced the dark during the evening game. The band had a blast performing it and the fans loved it, demonstrating as much with their standing ovation. Another halftime win came later that same year when USC hosted UCLA at the Coliseum. The one and only Maynard Ferguson stole the show and wowed the crowd when he joined the band on the fifty-yard line to play "Gonna Fly Now" from the year-old surprise box office hit *Rocky*. That was the first of many guest appearances the trumpet idol made with the band over the years, as he and Dr. Bartner had a kinship over their love of the trumpet. Perhaps one for the L column was in 1976 when Neil Sedaka sang "Love Will Keep Us Together" at the Notre Dame matchup. Bartner felt the performance could have been even better if Sedaka had been able to attend rehearsal. "You're only as good as you are during practice," said Dr. Bartner. "If practice is lousy, the show is lousy. If practice is great, the show is great. You can't win 'em all, but you can learn along the way and take what you can from each experience."

Over the years, many field shows had Hollywood themes and celebrity guests. One of Dr. Bartner's favorites appeared with the Spirit of Troy at the 1974 Notre Dame home game. When he was a kid, back in 1957, Art watched Carol Lawrence perform on Broadway as Marie in *Westside Story,* and he fell in love with the show. So, to have her sing the "National Anthem" with the band under his direction was like a dream come true. Then, at half-time of that game, Lawrence's husband, Robert Goulet, sang a song from the motion picture *The Little Prince.* A movie that hit the big screen in 1978 starred the TMB's home run actress, Diana Ross, as well as a young Michael Jackson and Richard Pryor. *The Wiz* (a contemporary remake of *The Wizard of Oz*) was the Hollywood buzz that year, and it made for great halftime entertainment at the Notre Dame home game, especially with a guest appearance by producer Quincy Jones and original cast members who danced while the band played music from the film. That was another for the win column. In fact, performing a montage related to movies always seemed to generate an enthusiastic crowd response, decade after decade.

Stirring emotion and sentimentality may not seem like something that would be in a marching band's repertoire, but when the TMB salutes successful USC alumni, it is. Perhaps the most meaningful show the band has ever done was a tribute to Olympian and World War II hero Louis Zamperini. His life story was told in the 2014 movie *Unbroken,* produced and directed by Angelina Jolie. She recorded a video introduction that played on the Coliseum big screen for the 2014 Notre Dame game halftime show. "Tonight, the Spirit of Troy pays tribute to an American hero. As a track athlete in the 1936 Olympic Games, alumnus of the University of Southern California, and esteemed veteran of the United States Army Air Force, Louis Zamperini had the kind of will and perseverance that is an inspiration to us all. I am honored to have known Louis and to help to tell his story in the upcoming film, *Unbroken*. But now, let us join in celebrating Louis' life. And as he would say, Fight On!" With black and white images of the late Zamperini and his family fading in and out on the stadium video screen, the band played unusually softly so the announcer could relay Louis' love for running as a young man. As a video clip from the movie showed Zamperini qualifying for the Olympics, the band formed Olympic rings while playing the Olympic fanfare. Shifting formation to a man running, complete with legs in motion, the band hit crescendo with Louis finishing the race, not medaling, but feeling triumphant, nonetheless. After the 1936 Games, the USC track team became Zamperini's family, which the band demonstrated by forming an outline of Trojan mascot, Traveler. The band maneuvered to have the horse rear up on hind legs. As a Trojan, Louis won an NCAA championship and set a national collegiate record for the mile, missing the world record by only 1.5 seconds. Then came the war. While the stadium announcer explained how Zamperini trained as a bombardier on the B-24, despite his fear of flying, the band played a cadence into concert formation. Wartime movie clips filled the big screen while the Song Girls did a swing dance in USO style uniforms to "Boogie-Woogie Bugle Boy." A diminuendo of the band's music allowed the narrator to tell of Louis' plane crashing, his forty-seven days lost at sea, his capture by the Japanese, and his time as a prisoner of war—during none of which did Zamperini's resolve ever break. The Spirit of Troy spelled LOUIS across the field, while Zamperini's proud, tearful children were recognized on the forty-yard line. Louis had passed away only five months before this tribute, at the age of ninety-seven. He was the epitome of what it means to be a Trojan, and this unique multimedia halftime show in his honor exemplified the power of a marching band to inspire tremendous pride.

Developing new field shows requires creativity and precision, and Dr. Bartner looks for a "certain something" to bring the audience to its feet. The *Star Wars* show of 1977 had it, and so did the reprise thirty-eight years later! In fact, this galactic halftime show received an NCAA award as one of the best halftime shows of 2015, out of all the college bands in the entire country. Dr. Bartner and his staff arranged a show to highlight the sci-fi saga's seventh in the series, *The Force Awakens*. The one and only Mark Hamill (Luke Skywalker) recorded an introduction for the halftime show at the USC-UCLA matchup. "A long time ago, but in a place not so very far away, a young graduate of the University of Southern California, named George Lucas, created one of cinema's most cherished and enduring film series... But today, I'm here to introduce The Greatest Marching Band in the History of the Universe as they pay tribute to the iconic music of John Williams and his score from *Star Wars*. So, (placing a Trojan Marching Band helmet on his head) may the force be with you and, 'FIGHT ON'!" The band took the shape of spacecraft, Darth Vader, Imperial Walkers trudging and collapsing, the planet being destroyed, and of course, Yoda. Midway through the field show came a crowd and band favorite: "The Dance Routine." The Trojan Marching Band has become known for its fancy foot moves, and in the Star Wars show, the band danced to "The Cantina Song"—much to the delight of fans in the stands, as well as George Lucas himself, who was on the sidelines to soak in the performance honoring his cinematic genius.

A few years later, Hollywood's Band performed a halftime show featuring another movie to recognize another 'SC alum. Kevin Feige is a graduate of the USC School of Cinematic Arts, and now the president of Marvel Studios—think *Avengers* fame. The audience loved the 2017 band's rendition of songs from Feige's fantasy sci-fi film, *Guardians of the Galaxy,* which kicked off with a formation of Rocket Racoon. The crowd exploded when the TMB took the shape of a rocket ship, complete with visible steam (from fire extinguishers) gushing from rocket boosters, propelling it across the field while it played "Brandy, You're a Fine Girl" by Looking Glass. Of the performance, the director of the movie, James Gunn, tweeted "Really fantastic work. It moved me."[2] Then in another theatrical, Disney-esque display in 2018, Hollywood's Band performed a tribute to one of its own with one of the more complicated and visually entertaining marching drills the band has ever done. Steve Bloom was a trumpet player in the TMB in the early eighties. Also a Cinema School alum, Bloom was the editor of Pixar's Oscar-award-winning animated feature film *Coco*. He introduced the halftime show in a video shown on the Coliseum big screen: "As a member of both the Pixar and Trojan families, I hope you enjoy the show. Fight on!" Then the band moved from straight lines into the shape of red race car, Lightning McQueen, and performed "Life is a Highway" from *Cars*, and "drove it" down the field with exhaust billowing from virtual tailpipes. The montage also included "Remember Me" from *Coco*, with the band in the formation of a calavera. The TMB then transitioned into the shape of a house to play "Memories Can Weigh You Down" from *Up*, in which the Silks put down their flags and picked up umbrellas to be the balloons that visually lifted the house as the band marched a backwards diagonal and held the shape. Then, as if that weren't enough, the next formation was Slinky Dog from *Toy Story*, and the band made it look like the dog's back end had to catch up to the front while they played "You've Got a Friend in Me." For the finale, the band lined up to form the logo of Mr. Incredible and played "Incredibles" from the movie by the same name. It really was an incredible performance.

Dr. Bartner has created literally hundreds of halftime shows, entirely too many to describe in detail. Suffice it to say the celebrity guest list is immense. One of his favorites, who performed in 1989, was Grammy Award-winning *Tonight Show* band leader Doc Severinsen. He joined the Spirit of Troy on the field and performed trumpet as an honorary member of the band. In the 1990s, shows included stars like Broadway singer Jennifer Holliday; the cast of the original Star Trek series; Latin jazz percussionist Poncho Sanchez; and Bozo the Clown, who under the makeup was former TMB drum major, Larry Harmon. Some other Hollywood connections who took part in a halftime show during the 2000s, whether performing, conducting, or simply hanging out on the sidelines were people like: 'SC alum and movie director Robert Zemeckis of *Back to the Future* and *Forrest Gump* fame; 'SC alum and lead singer of the rock band Offspring, Dexter Holland; KC and the Sunshine Band; Henry Mancini's daughter, Monica Mancini; Rapper Snoop Dogg; George Clinton Parliament Funkadelic (P-Funk); alternative metal group System of a Down; former Guns N' Roses lead guitarist, Slash; and Sam Harris, lead singer of X Ambassadors—just to name a few. The list really does go on and on.

While there may not be a specific award for amazing halftime shows (though if there were, Hollywood's Band would likely win it), Dr. Bartner and the Trojan Marching Band's halftimes led to some nominations, including a Heisman Trophy nod, if only in jest. Every university has its nemeses, and USC is no different. One Trojan rivalry is Stanford, a.k.a. "The Farm," so nicknamed because the campus was built on donated farmland. The university marching ensembles are no exception to the friendly competition and regularly engage in a "battle of the bands." *Los Angeles Times* columnist John Hall witnessed the exchange at the 1977 game, which included Stanford mocking the Trojan stallion mascot by presenting a Shetland pony on the field. Then USC kidded Stanford's multiple mascots with a parade of Indians, gorillas, trees, and Cardinals, whereupon Traveler's rider dismounted, ran to centerfield and playfully "slew them all" with his Trojan sword. Of the performance, Hall wrote: "The Trojan Band has gotten so large (250+) and strong, plays so well (it now does the National Anthem like nobody ever) and works so hard (earlier halftime shows included reproductions of *Star Wars* and *Rocky* in bigger than Busby Berkeley splendor) that we've once again, with apologies to Ken MacAfee, got to nominate Art Bartner's mob for the Heisman Trophy." The quote below the headline read, "On behalf of the Trojan Marching Band and myself, I would like to thank you very much for your nomination of us for the Heisman Trophy. - Dr. Arthur C. Bartner"[3] (Earl Campbell of the Texas Longhorns actually won the Heisman that year.) It was another Stanford matchup that led to Dr. Bartner's "Best Coach nomination." The other northern California school, Cal Berkeley, had beaten Stanford with a wild display of frantic lateral passes that led to a game-winning touchdown, even with the Stanford Band blocking the endzone. That 1982 moment in college sports history was dubbed "The Play"—and it was that play that the TMB re-enacted during halftime of the USC versus Stanford game in 1983, which ironically, the Stanford Band attempted to interrupt by crowding the endzone once again. The day after that performance, *Los Angeles Herald Examiner* columnist Allan Malamud declared "the best coaching job on campus this year again is being done by Dr. Arthur C. Bartner. Bartner may be the greatest band leader to grace Hollywood since Glenn Miller."[4] The following year, the TMB's celebrity identity was definitively pronounced by journalist Jon Krampner, when he wrote, ". . . the Trojan Marching Band has acquired the unofficial title of 'Band of the Stars'. If the Dallas Cowboys are America's Team, then this is *Hollywood's Band*."[5] So, there it was, in black and white: validation for years of very hard work on and off the field.

As much as Dr. Bartner loved the entertainment value of these celebrity-filled shows and the recognition and expansion of the band because of them, none of it would have happened if it hadn't been for one man: Hank Ehrlich. "He was a friend of and advocate for me and this band from the beginning. Look at what he started," said Dr. Bartner. Diana Ross was only the first of many, many introductions that Uncle Hank provided for Dr. Bartner. Their personal and professional relationship grew stronger through the decades, mutually beneficial as it was. Their collaborations behind the scenes made for fantastic displays that put Hollywood's Band on big and small screens and brought celebrities to the front of their field. Hank Ehrlich passed away in 1992. "He hustled for us till the day he died," said Dr. Bartner. "I'm forever grateful."

## Postgame!

Even after driving it hard and playing it loud for the halftime show, the band's job is far from over. The Spirit of Troy has the whole second half of the football game to go. Everyone—the band, the team, and the fans in the stands—all get a morale boost between third and fourth quarters when the Spirit of Troy performs "The Lone Ranger." The stallion Traveler charges around the stadium and the Olympic torch lights up, honoring Olympians and war veterans. "It's one of those wow moments, a great Trojan tradition!" said Dr. Bartner. Like the team, the band never quits, no matter how tough it gets. Some games are blowouts, with the Trojans taking an early lead and keeping it together all four quarters. Other times, it's back and forth with the lead changing hands, or in some cases, the Trojans have to come from behind and play all out to win; sometimes they do and sometimes they don't. Whatever happens on the field, Dr. Bartner and the Trojan Marching Band always back the team one hundred percent.

With the game done, win or lose or draw, and with the pressure to perform a perfect halftime show now behind them, the band members get to cut loose with their famous "Postgame Concert." Dr. Bartner sends the musicians down to set up on the field below the student section, and they rock it out for all the fans who didn't leave early to beat the traffic. After a loss, the stands are a bit emptier, but after a big win, the crowd is packed. That may be because they stay to see which football team player will get to take the ladder and wield the sword for the band to play the Trojan victory song "Conquest." The powerful moment is proof of the tight bond the band and the team have formed over the decades. The second song to be played is "All Hail," a slower, nostalgic, lingering tune that honors the alma mater. Dr. Bartner loves the showmanship and pacing of the postgame concert. He and the band feed off the energy of the crowd, playing rock charts for ten, fifteen, maybe even twenty minutes. Each section has its own coordinated dance moves to different songs, so the sights are as entertaining as the sounds—especially when they play "Tusk." The horn swings and dance moves have the entire band in motion. Certain tunes feature specific instruments, like trumpet for "Heartbreaker," drums for "Sing, Sing, Sing," and the tubas who stay lying on their backs after the whole band kicks their feet in the air for "Animal House." Finally, Dr. Bartner leads the crowd for a "SoCal Spell-Out"—and then it's time for the drum major to stand atop the ladder for the band to play "Conquest" once again. This time they play it to the audience, the fans, the alumni—without whom none of these traditions would even exist.

With their energy still surprisingly high, one would never realize they'd been up and driving it since the early morning, but the band can start to wind down on the march back to campus. Climbing up the peristyle stairs and out the Coliseum gates, the hundreds of band members have a more casual traipse across Exposition Boulevard, past the flagpoles, on their way to Tommy Trojan, where they play one last rendition of "Fight On!" and "Conquest." Finally, after a very long, strenuous, exciting day, Dr. Bartner at last can say, "Thank you, band... Band DISMISSED!" The Trojan Marching Band would meet quickly with their section leaders and then disassemble to go out and celebrate the victory, drown their sorrows for the defeat, or simply go home to sleep. They best rest their chops because odds were they'd be playing a celebrity gig that next week.

## High Note: Be Diverse

Traditions are the common thread that binds together the band, the team, and the fans. The stronger the traditions, the stronger the bond—which is what Dr. Bartner desired to develop from the beginning. From kicking the pole and kissing police to emerging from the tunnel and playing for the team, to standing in the stands and playing "Tribute to Troy" over and over and over again; from doing dance routines and driving it off the field to playing "Fight On!" for touchdowns and "Charge" for third downs—these elements are all part of putting on a show. For the consistency traditions provide, each show is also an opportunity to develop a variety of themes, styles, and emotional connections for the audience. Dr. Bartner invited student suggestions for tunes and shows and then he created, and the band learned, a new combination of music and marching for nearly every home game. ***Keeping traditions alive while also breathing new life into an organization contributes to excellence.*** Dr. Bartner realized that arranging and playing new music keeps the program on the cutting edge and keeps band members and crowds engaged. Welcoming diversity in band performances—and in the ranks of the band—builds value and appreciation for the program. *Be diverse.*

# 9

# BEING STARSTRUCK

*Remembering musical moments like "Tusk," Lindsey Buckingham of Fleetwood Mac performed at Bovard Auditorium, where Dr. Bartner gifted the guitarist a second Trojan helmet, 2015.*
Courtesy: Benjamin Chua

# CHAPTER NINE

## BEING STARSTRUCK

"I've always been starstruck," said Dr. Bartner. He sees himself as just a regular guy doing his job, and yet, he's surrounded by Hollywood. By the early 1980s, the buzz in the band biz was all about Dr. Bartner and what he would do next as the invitations for celebrity related performances kept rolling in. It seemed that each appearance on a television show or movie only magnified the magnetism of the Trojan Marching Band. Hollywood's Band was in demand! And so was Dr. Bartner. His gift for recognizing talent and for directing hundreds of students into one cohesive production was garnering requests left and right. He already had a full plate of responsibility with the Spirit of Troy and the Disney All-American College Band, and he still had a very limited budget and not enough staff to help him keep everything organized. Something was going to have to change, and quick, because he couldn't say no to these incredible opportunities.

### Seen On Screen

It never hurts to have friends in high places. Dr. Bartner and Hank Ehrlich, the Public Relations Director for Paramount Studios, developed a great friendship after the 1973 Diana Ross Rose Bowl home run. Their relationship led to multiple mutually beneficial performances, being good P.R. for both the movie studio and for the band. The Trojan Marching Band was asked to perform at the 1978 premier for what would become a perennial world-famous favorite, *Grease*. Hollywood's Band members played tunes with Olivia Newton John, John Travolta, and other cast members. Four years later, it just so happened that producers needed a marching band for a scene in *Grease II*, and the TMB was available. Instead of their usual cardinal and gold caped uniforms, the band members put on white tunics with red accents to play the part of the Rydell High School Marching Band. They filmed at an out-of-service Excelsior High School in nearby Norwalk, California. The 1982 sequel with a very young Michelle Pfeiffer and Michael Caulfield may not have been quite as successful as the original, but it was still fun for Dr. Bartner and the band to be part of its third motion picture.

In fact, it was a whole lot easier than what the band endured for the filming of its second movie a few years earlier. In coordination with Universal Pictures, the Trojan Marching Band got to play all three choruses of "Fight On!" while a helicopter took aerial shots of the scene for *The Gong Show Movie*. Chuck Barris starred in and directed the 1979 film, based off his popular television show. Toward the end of the storyline, Barris was having a nervous breakdown, sitting cross-legged in the desert of Morocco (actually the dunes near Pismo Beach, California) and his friend, Buddy Didlo (played by James B. Douglas) blew a whistle. "TWEEEET! TWEEEEET!" And it echoed, "Tweeeee-EEET! Tweet, Tweet, Tweet, Tweet!" That was the cue, and over a tall desert hill appeared about one hundred fifty members of the band, driving it down a steep, soft, sand dune. Eight USC Song Girls with pom-poms, two baton twirlers, the drum major in gold chest plate, twenty-one Silks with waving banners, and the whole ensemble swinging their instruments, all tried to keep straight ranks with sand flying everywhere. It was a total of forty-eight seconds on screen, but it felt a lot longer than any torture drill they'd ever done. It was a good thing the moon boots and uniforms were getting replaced the next year, because band members kept finding sand everywhere for months. "The night before that gig, we stayed overnight in Army barracks," recalled Dr. Bartner. "And it was the most uncomfortable bed you've ever slept in. Then that morning, they fed us green eggs, and you can imagine how well the band took that. Oh! What a funny memory!"

Filming the Chuck Barris movie took place less than four months after the band had recorded the music video for "Tusk" with Fleetwood Mac. That tune was on fire and cranking up the charts, so much so that it made news on the music countdown television show *Solid Gold* that premiered in January of 1980. Grammy Award-winning artists Dionne Warwick and Glen Campbell hosted the two-hour special highlighting the Top 50 songs of 1979. The pair introduced the Trojan Marching Band playing "Tusk" as the Fleetwood Mac music video played. The full-uniformed TMB filled the several circle-shaped stages usually reserved for the Solid Gold Dancers. That pilot show did so well that eight months later, this Paramount Television production became a weekly presentation of Solid Gold Dancers grooving to the top music charts of the week. "Tusk" continued to be instrumental in Hollywood Band's growing visibility, something Dr. Bartner could never have predicted but was ecstatic about, nonetheless, because *Solid Gold* was only the first of many television cameos in the 1980s. Some of the shows in which they performed received better reviews than others.

Audiences loved the original version of the ABC television series *Omnibus* in the 1950s, because as it claimed, it had something for everybody. The focus of the weekly Sunday afternoon show appealed to viewers interested in dance, theater, pop science, music, and art. So, it was only natural that when the network revived the show in 1981, a feature on the Trojan Marching Band would be perfect, sharing the hour with other stories about David Bowie, Larry Hagman, Don Meredith, and Bea Arthur. And it was indeed a great segment. Unfortunately, the show itself went head-to-head with *60 Minutes* and didn't last very long. However, an entity that has stood the test of time is Disneyland, and the USC Trojan Marching Band played a key role in its *30th Anniversary Celebration Television Special* that aired (live-to-tape) on NBC on February 18, 1985. Of course, at this point, Dr. Bartner felt quite at home in the Magic Kingdom, with his work with the All-American College Bands, but this performance was for the Spirit of Troy. The two-hour broadcast hosted by John Forsythe and a ten-year-old Drew Barrymore. The show carried viewers from superstar to superstar all throughout the theme park, including David Hasselhoff, who rode his tricked-out car, KITT, to Tomorrowland; Marie Osmond, who sang at Sleeping Beauty Castle; Julie Andrews, who performed "When You Wish Upon a Star" in Fantasyland; and many other celebrities of the era. The all-star cast of performances culminated with the USC drum major leading the Trojan Marching Band in a parade down Main Street. Minnie Mouse and company followed the procession until the band split to line both sides of the crowded street to make way for a gigantic birthday "cake big enough for the whole USA" with Mickey Mouse waving from atop. As one would expect, fireworks filled the skies for the finale. Dr. Bartner was proud and happy with the television special that created lasting memories for the band members, the live audience, and television viewers, young and old alike. It was a historic event, after all! The program also earned a nomination for a Primetime Emmy Award for the USC band's music arranger. As one of four principal arrangers for the production, Tony Fox was nominated for Outstanding Music Direction. Once again, it was evident that Dr. Bartner and the USC ensemble had something magical happening as it developed its reputation as Hollywood's Band.

The Disney performance was significant because it demonstrated how the band's small parts in obscure movies were turning into bigger appearances in more popular shows and larger events. The roles evolved from marching into a drug store to celebrate a young man's purchase of health protection items in *Amazon Women on the Moon* to trampling a criminal mastermind who was already hit by a bus and flattened by a steamroller in the slapstick comedy *Naked Gun: From the Files of Police Squad.* Hank Ehrlich (affectionately called "Uncle Hank" by band members) invited Dr. Bartner and the band for a private screening of the Leslie Nielson movie at Paramount Studios in December of 1988. Band members went wild when the ensemble came on screen for ten seconds. (Rumor has it that when it played in the Westwood movie theaters, UCLA fans booed the band.) A few months before that, the world-renowned band, Kansas, had the TMB arrive on set as they were recording their music video for the song "Can't Cry Anymore," which did alright on the charts but was never as big a hit as "Tusk." Next thing Dr. Bartner knew, the Trojan Marching Band was asked to march on stage playing the theme for *America's Funniest Home Videos* on their finale $100,000 award show, and then to be part of a two-minute party scene welcoming a new named partner on *L.A. Law,* and then help Neil Patrick Harris invite Wanda to the prom in *Doogie Howser, M.D.* One of the big bass drums had a blue "WANDA" decal on it, and as the drummer turned sideways, other band members held up a matching banner saying "Go to the prom," and then a tuba player spun around with a "Please" cover over its bell. The band even had a speaking part, shouting "Wild Thing" when Wanda accepted. Aside from the six-minute Disney special finale, these TV show roles were the band's longest screen time performances yet! Meeting celebrities and taking photos with them on a movie set or in a television studio is not something any other college band got to do. Granted, the actual taping of the shows was a lot of what band members laughingly call "hurry-up-and-wait!" That is, it could take many hours of standing around just to capture the few moments required for the show, but Dr. Bartner encouraged them to do homework while waiting on the set. Then, when the recording was done, and the performance went public a few months later, band members would gather and have a watch party to view their time in Hollywood's Band captured on film forever.

## Ceremonial Scenes

Dr. Bartner loved seeing band members unite with a purpose and perform with heart and spirit to entertain famous people in venues that would never have crossed his mind, until he got a call to have the Spirit of Troy attend. Of course, it made sense to play fight songs on the USC campus when in 1976 President Gerald Ford campaigned for reelection from the steps of Doheny Library before a crowd demonstrating mixed opinions. But it was another thing entirely to receive an invitation four years later to be part of a red carpet ceremony for President-elect Ronald Reagan. Los Angeles Mayor Tom Bradley and the city council declared January 13, 1981 to be "Ronald Reagan Day." He hosted a farewell event for the former actor to offer good luck wishes as Reagan and his wife departed for his inauguration and life at the White House. Some eighty mayors from the cities in Los Angeles County, plus two hundred seventy other government officials were invited to the ninety-minute program at city hall to celebrate Reagan as the first L.A. area resident to be elected to the nation's highest office. It was ironically fitting that the former Hollywood actor be treated to a performance by Hollywood's Band.

While his farewell party was a big deal, Reagan's welcome home after eight years in office turned out to be an even bigger one—at least for the Trojan Marching Band. Air Force One brought the president and First Lady Nancy home to Los Angeles, and as the plane taxied to its parking space on the LAX tarmac, the USC Trojan Marching Band could be heard entertaining the waiting crowd. The aircraft door opened and when the Reagans stepped out to the stairs, they were greeted by a loud assemblage of supporters, including dozens of young students in "Just Say No" green shirts. (The anti-drug message was one of Nancy Reagan's platforms while at the White House.) Filling bleachers off to the retiring president's left was the TMB. Reagan gave a short speech, reminding the audience that he wasn't done campaigning on the "mashed potato circuit" because he still had things to do that didn't get done in office. Suddenly, cheers from the bleachers got his attention and his staffer said, "What? You want to give me a helmet?" More cheers in the affirmative, and then a cardinal feather plume flew about ten feet from the stands to the platform setup in front of the president's plane. The staffer caught it, pretended to put it on, and then handed it to Mr. Reagan. Newspaper photographers captured the image of President Ronald Reagan waving while wearing a Trojan helmet and a broad smile—an image that made the newswires and was printed around the country. The retired Commander in Chief autographed a photo and sent it "To members of the USC Trojan Marching Band - With appreciation and admiration, Ronald Reagan." That helmet sits on permanent display at the Reagan Presidential Library in Simi Valley, California. Reagan may not have worn the helmet again, but he did have Hollywood's Band perform a few years later at his star-studded 80th birthday celebration at the Beverly Hilton in 1991. Nearly a thousand guests attended the black-tie affair to honor only the second U.S. president to reach his octogenarian (Harry Truman was the other). The dinner and roast raised two million dollars to support his presidential library.

Speaking of presidential libraries, the TMB was on hand for the dedication of another one a year earlier: President Richard Nixon's. His privately funded twenty-five-million-dollar complex was dedicated on July 19, 1990 in his birthplace of Yorba Linda, California. Dr. Bartner and the band stood on bleachers stage right and paid tribute as each of four presidents and first ladies were presented to the fifty thousand spectators. Trojan Trumpets blared the University of Michigan fight song "The Victors" as the 38th President Gerald Ford and First Lady Betty were announced. (Michigan is Ford's alma mater—and Dr. Bartner's!) Then, when the 40th President Ronald Reagan and First Lady Nancy came to stage, the band played "The Victory March," Notre Dame's fight song, reminiscent for Nancy as her childhood home was in Chicago. As the 37th President Richard Nixon and First Lady Pat took the platform, of course the Trojans played "Fight On!" since Pat was a USC alum. And finally, Trojan Band members craned their necks to try to see then-current President George Bush and First Lady Barbara as they were presented to the stage with the U.S. Marine Band playing "Hail to the Chief." Dr. Bartner recalled it being such an incredible honor to play in the presence of four living U.S. presidents at one time. Even the Eisenhower administration was represented by his grandson, David, who had married Nixon's daughter, Julie. Former President Jimmy Carter and First Lady Rosalynn were the only living executives unable to attend due to a prior commitment. The Spirit of Troy stood by while Reverend Billy Graham gave the convocation that opened the two-and-a-half-hour ceremony full of presidential speeches before it concluded with thousands of red, white, and blue balloons filling the sky to the sound of Vikki Carr singing "God Bless America." "It's one of those thrilling things you never forget," said Dr. Bartner. "What a privilege to be able to give the students an experience like that." This prestigious presidential performance was after they'd already played at ceremonies for high-level clergy.

Among the international delegations that made good will tours to the United States in the 1980s was the pontiff, Pope John Paul II. As the first non-Italian to become Pope in more than four hundred years, his world tours attracted people by the thousands. In 1987, he traveled across America to hold mass in seven cities, including Los Angeles. On September 15, His Holiness filled the Los Angeles Memorial Coliseum, and on Wednesday, September 16, a record-setting crowd of sixty-three thousand people filled Dodger Stadium to hear him present mass. Not even a World Series baseball game filled Dodger Stadium like that. Before the Polish Pope's arrival by helicopter, the Church of Los Angeles held a ninety-minute "pageant" that was emceed by Ricardo Montalbán. The pre-liturgy celebration began with a papal fanfare, played by musicians and Silks from the Trojan Marching Band, billed as the "University of Southern

California Herald Trumpets, Tympani and Flag Unit." Rather than traditional Trojan garb, the band wore white robes bearing the Pope's coat of arms. While thrilling, it was also one of the more solemn, dignified performances the Spirit of Troy has ever done.

## Playing on the Set

Anytime a celebrity TV show wanted a display of pomp and circumstance for any reason, they knew who to call: Hollywood's Band! Talk show and variety show hosts like Arsenio Hall, Leeza Gibbons, Rosie O'Donnell, Donny and Marie, Wayne Brady, Tyra Banks, Joan and Melissa Rivers, Queen Latifah, Dr. Phil, and even Ellen DeGeneres all requested the Trojan Marching Band perform during their show. Dr. Bartner remembers when the band was in the peanut gallery on the *Arsenio Hall* show. "We had a thing going back and forth the entire show, because Arsenio was cracking jokes with the band the whole episode," said Dr. Bartner. Then members of the band played a few tunes on stage with Cheech and Chong.

It doesn't matter the time of day, because the band will always play, as it has for *The Talk, Extra, Good Day LA,* and even *Good Morning America*. On the late-night spectrum, the TMB performed on set with Carson Daly, Conan O'Brien, Jay Leno, James Corden, and Jimmy Fallon. "Fallon did a bit with the audience where he'd have them fill out a card with an answer to a question," said Dr. Bartner. "And that night he asked, 'What's your favorite thing in Los Angeles?' and someone answered the USC drumline—and that was the cue for the drummers to come out!" Snare percussionists traded cadences with the Tonight Show Band, much to the audience's delight!

The popularity of talent competition shows grew over the decades, and Hollywood's Band was part of that trend as well, with invitations to perform on *American Idol, America's Got Talent, America's Next Top Model, The Voice,* and Dr. Bartner's favorite: *Dancing with the Stars*. In full uniform, the band stood at attention outside the studio, and with a live introduction, the drum major led the band through flashing cardinal and gold spotlights to a dance floor where they crisscrossed their way to the elevated stage. Once in position, Hollywood's Band hit it with "Get Down Tonight" for a group of break-dancers to spin on their heads and leap over one another. "It was awesome, because we got tremendous viewership on that popular show."

Not to be forgotten are the comedy shows like *Last Comic Standing, Hilarity for Charity* with Seth Rogen, and *Carpool Karaoke* with James Corden and guest star Will Smith. In the latter, the comedians cruised through L.A. singing Smith's song "Gettin' Jiggy Wit It." Then Corden halted the car and quit singing, to Smith's dismay. Corden explained he was experimenting with a new type of surround sound, rolled down the window, and said, "Hey Fellas!" Next thing Smith knew, about a hundred members of Hollywood's Band surrounded the car, and Smith and Corden popped up through the sunroof to sing while the BAND got jiggy with it. That performance was one of the most popular episodes of the show, with more than twenty-four million views on YouTube.

The TMB has even serenaded game show winners for *Hollywood Square* and *Jeopardy!* Alex Trebek flaunted a Trojan helmet during that Jeopardy college championship series. Of course, with the football team connection, the Trojan Marching Bad made multiple appearances on sports TV shows including *Rock N' Jock Diamond Derby, The Best Damn Sports Show-Period* (hosted for a time by USC QB Rodney Peete), *SportsCenter, College Football Live, College Football Now,* and *Sports Illustrated Swimsuit Edition* for television.

Bestowing accolades on celebrities is one more way the TMB received airtime. Hollywood's Band made its first award show performance for the 48th Annual Academy Awards, where Dr. Bartner met famous composer John Williams—a connection that would lead to future Hollywood opportunities. Paramount hosted the 1976 Oscar ceremonies, and Bartner's friend from the studio, Hank Ehrlich, was instrumental in securing the band's invitation from the show's producer, Howard Koch. The March 29 finale performance almost didn't happen, though, because it was the one time in Dr. Bartner's career that he misjudged the timing of the show. He thought he had more time to get the four miles from rehearsal on campus to the Dorothy Chandler Pavilion in downtown Los Angeles. "The kids literally had to run from the buses to their positions," recalled Dr. Bartner. "But we got there in time, and it all worked out. And I was less than five yards from Jack Nicholson, who won the Oscar for Best Supporting Actor in *One Flew Over the Cuckoo's Nest.*" What Dr. Bartner remembers most, though, is that Elizabeth Taylor and Gene Kelly introduced the band to play "America the Beautiful" in honor of the nation's bicentennial. "I think this performance really established us as Hollywood's Band, because the Academy Awards is the biggest night for Hollywood."

Since that time, the Trojan Marching Band has appeared on two more Academy Award Shows, including 2009 when the band wore tuxedos and top hats while playing Broadway classics on stage with Hugh Jackman, Beyonce, Zac Efron, and other stars. Brad Pitt and Angelina Jolie leaned forward to tell band members, "Great show!" Later came two Grammy Award Shows, the BET (Black Entertainment Television) Awards, the Kids' Choice Awards, the American Film Institute Life Achievement Awards, the ESPY Awards, and the CBS Sports Courage in Sports Awards. Hollywood's Band has continued to play on the sets of popular television shows like *Scrubs, How I Met Your Mother, Hell's Kitchen, KC Undercover,* and *Glee* (as McKinley High School Marching Band.) As for major motion pictures, the TMB played the Alabama Marching Band in *Forrest Gump* with Tom Hanks and the Texas Longhorn Band in *When Billie Beat Bobby.* They also had a small role in the remake of *The Little Rascals* and later a much larger role in *The Last Boy Scout* with Bruce Willis. "*The Last Boy Scout* was a really amazing gig," said Dr. Bartner, "because it was filmed in the Coliseum like a real football game, with the Trojan Marching Band in the stands." Hollywood's Band has also contributed to multiple movie soundtracks including *The Sixth Man, Boys and Girls, The Longest Yard,* and the band recorded the heart-racing opening scene music for the movie *Croods*. All these appearances may seem like a lot, but in reality, it is by no means an exhaustive list—only the highlights of a very impressive catalog of credits.

## Star of the Show

The Spirit of Troy may have been running around Hollywood like it owned the city, but the Trojan Marching Band certainly did not get paid like a celebrity. To the contrary, many of the special events the band did were simply voluntary, meaning, they didn't get paid to perform. Even when they did, Dr. Bartner didn't get to keep all the funds for his program. The budget for the band was held in the School of Music, and a portion of any contribution or payment to the band would go to the department.

Removing those funds from an already essentially non-existent band budget (a whopping five thousand dollars per year) made it arduous for Dr. Bartner to manage everything required to run a thriving, expanding program. Through his first decade as band director, Dr. Bartner had seen some serious success, from Diana Ross to Fleetwood Mac and everything in between. The Trojan Marching Band was bringing sensational visibility and stardom to the University of Southern California, certainly on par with the attention the football team brought by winning championships and Rose Bowls. Besides, wherever the team was, the band was also. (And not just the football team, by the way!) Dr. Bartner had developed the band in numbers, in quality and quantity of performances, and in the respect, pride, and tradition befitting of a prestigious university like USC. If this progression was going to continue, Dr. Bartner needed more staff and financial support. That fortification finally came with the transition of the university executive administration.

USC's eighth president, John R. Hubbard, retired at the end of 1980 at the culmination of the university's centennial celebrations (1880-1980). Inaugurated on May 10, 1981 as the new president was James H. Zumberge, even though he had officially taken over the post nine months earlier. He took his time rebuilding his executive staff, bringing in professionals from outside the university, with the goal of stimulating fresh thinking and new ideas. He also reduced the number of senior vice presidents from nine to three. One of the three was a vice provost and chemical engineering professor from Cal-tech in Pasadena, Cornelius (Neil) Pings, and he joined the Trojan family as provost and senior vice president for academic affairs. He would oversee the College of Letters, Arts and Sciences, the administration of all academic programs and research at all levels graduate and undergraduate, as well as all student affairs. With the reorganization of the administration, Dr. Bartner saw his opportunity and took it.

"I went to Neil Pings and made my case," said Dr. Bartner. "Every year, the team would go to either the Cal or Stanford game, and I'd have to go to the provost and beg for money for the band to go, too. We didn't have money for band camp. We didn't have money for a band awards banquet. We didn't have money for uniforms. We didn't have money for anything. And whatever money we did get, we had to give part of it to the music school." Pings listened, and he heard Dr. Bartner. The provost moved the band budget out of the music school and into his student affairs office, and he gave the band a budget of one hundred fifty thousand dollars. "This was HUGE. This was CRUCIAL. He basically saved the Trojan Marching Band." The funding would allow Dr. Bartner to cover travel expenses to Northern California games, the costs for an annual awards banquet to honor his students, and most importantly, it would pay for the investment in the students at band camp, the essential training week for the Spirit of Troy. "Pings made an enormous contribution to the Trojan Marching Band, and I'm forever grateful for that. My wife, Barbara, and I became great friends with Neil and his wife, Margery, during his time at USC." Dr. Bartner said Pings was the only administrator to ever come to one of the TMB's end-of-the-season banquets. When he was invited to speak, he came to the front of the room, reached into his tuxedo pocket, pulled out a pair of sunglasses, and put them on. "The band went hysterical. And from that moment on, he OWNED the Trojan Marching Band," Bartner remembered. "Pings was a riot, tongue-in-cheek, making fun of the band, and at the same time, making sure they represented the university in its highest values. It wasn't a lecture, but his points were well made in such a clever way." Thanks to his provision and foresight, Provost Cornelius Pings paved the way for the Spirit of Troy to march on solid ground as it became the most respected and visible college marching band in the country.

## High Note: Be Connected

Dr. Bartner and band members were having their pictures taken with all sorts of celebrities before selfies were even a thing! It seemed every time he turned around, another amazing opportunity was offered for Hollywood's Band to perform—whether it was a fancy affair for high level dignitaries or a guest appearance on a late night, early morning, comedy, reality, sports, awards, or game show—or movie! Regular repeated requests like that don't happen by accident or by reputation alone. ***To attain ever greater levels of excellence, develop sincere relationships with connections who share a mutual interest for mutual benefit. The most successful partnerships are win-win.*** The connections and networking within the Trojan band family last a lifetime. Beyond generating synergy with Hollywood entertainment producers like Uncle Hank, Dr. Bartner also sought to expand the band's level of support on campus. He put it all out on the table with the new university administrator, Neil Pings, explaining the collective interests for the band, the team, and the university. The cooperative, symbiotic relationships contributed to elevating the status of them all—with the added bonus of building lifelong friendships as well. *Be connected.*

# Dr. Arthur C. Bartner and Hollywood's Band Through the Decades

In his youth, Art Bartner was passionate about two things: basketball and trumpet. He earned a place on the all-star basketball team and all-state band.
*Courtesy: Dr. Arthur C. Bartner*

Top: Art Bartner with his brother and sister, circa 1950.

Middle left: Art and soon-to-be-wife Barbara.

Middle right: Arthur's prom picture from the late 1950's.

Left: Art with his son and daughter, Steven and Debbie, in the 1960's.

*Courtesy: Dr. Arthur C. Bartner*

Arthur Bartner of 452 Richmond avenue, Maplewood, sho above right, and Gary Kocher, drum major, are members of University of Michigan Marching Band.

Realizing that college basketball was not going to work out for him, Art played trumpet in the University of Michigan Marching Band while earning his degree and his master's in education, late 1950s.

Mr. Bartner's first teaching job was at North Adams High School in Ann Arbor, Michigan, 1960s.

**Bandsmen March To New Master**

A [illegible] of sophomores on Coach John McKay's USC football team won't be the only rookies making their first appearance before a Coliseum crowd tonight.

A new director of the Trojan Marching Band will make his debut tonight, too. He's Arthur C. Bartner, a 30-year-old graduate of the University of Michigan.

Bartner specializes in arranging music for marching bands and writing original shows that combine pageantry and instrumental features with precision drills and dance routines. He was a member of the highly touted Michigan marching, symphonic, varsity and jazz bands.

*Arthur Bartner*

For the past five years Bartner has been director of bands at Davison High School near Flint, Mich. Last year his musicians were one of the top-rated bands in the state and appeared on nationwide television during the half-time show at a Detroit Lions football game.

Bartner will also assist the conductor of the USC Wind Orchestra and serve as a visiting professor of music and music education in the School of Music and School of Performing Arts. He teaches trumpet, music theory, history and education. He was selected as the outstanding educator in the Davison school system for 1968-69.

Photo of the student newspaper announcing the arrival of the new director for the Trojan Marching Band, 1970.

*Courtesy: Dr. Arthur C. Bartner*

Dr. Bartner with his children and TMB drummer Bill Dutton on the set of *Mitzi & 100 Guys*, 1975.
*Courtesy: Dr. Arthur C. Bartner*

John Wayne with members of the TMB who taped a promotion for *Super Night at the Super Bowl*, 1977.
*Courtesy: Jeannine Zakaryan*

Left: Members of the Trojan Marching Band at Dodger Stadium while recording "Tusk" with Fleetwood Mac, 1979.
*Courtesy: Scott Steele*

Bottom Left: Dr. Bartner and Mick Fleetwood and members of the Trojan Marching Band cheer after a gig, circa 1991.
*Courtesy: Jennifer Sorgatz*

Above: Jock rallies moved from the basement locker room to the practice field to behind Heritage Hall, 2016. Below: Dr. Bartner and the band emerge from the Coliseum tunnel to the field to play for the team during warm-ups, 2019. *Courtesy: Benjamin Chua*

Top: As it has periodically throughout five decades, the Trojan Marching Band descends the peristyle steps of the Los Angeles Coliseum, 2014.
*Courtesy: Benjamin Chua*

Middle: The TMB spells out "Trojans" as they play "Conquest" during preshow, 2019.
*Courtesy: Ling Luo*

Bottom: The Trojan white stallion mascot, Traveler, gallops around the field at home games after the USC team makes a touchdown, 2019.
*Courtesy: Ling Luo*

Left: Band members became costume designers for this halftime show rendition of the new box office hit movie *Star Wars*, 1977.
*Courtesy: Jeannine Zakaryan*

Right: Trojan band members place their instruments on the field to perform a crowd favorite dance routine, 2019.
*Courtesy: Benjamin Chua*

Middle: The TMB creates a multitude of different formations in each show, and most shows are new each week. Here, the band takes shape as a rocket complete with rocket boosters, 2019.
*Courtesy: Ling Luo*

Bottom: After a winning game, USC Quarterback Sam Darnold ascends the ladder and wields the sword as part of the band's postgame performance, 2016.
*Courtesy: Benjamin Chua*

The note that former President Ronald Reagan sent to the Trojan Marching Band with the photo of him wearing a band helmet at the Los Angeles Airport tarmac on January 20, 1989.
*Courtesy: Cheryl Cox*

TMB members marched through the desert (sand dunes near Pismo Beach, California) for the filming of *The Gong Show Movie*, 1979.
*Courtesy: Scott Steele*

Below: Trojan band members dressed in Alabama uniforms watch and wait to perform as camera crews prepare the set during the making of *Forrest Gump*, 1994.
*Courtesy David Dibble*

Top right: Evidence of the growing bond between the band and the team after USC beat Notre Dame on their Irish home turf, 1979.
*Courtesy: Scott Steele*

Lower right: Without space in the stands, the band fills the sidelines at a Notre Dame matchup, 2007.
*Courtesy: Benjamin Chua*

Top left: The TMB makes an annual trip to the Bay Area for matchups against either Cal or Stanford. The band plays the stage while Dr. Bartner pumps up the crowd of fans filling San Francisco's Union Square the evening before a USC football game, 2014.
*Courtesy: Benjamin Chua*

Lower left: Dr. Bartner fulfills a lifelong dream to conduct on Broadway in Times Square, New York City in advance of the USC-Syracuse game, 2012.
*Courtesy: Benjamin Chua*

Right: Goux's Gate is the walkway to the USC football team practice field, named in honor of Coach Marv Goux.
*Courtesy: Tylar Hedrick*

Middle left: Former USC Head Coach Pete Carroll brings the Trojan team to the Trojan band after beating Notre Dame, 2005.
*Courtesy: Benjamin Chua*

Middle center: Former Trojan football player and USC Athletic Director Lynn Swann receives the honor of being the first recipient of a drum major sword during halftime, 2016. *Courtesy: Benjamin Chua*

Middle right above: Former Head Coach Clay Helton and Dr. Bartner greet after a game, 2019.
*Courtesy: Ling Luo*

Left: Jake Olson first climbed the ladder with his twin sister as a fan in 2008 before losing his sight. Then in 2015, he made a second trip up the ladder, now as a member of the Trojan team and college football's first blind player.
*Courtesy: Benjamin Chua*

Dr. Bartner directs the Olympic All-American College Band for Opening Ceremonies of the 1984 Olympics at the Los Angeles Coliseum. Some eight hundred members fill the field, culminating in the outline of the shape of the host nation, the United States of America.
*Courtesy: Tim Seno*

Left: Dr. Bartner wanted a picture of the whole band after performing at the Grand Place in Brussels, Belgium, 1990. (The author is pictured standing in the center behind the twirler, just to the right of the light post. Also, below at the Berlin Wall.)
*Courtesy: Christy Stansell*

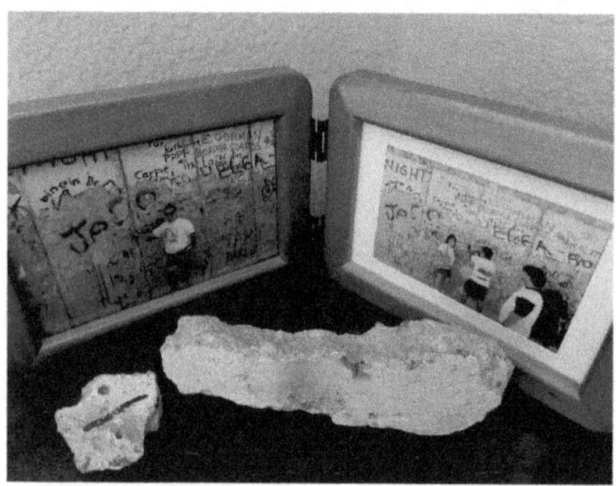

Above: Pieces of the Berlin Wall on display after they were chiseled from Checkpoint Charlie crossing.
*Courtesy: Cheryl Cox*

Right: The TMB performs in West Berlin in front of the modern portion of the Kaiser Wilhelm Memorial Church.
*Courtesy: Christy Stansell*

Top left: Paris, 1994
*Courtesy: Cheryl Cox*

Top right: Madrid, 1994
*Courtesy: Dr. Arthur C. Bartner*

Left: Normandy, 1994
*Courtesy: David Dibble*

Lower left: Blarney Castle, 2018
*Courtesy: Benjamin Chua*

Lower right: London, 2012
*Courtesy: Benjamin Chua*

Above left: Dr. Bartner calls the tunes during a baseball game at Dodger Stadium, circa 1975.
*Courtesy: Jeannine Zakaryan*

Above: As director of the All-American College Band at Disneyland in California since 1977, Bartner leads musicians from venue to venue, circa 1997.
*Courtesy: Cheryl Cox*

Right: The Trojan Marching Band marches the Tournament of Roses Parade in Pasadena, California, 2017.
*Courtesy: Benjamin Chua*

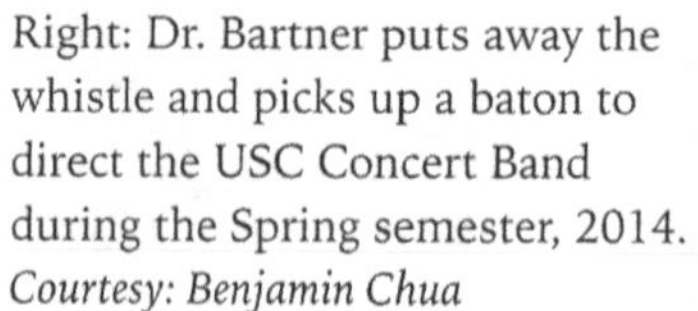

Right: Dr. Bartner puts away the whistle and picks up a baton to direct the USC Concert Band during the Spring semester, 2014.
*Courtesy: Benjamin Chua*

Above: Dr. Bartner dives in for Swim With Mike, circa 1990.
*Courtesy: Cheryl Cox*

Above right: TMB on Catalina Island for Fourth of July, 2007.
*Courtesy: Benjamin Chua*

Right: The band plays at the wedding of TMB alumna Ashley (Kuhnert) Hatcher, 2015.
*Courtesy: Rhonda Rogers*

Below left: Former USC Head Coach John Robinson, his wife Beverly, and Barbara Bartner join in honoring Dr. Bartner at his induction to the USC Hal of Fame, 2012. *Courtesy: Jeannine Zakaryan*

Below right: The band's former assistant director and music arranger Tony Fox and his wife Nolcha join the Bartners, as well. *Courtesy: Benjamin Chua*

Above right: Dr. Bartner walked the commencement procession to receive his honorary Doctor of Music from the University of Southern California, 2019.
*Courtesy: Benjamin Chua*

Above left: USC alumni and TMB supporters Steve and Rosemarie Johnson join Dr. and Barbara Bartner for the grand opening of the Dr. Arthur C. Bartner Band Pavilion on the USC campus, 2018.
*Courtesy: Benjamin Chua*

Left: The TMB elected its first ever woman drum major the year of Dr. Bartner's retirement, 2019. *Courtesy: Ling Luo*

Left: Flowers after his Final Curtain spring concert are the least anyone could do for Barbara Bartner for her decades of support of Dr. Bartner and the Trojan Marching Band.
*Courtesy: Benjamin Chua*

# 10

# ON THE ROAD AGAIN

*Dr. Arthur C. Bartner engages the fans at Navy Pier in Chicago during a rally in advance of the Notre Dame game, 2015.*
Courtesy: Benjamin Chua

# CHAPTER TEN

## ON THE ROAD AGAIN

Traveling across town to a movie set is one thing. Loading up a bus or flying across country for an athletic event is another. The Trojan Marching Band has not missed a single USC football game since 1987. In a conversation with Dr. Bartner, then-head football coach Larry Smith made a special request to have the twelfth man on the field at EVERY game, home and away—including Notre Dame in South Bend, Indiana every other year. By the time Dr. Bartner retired, he had a streak of more than four hundred football matchups and nearly six hundred gridiron games altogether in his full USC career. That included thirty-six bowl appearances, about half of which were of the Rose variety. In fact, during his fifty-years directing the TMB, there were only a dozen where the Trojan football team did not earn a bowl game berth. Wherever or whenever the team played, coordinating as many as three hundred musicians for travel is a challenge, logistically, financially, and mentally. Anyone's patience would be tested when traveling with a group of young people of varying maturity levels. Even so, it was well worth it to Dr. Bartner to provide his students with so many memorable experiences, especially road trips.

### Bus Business

As the band numbered between two hundred fifty and three hundred band members, long distance travel was complicated at best and clearly not something Dr. Bartner could coordinate on his own. At least now there was a little less stress, because with Pings' budget increase and the fundraising efforts getting better and better results, he could more easily afford the trips. Dr. Bartner incorporated his philosophy of student leadership to help organize the travel information for the monstrous group. The band director is only one man with two eyes, so the band hierarchy became very important. Section leaders each took responsibility for the members of their own section, from the planning phase until they got home. They are expected to set the example of Trojan Spirit and behavior. By the 1980s, Dr. Bartner finally had a few more teaching assistants who could synchronize arrangements among section leaders and the band manager, including bus reservations, departure times, roommates for hotel stays, meals, snacks, water—oh, and all the equipment and uniforms. He invited students who wanted to be part of the band but not play an instrument to serve as a prop crew to help take care of extraneous but important things, like his ladder. Eventually, Dr. Bartner was able to hire an operations manager to handle the coordination efforts, which made travel planning much easier. Regardless, the leadership would still have additional staff meetings beyond the regular practices, so they had to be very detail-oriented and devoted to their jobs. Dr. Bartner believed in developing the students' leadership qualities with this level of management duties, while also realizing that the trips were ultimately his own responsibility. The chain of command always ended with him, so the more planning and preparation together, the better.

Participating in away games required strategizing, even if it wasn't always the full band going. Besides the biennial Notre Dame game for the full band, each class would get their own special road trip, depending on the football schedule that year.

Some years, seniors would get to go to Oklahoma, Texas, or maybe Hawaii or New York City—they would collectively get first choice of destinations. Juniors would get to go to the game the seniors didn't want, like Washington or maybe Utah, sophomores to Arizona or Oregon, and freshmen would join the rest of the band for the San Francisco weekender, when USC played either Stanford or Cal. That game alternates each year, and it's a trip the entire band—and Trojans everywhere—look forward to all year.

Occasionally, USC played a Friday night game to accommodate television coverage, but they typically played on Saturday. Kickoff time varied, too, depending on what slot worked best for the network broadcasting the contest—and that's determined by the rankings of the football teams. The least favorable time is the 7:30 p.m. Pacific slot, because the late games are, well, very late. Dr. Bartner would rather have 12:30 p.m. Pacific kickoff. But the best is when the team is winning and at the top of the polls to get the primetime slot of 5 p.m. Pacific/8 p.m. Eastern. No matter what time the Bay Area game started, when headed for an away game, the band hit the road early Friday morning. Students loved having a viable excuse to miss class, as it would take the entire day to ride up the length of the state. Band members arrived on campus with all their gear to load up onto one of half a dozen buses, or maybe seven when the Song Girls and spirit squads traveled with the band. Each motorcoach (the fancy term for buses that had televisions above the seats) could carry a section or two. Which musical instrument groups got paired up depended on the size of their section that year. Sometimes tubas and Silks shared, and another bus for flutes and clarinets. But they learned early on, never, ever put alto sax and tenor sax on the same coach, because they have a bit of a rivalry. Same with trumpets and trombones—that's a no-go. Besides, the trumpet section was often big enough to fill its own bus. So was percussion. For many years, Dr. Bartner also provided a "study bus" so that studious students could get some homework done on the road. Some scholars would even take proctored exams to fulfill class requirements, if necessary. A few minutes before departure, Dr. Bartner would hop aboard each bus, one at a time, for a quick pep talk and reminder to behave, and then he'd saunter back to the study bus, where he could enjoy the requirement of peace and quiet for the eight-hour trek up I-5 through central California. (Although in later years, he "aged-out" of the bus ride and followed behind the caravan in a private car.)

It was the opposite of peace and quiet on the other buses. Even early in the morning, many band members were exuberant and in the mood to goof off. The extent of the clowning around had to be toned down over the years, as it could easily get out of hand, something Dr. Bartner trusted the section leaders to handle and enforce the rules in the student handbook that each member was required to read and sign at the beginning of the season. Each section had their own set of road trip traditions, like serenading the bus driver to make them feel welcome in the Trojan family or taking turns singing fight songs while holding the chair at the front of the bus. (That's not actually holding *a chair* on the bus. Remember, it's the phrase for standing with one leg held in marching position, in the shape of a chair.) The band members made it fun, even coordinating clever trip themes, complete with costumes and/or specially designed game-specific t-shirts. A few hours into the drive, band members would settle down in their seats to snack and chat with their friends, at least until they started to get antsy. Before long, they needed to stretch and eat lunch. The buses would descend upon the

Buttonwillow rest stop, where other unsuspecting travelers would hurry up and get back in their cars to leave when they saw hundreds of students getting off multiple buses. Some guys would toss around a football across the parking lot while others would play hacky sack. Using the restroom—even a rest stop restroom—in a building instead of the back of a co-ed bus was always a good idea for the ladies in the band. After about an hour of fresh air and limbs in free motion, it was time to reboard the buses for the rest of the journey to the Bay Area.

## Time to Rally

Finally, the buses rolled up to the hotel by late afternoon, just in time for the band to quickly check into their rooms, grab and eat a band-provided sack of food, then put on their uniforms, because it was time to rally! No rest for the road-weary, Dr. Bartner and the Trojan Marching Band got back on the buses to head to Union Square for an enormous pep rally. This half-hour-or-so performance was one of Dr. Bartner's very favorites, because he emceed it in front of a massive, fired-up crowd that filled the entire square. Standing at attention on steps above an audience awash with cardinal and gold spirit gear, the Trojan Marching Band ignited passion with a chill-bump raising, powerful blaring of "Tribute to Troy." With Silks swirling on the steps stage right, tubas bellowing from the back, and USC Song Girls leaping front and center in front of the drummers, onlookers responded with shouts of "Fight on!" and victory fingers held high. Then, the band got down to business, playing rock chart after rock chart. With his showmanship expertise, Dr. Bartner called the shots, paying attention to the crowd reaction, instinctively knowing what tune to play next. Even with limited space, the solo twirler could toss batons sky high and catch them behind her back or in the middle of a high dance kick. In between numbers, the drumline played cadences to engage the fans with the chant "Beat the Farm!" or "Beat the Bears!"—depending on which Bay Area team was on the schedule that year. For decades, the climax of the rally was a famous cheer led by an alumni Yell Leader (the guy version of Song Girls.) "This is a tradition that's been going on since before I started here in 1970," Bartner said in front of the cheering crowd. "And to prove it, I'm going to bring out a guy who is older than I am!" Bartner ribbed the guest with a playful grin as the audience laughed in disbelief. "He was one of the great Yell Leaders of all time and the executive producer of the hit show *Cagney and Lacey*. He leads the best SoCal Spell-out in the history of SoCal Spell-outs. Welcome to the stage, Barney Rosenzweig!" The award-winning television producer bounded on stage to say a few words rousing words about the Trojan's opponents and then led the cheer: "S! O! U! T! H-E-R-N! C! A! L! I! F-O-R-N-I-A! Southern! Califooooooooornia!" With thunderous applause, surrounded by luxury retail storefronts of Saks Fifth Avenue, Tiffany & Co., Bloomingdale's, Louis Vuitton, and others, the Spirit of Troy put a figurative sword in the ground, claiming San Francisco for its own. The next day, before kickoff, the Trojan Marching Band drum major would lead the band onto the opponent's turf, and literally stab the football field for GAME DAY!

It was a similar scene in most cities where the band followed the team for a game. It's especially impressive in Chicago for the Notre Dame game when the full three-hundred-plus band performs a pep rally on Navy Pier with blue waters of Lake Michigan in the background—a sight and sound enjoyed by several thousand people who attend that assembly. Sometimes the rally would be in a hotel ballroom and the walls would vibrate from the intense volume of the horns and drums. The audience could feel the pounding in their chest, louder and stronger than their own heartbeat. That is the kind of performance Dr. Bartner thrives on—all in the name of building the spirit and pride of the Trojan Family, no matter where the band goes.

## Traveling Band

The first time Dr. Bartner took the band anywhere of significant distance was the 1973 Notre Dame game, thanks to the idea suggested by his core group of students and the generosity of his friend, Ken Cotler, who hosted the fundraisers to help pay for the ensemble's trip to South Bend. The band used up its bank account to make that Notre Dame excursion again in October of 1975, and then turned around two months later for an adventure to the Liberty Bowl in Memphis, Tennessee. There's no way that would have been financially possible if it weren't for the payout that the conference gets from the bowl organizers. Anytime a team earns a berth in a bowl game, the event organizers and sponsors compensate the team's conference, which then divvies up the money among the schools in that conference.[1] That payment also covers travel expenses for the winning team, which then directs funds to the band and other spirit squads to be able to attend as well. In the 1970s, that funding was in the hundreds of thousands of dollars, and these days, it is well into the multiple millions. Teams strive to get to the Rose Bowl because it has always had one of the top payouts, but the 1975 Trojan team would not get its fourth consecutive Rose invitation. After going undefeated that season and beating Notre Dame, the

Trojan team lost heart and fell apart, losing four games in a row after coach and athletic director John McKay announced his resignation. He was going pro as head coach of the NFL's first expansion team, the Tampa Bay Buccaneers. So, the Trojans went to the Liberty Bowl instead, where they shut-out Texas A&M 20-0. The Trojans did return to the Rose Bowl for the 1976 season, winning 14-6 against Dr. Bartner's alma mater Michigan, but in 1977, they would make their first and only appearance in the Bluebonnet Bowl. Dr. Bartner took the band to perform at the Astrodome in Houston, Texas, where the Trojans easily won the Texas A&M rematch, 47-28. The next year, it wasn't a bowl game, but a regular season game that took the band to Hawaii for the first time for the 1978 Trojans to beat the Rainbow Warriors. The next few years would see USC go to a couple more Rose Bowls, and also to Arizona, Hawaii, and Florida, to lose the Fiesta, Aloha, and Citrus Bowls. Can't win 'em all—but the conference still gets paid anyway, so it's okay. "Whether the team wins or loses, it's about the experience we give the students," said Dr. Bartner. "We will go anywhere to support the football team, rally the fans, and entertain the crowds. That's why we travel!"

In the middle of all that was the Mirage Bowl. [2]It was not a postseason game, but rather a regular season game played in an irregular place: Tokyo, Japan. This 1985 matchup between the USC Trojans and the Oregon Ducks was the only time that USC has ever played a football game on foreign soil. It was also the first time the TMB traveled internationally. The creator of the game was a Japanese man named Atushi Fujita. He had seen a Rose Bowl on TV while working for a Japanese television station and loved the pageantry of it so much that he decided Japan needed its own bowl game, even though the culture knew little to nothing about how the game is played. He got Mitsubishi to sponsor the event, thus the name of the game being "Mirage," coined after the model of the carmaker's latest vehicle release. Mitsubishi even displayed one on the field near the endzone. The sponsors paid big bucks plus expenses for the teams and bands to make their way to the Orient for the exhibition game held at the Tokyo Dome, home of the 1964 Olympics. During contract negotiations, organizers indicated they would pipe-in Japanese music during the game, to which Dr. Bartner obviously objected. "This should be like any other American football game. This should not be a circus that will interfere with the game." He suggested that if the Japanese really wanted to experience a true football game, the only music in the stadium should be played by the bands. The Spirit of Troy got to do the halftime show, along with the Grambling State University Band, which attended because the Ducks band did not. "The Grambling Band had tremendous showmanship," Dr. Bartner recalled. "It was a great exhibition because we were two bands with very different cultures and styles. It was very entertaining." The Japanese audience of about sixty thousand would learn how the game was played by reading signs telling them when to cheer, with half the stands getting green and yellow pom-poms and the other half getting cardinal and gold. The team, Song Girls, one hundred members of the band, a handful of USC administrators, and about a thousand fans made the eleven-hour flight around the world to view the spectacle. Doing their best to welcome the guests, sponsors kindly provided band members with meal tickets labeled "bleakfarst" (breakfast) and ball caps embroidered with "Torojons" (Trojans). While sightseeing was limited, the hotel accommodations were less than stellar (and in fact were horribly cramped, especially for two-hundred-eighty-pound football players), and the practice field was full of mud and weeds, the Spirit of Troy did what it does best and played the Trojan team to victory. With the Japanese interpreters repeating the English calls on the field, quarterback Rodney Peete led the team to a 20-6 win over the Ducks. In one last demonstration of cordiality, the scoreboard read, "Congraturations USC." (No joke! And no offense. It was the thought that counts.) After spending Thanksgiving weekend in Tokyo, the Trojan delegation was delighted to return home for the rest of the holidays, full of memories from a once-in-a-lifetime junket to Japan. Turns out, that would not be the only international affair to which the Spirit of Troy would be invited.

## High Flying Band

Before going overseas again, the band would get to travel domestically for other events, because remember, wherever the team goes, so goes the band. While a bus is the usual mode of affordable transportation, some events are simply too far, so they get to board a plane. Dr. Bartner's staff worked with travel agents to get the best bulk deals on airfare, usually flying the airline that doesn't charge for baggage—because there's a lot of that! In fact, for West Coast travel, he usually had assistants drive a truck with the equipment, because it saved the budget. But he and the band took to the skies. Back in the day, before air travel became old hat, band members got dressed up for flights. Trumpet players still "fly fancy," but for many young people, times have changed, with flip flops replacing dress shoes and sweatpants replacing slacks. While Dr. Bartner didn't dictate a dress code, he hoped band members dressed as respectfully as possible, while remaining comfortable, because they still represented not only the Trojan Marching Band but the University of Southern California, too. He also expected the students to be on their best behavior and mind their manners. That may sound like an odd request to make of young adults, but some kids learn lessons the hard way, and Dr. Bartner can't be the parent to three hundred students, especially when they're divided among three or four different airplanes. Once again, the section leaders and teaching assistants earned their keep for maintaining decorum in their ranks while still having fun. Speaking of which, before extensive post-9/11 security measures went into effect, there was one Trojan travel tradition that left quite an impression on non-band passengers on the plane. It had to do with a carryon item that each band member brought with them. As the aircraft pulled back from the gate and began to taxi toward the runway, band members got ready, and when the plane was almost aligned and ready to hit the throttle for take-off, the appointed musician would yell "HELMETS ON!" and the entire band strapped on their golden uniform helmet, plumes and all, as the plane launched into the sky. They wore them until the aircraft reached cruising altitude, and then stowed them again for the rest of the flight. It was quite a memorable and amusing sight for the passengers and flight attendants, who would always remember they flew with Hollywood's Band.

Whenever the band went somewhere new, Dr. Bartner made an effort to ensure the students got a chance to do something unique to the location, learn a little bit of culture, or even explore on their own. For example, every other year, when the Trojans played the Irish, the band flew into Chicago and stayed in the city (until in later years it became cost-prohibitive and they'd get suites at a property near the airport.) Regardless, with their scheduled free time, groups of friends grabbed a bite to eat at Chicago's legendary "Gino's East Pizza" and carved their name into the wooden tables, walls, or ceilings. No cause for alarm, though, because the graffiti-type artwork is expected and part of the draw and decor of the restaurant (in addition to the ridiculously cheesy, super saucy, deep-dish, delicious pizza.) While there, the drummers entertained fellow band members and others at the pizza purveyor by playing cadences on their plates and glasses. Afterwards, they'd get to go sightseeing and usually visit the one-hundred-ten story Willis Tower (formerly Sears Tower). Standing 1,451 feet in the air, it was once the tallest tower in the world, but is now twenty-first on the list. (For comparison, in downtown Los Angeles, the former Arco Plaza, now called City National Plaza, is fifty-two stories standing seven hundred feet tall.) Regardless, the tallest building in the windy city still has spectacular views, day or night.

Another tall sight worth seeing almost didn't happen, until Dr. Bartner made an executive decision, a selfless act of which no one in the band ever knew. In 1990, the Trojans were offered a half-a-million-dollar payout with the invitation to play in the College Football Kickoff Classic at Giants Stadium near New York City. The team accepted and the whole band got to go along for the pre-season game. USC Quarterback Todd Marinovich led the team to a 34-16 win over the Syracuse Orangemen. During the visit, Dr. Bartner and the band were on buses, headed to visit the Empire State Building, but "the traffic was SOOOO BAAAAD, bumper to bumper and not moving" that he just let the students out. He wanted students to see some Big Apple sights of their choice, like Grand Central Station, Central Park, the United Nations, Wall Street, and even the World Trade Center twin towers (eleven years and eleven days before the 9/11 tragedy.) At a predetermined time, the band was to meet up back at the buses so they could go to New York City's other most famous landmark, the Statue of Liberty. They were going to take the ferry across to Ellis Island and climb up the narrow, winding staircase through the gown, up to crown, where a small window delivered a majestic view of the harbor and Manhattan skyline. However, upon arrival, Dr. Bartner learned that in order to buy that many tickets, one must be a member of the Statue of Liberty foundation historical society. He could have declined and left a few hundred kids disappointed, but instead, Dr. Bartner pulled out his personal credit card and purchased a (not inexpensive) membership and the tickets for the band to get up close and personal with Lady Liberty. This is just one more example of how Dr. Bartner has always been committed to giving his students a wonderful experience and lifelong memories, no matter how far or near the band had to go to create them.

Another visit to New York City some two decades later afforded Dr. Bartner an opportunity to make one of his own childhood dreams come true, while simultaneously providing an incredible adventure for band members. Art grew up in New Jersey, a mere twenty minutes from New York City (not counting modern day traffic.) As a young teenager, he would take the train, ferry boat, and subway from Maplewood to Manhattan to take private trumpet lessons at Radio City Music Hall. Less than half a mile and around the corner from there was the infamous Times Square, which even in the 1960s was a frenetic hub of lighted signs and bustling activity. The only difference is that back then, cars could still drive down the streets. Beneath the high rises where the ball drops on New Year's Eve is Duffy Square, which is really more like a triangle at the intersection of Broadway and 46th and 47th streets. Nowadays, it is blocked to vehicles and only pedestrians move through the area, which tens of thousands of people do every day. In the square is a low-cost ticket booth that sells seats for Broadway shows. By the booth is a set of bleachers/stairs where visitors sit and rest—and sometimes take in a concert—which is what thousands of people did when Dr. Bartner and the Trojan Marching Band performed there in 2012. Number-2 ranked USC was playing Syracuse on September 8, and of course the band went to support the team. The day before the game, the Spirit of Troy filled the Broadway portion of the Times Square intersection for a rally. This is where Dr. Bartner's childhood vision became reality. "My goal growing up was to conduct an orchestra on Broadway," said Dr. Bartner. "Even though it wasn't on a stage or in an orchestra pit, I GOT TO PERFORM ON BROADWAY! It was a dream come true!" In the glow of flashing video screens and vibrant billboards, with the sounds of sirens blaring down side streets, Dr. Bartner took to his ladder beneath the Coca-Cola sign and lifted his hands to conduct the Trojan Marching Band. Even more animated and elegant with his direction than usual, this was no ordinary rally as the musicians played song after song, including dance routines with Song Girls, spirit squad, and twirlers. It was better than a Broadway stage because the crowd was shoulder to shoulder around the band. From atop his platform, all Dr. Bartner could see was three hundred sixty degrees of smiling faces, clapping and dancing to the music. Hollywood's Band was on Broadway, and he loved it—almost as much as he loved the football team and coaches. (By the way, icing on the cake of that Broadway event: USC beat Syracuse 42-29!)

## High Note: Be Passionate

If one were to tally the distance that Dr. Bartner and the band traveled during his fifty years directing, the total would be in the hundreds of thousands of miles—giving another whole meaning to *Drive It!* Whether by bus or plane or automobile, and whether it was for a gig or a game, band members must be willing to get up and go—and give it their all once they arrive. That's exactly what Dr. Bartner and the TMB did every time—because they love to entertain and engage with crowds. ***When you truly love what you do, you more easily perform at a higher level of excellence, and it shows in the response and results you receive.*** Whether it's a road trip to the Bay Area or a cross-country flight to Notre Dame, the goal is to inspire a love of music for performers and audience alike. The pride Dr. Bartner has for putting on a great performance is secondary to the passion he feels for providing once-in-a-lifetime experiences for his students. The memories they have from these unique opportunities endure long after the final note of the show. *Be passionate.*

# 11

# HEARTBEAT OF THE TEAM

*Dr. Arthur C. Bartner during a jock rally on the practice field with former USC athletic director, Lynn Swann (L), and former USC defensive line coach and mentor Marv Goux (R).*
Courtesy: Dr. Arthur C. Bartner

# CHAPTER ELEVEN

## HEARTBEAT OF THE TEAM

The USC Trojan Football Team and the Spirit of Troy are inseparable. The one exists for the other, and neither would be what they are without the other. The symbiosis is never more obvious than after the Trojans win a game. As soon as he can get away from the media, the head coach and the team head straight for the band, which has descended from its end zone bleachers to perform a postgame concert. All one hundred or so football players shift down the sideline to take a position in front of the musicians. One player, an MVP of sorts, is selected for a distinct honor. He is handed the drum major's sword and ascends the band director's ladder to direct the TMB as it plays the Trojan battle cry "Conquest." Sometimes that most valuable player is the coach himself. It's an intense, often emotional moment of pride for both the team and the band. Dr. Bartner has lost count of how many players and coaches have stood atop that ladder, because in the fifty years he has been at USC, some extraordinary men have come through the Trojan program. Dr. Bartner is honored to have had such a close relationship with so many of them, especially because they've had considerable impact on the Spirit of Troy.

When he first came to campus in 1970, Bartner was still only Mister. He was young, naive, and very green, even with seven years of high school band directing under his baton and his doctorate well under way. He also had no idea what he was getting himself into. What he did know—besides the white horse mascot—was that the University of Southern California had a powerhouse football team led by an audacious group of coaches. The Trojans had just beat his alma mater in the Rose Bowl, the biggest game in college football, so the team was already in the national spotlight. It didn't take Mr. Bartner long to realize that the marching band was not in that league—yet. It wasn't the students' fault because they hadn't necessarily been set up for success. And it wasn't the prior band director's fault, either. It was just the culture and the way things were done back then, because up until his arrival, no one on campus—administrators, the team, the fans, not even the students—really cared about the band. But Bartner was ambitious and had a vision, and thankfully, that commitment to excellence and perfection was shared by the USC football coaches.

## Coaching Colleagues

When Bartner came on board, John McKay was in his tenth season as the Trojans head coach. He had an astounding seventy-two percent winning record, 72-24-4, including three Rose Bowl wins. What is interesting is that in his first two schedules in 1960 and 1961, McKay had a dreadful losing record, winning only four games each season. Finally, in his third year, something clicked, and the Trojans went undefeated to claim his first national championship in 1962. This is oddly parallel to Dr. Bartner's first three years at USC. McKay's Trojans were once again in a bit of a slump, going 6-4 in both the 1970 and 1971 seasons. During that same period, Bartner and the band also struggled to gain focus and footing. Then, in the third year, 1972, once again something clicked, and not only did the Trojans go undefeated to claim another national championship and Rose Bowl title, but Dr. Bartner also hit the home run with the Diana Ross halftime show. Both the football team and the marching band had hit their stride at the same time, and it was a splendid synchronicity. Since then, both the team and the band have had their share of ups and downs—all part of the nature of the business. By the time McKay left for the NFL in 1975, his Trojan game total was 127-40-8, a seventy-five percent winning record, including four national championships, earning him a place in the USC Hall of Fame and the posthumous title of "The Pac-12 Coach of the Century." Coach McKay passed away in 2001 at age 77, having left a legacy that would perpetuate Trojan Spirit for decades to come.

While Coach McKay and Dr. Bartner didn't really get to know each other very well in those early years, it was one of McKay's assistant coaches who really made a lifelong impact on Dr. Bartner, the band, the team, and consequently, the entire University of Southern California. Defensive line coach Marv Goux was absolutely one of the best friends Dr. Bartner ever could have asked for, embracing him (literally around the neck once) from the very beginning. "He certainly had a way with words," Dr. Bartner said. "He was always screaming and hollering." A former player coached by Goux recalled a fiery speech he gave the night before a Notre Dame away game. "[Forget] the score, we came here for more than that. Tomorrow, we take a program's heart and tear it to pieces with our bare hands. Tomorrow we play with Pride and Dignity. Every play, every player on the field for Notre Dame gets knocked to the ground. All of them, every play. Then you reach down to help them back up. That's who we are. Tomorrow we play like MEN. Tomorrow we play like TROJANS."[1] Goux's vibrant personality and black-bushy eyebrows even earned him a few small parts as a football coach in television shows like *Columbo* and *Banacek*. As colorful and occasionally crude as he could be, Goux was the brightest light and biggest heart on the field, and Dr. Bartner loved that about him and aspired to leave the same impression. "I became the Marv Goux of marching band directors, very passionate and very intense," Dr. Bartner reminisced. "Marv was very passionate about Trojan football, and he was the most intense guy you'd ever meet. His eyes would melt you down, even the big football players. So, I became this guy. Marv yelled a lot. I yelled a lot. Because we're both perfectionists." The love of their game had given both men the drive to succeed, whatever it took. In 1994, Goux was inducted into the USC Hall of Fame, recognized for his years as a star Trojan player and twenty-six years as an assistant coach. "He was the embodiment of Trojan Spirit." Since then, the walkway onto the Trojan football team practice field has been marked with a plaque naming it "Goux's Gate," perhaps symbolic for all the doors of opportunity that he opened for hundreds of football players in his career. Goux was only sixty-nine when he passed away in 2002 after battling cancer, a fact that Dr. Bartner still tears up about, even decades later. "He was the spiritual leader of the team and consequently, the band, too. He united us all in a way that left a lasting impact."

## Leadership and Life Lessons

No one could ever replace Goux, but several other coaches who made USC their home team easily embraced, and even enhanced, the Trojan Family culture. When John McKay retired after sixteen seasons (including the last five simultaneously as athletic director), his assistant John Robinson took over as head coach. "Robinson had an easy way about him, so relaxed and down to earth, kind of like a favorite uncle," Dr. Bartner said.

"Everything he did was constructive, all about improving, and I learned a lot from him about that." Dr. Bartner remembers being incredibly impressed with Coach Robinson at the celebration banquet hosted by Los Angeles Mayor Tom Bradley after USC won the 1977 Rose Bowl. "I sat with John and some students at the USC table, and you know what?" said Bartner. "John talked about everybody but himself. He talked to students, to faculty members, to alumni, everyone at the table, and never once talked about himself. He was really interested in them and everything to do with USC."

Ironically, Robinson once called Dr. Bartner the most intense man he'd ever met. Dr. Bartner admits that the perfectionist in him had a tendency to "go off" in a not-so-relaxed manner when he heard an off-note or saw an off-step, especially when it happened while the band was playing for the team. "The Jock Rally is the most important performance the band ever gives," Bartner said, "because it's for THE TEAM!" Coach Robinson saw that intensity come out once during a Jock Rally and commented to Dr. Bartner about it. The band director has never forgotten that discussion and has used it as a turning point in his teaching methods. "This is what I think makes me a better band director. You never stop learning, and you learn from other people, and that's what I learned from Robinson." This coach and the band director also shared a parallel pinnacle moment in their careers, when Robinson led the Trojans to the 1978 co-national championship, and just months later in 1979, Dr. Bartner scored the "Tusk" recording gig with Fleetwood Mac. Two big coups for the Trojans! Robinson carried on his predecessor's winning record, compiling four Rose Bowl wins in his 104-35-4 record, over two separate stints, first in 1976-1982 and again from 1993-1997. That's seventy-four percent, just one percent off McKay's.

Bartner shared how Robinson tells the story about giving credit to him and the band for "saving his job." His top-ranked Trojan team had been routed in its first game of his first season (losing to Missouri 25-46), and players were in a very negative place during practice, especially following murmurs of rumors of throwing out the head coach. Dr. Bartner decided to have the band show up unannounced on the football practice field. He got the team dancing to rock charts and entirely shifted the mood. That was the turning point lesson for Coach Robinson, and the Trojans went on to win the next eleven games and the Rose Bowl. That's just what the band and the team did for each other. Decades later, long after Robinson left USC for the second time (to take a three-year stint coaching the L.A. Rams), Dr. Bartner was invited to a going-away party for Robinson before he departed for Louisiana. Dr. Bartner said it was such a warm, welcoming, special occasion with other former coaches from his era, present as well. The head coach and the band director relived the old days and shared their appreciation and admiration for one another, and to end the evening, Dr. Bartner had the band play for Robinson, one last "Conquest."

Not only was the Trojan winning tradition reignited when Larry Smith took the reins, but he also played a critical role in the relationship between the football team and the marching band. Smith was the first "outsider" to become the USC's head coach in sixty-two years—that is, he was someone who did not already have ties to the Trojan family in one way or another. (The only other outsider came to USC in 1925 with the arrival of Howard Jones. The practice field named in his honor is on the other side of Goux's Gate.) Smith was known for taking struggling teams and putting them back on track. USC had flailed a bit under Ted Tollner. Even though he did get the team to the

Rose, Citrus, and Aloha bowls—winning the Rose but losing the others—he also had back-to-back losses to Notre Dame and UCLA that wound up ending his head coaching career. So, when Larry Smith came in, no one, including Dr. Bartner, really knew what to expect from him or how he would fit in with the family. He showed the Trojans that he had what it takes when he got the team to the Rose Bowl his first year out and then the next two years as well. But he did not have an easy start to his Trojan career in 1987.

Coach Smith's debut football game was televised as the college football opener on *ABC Sports*, a matchup between the Pac-10 and the Big-10. USC had not lost to a Big-10 school since the Rose Bowl thirteen years prior. The Trojans were guests on the Michigan State Spartans field in East Lansing, Michigan. The Big-10 had the home advantage with a sold-out crowd of nearly seventy-eight thousand—very few of which were dressed in cardinal and gold. The Spartan Marching Band could be heard playing their fight song as the team took the field for the first night game ever held in their stadium, but there was no such fight song welcome for the Trojan team, because the TMB was not there. After kickoff, the green and white jerseys scored the first touchdown. Then a Spartan fumble gave the Trojans position to get a field goal. The teams traded field goals and it was 10-6 at the half. Spartans came back charging for a touchdown at the top of the third quarter, making it 17-6. Michigan State took advantage of a Trojan fumble and made it 24-6. The Trojans had a few chances for touchdowns, but passes landed as interceptions instead. Spartans got another field goal, making it 27-6 with less than five minutes in the game. One lucky touchdown for USC ended the game at 27-13, but it was much worse than the score let on. Coach Smith was beyond frustrated with the team's mistakes on the field. He and the team returned to Los Angeles embarrassed, getting raked over the coals by the media. That's when Larry Smith learned the power of "Driving It" and "Fighting On!"

Dr. Bartner said Smith's style was tough, organized, and disciplined, and he cared about the team as people, not just football players. He truly cared about the band, too, because soon after he returned from the Michigan State defeat, Smith said he would never go on the road again without the Trojan Marching Band. "That's a perfect example," said Dr. Bartner, "of how much the band has come to mean to the spirit of the football team. Since that time, we have some portion of the band at every game, home or away." Smith went on to have a long string of victories with nineteen wins in a row, even stepping atop the band director's ladder a time or two. Unfortunately, that streak came to an end and took a bad turn, with USC ending Smith's contract three years early after a 3-8 losing season, followed by a poor showing against Fresno State in the Freedom Bowl. Despite the disappointing departure (and 44-25-3 USC record), he still left his mark on the Trojan family, no longer as an outsider. Smith went on to coach elsewhere and did a stint as a Fox Sports commentator before passing away in 2008 at the age of sixty-eight. Dr. Bartner appreciates Smith's contribution to USC and the TMB. It's because of his personal request that Dr. Bartner and the Spirit of Troy have attended more than four hundred consecutive college football games—a record in its own right. Win or lose, the band plays for the team no matter what.

"Win Forever" is a life motto and title of a book that Pete Carroll published in 2010, based on his lifetime of coaching football, including a nine-year run at USC. Carroll became the Trojans head coach in 2001, after a tumultuous eighteen-day search to replace Paul Hackett, who was fired for one of the worst Trojan records in forty years. On the tails of Hackett's double losing seasons, fans were skittish about Carroll, given that he hadn't been in college athletics for twenty years, let alone on a football field at all for about a year. He was actually USC's fourth choice for a new hire. Carroll nearly proved his critics correct, by going 5-2 in the beginning of his first season. He evened it out to 6-6, but then lost to the Utah Utes in the Las Vegas Bowl. Carroll's first season was the first time in fifty years that the Trojans never saw a spot on in the polls. Then, a familiar voice of wisdom spoke to Carroll: Marv Goux. He sternly told Carroll if he wanted to know about Trojan Spirit and tradition, go talk to Art Bartner—because this football team should be much better. And it did get better, MUCH better. In fact, Carroll went on to create the longest home game-winning streak the Trojans ever knew—thirty-five games in a row at the Coliseum, over six years from 2001-2007. In the middle of that, from 2003-2005, was thirty-four consecutive wins, home AND away. (Unfortunately, fourteen of those were later vacated by NCAA sanctions, but still!) Carroll led the Trojans to two national titles, seven Pac-10 championships, seven bowl games, three Heisman Trophy winners, and a total of ninety-seven wins in one hundred sixteen games—an eighty-four percent winning record! (That's pre-sanction, but still!) Carroll credits the Spirit of Troy under Dr. Bartner for helping to create that victorious atmosphere. "The Trojan Marching Band is the magnetic force that brings the Trojan Family together, unifying us all with the battle cries, the stabbing of midfield, the rendition of 'Tusk,' the shiny gold helmets, the unwavering shouts of 'Fight On!'" said Carroll. "The band's energy fuels our fans and university in tremendous ways, and it's one of the most important traditions of this fine institution."[2]

For his part, Dr. Bartner credited the success to Coach Carroll for making football fun. "He'd bring the team to band practice and have the players surround us, and then he'd tell stories and make fun of me," recalled Bartner with a smirk. "He was always encouraging. If a player dropped a pass, he wouldn't yell at him, but instead tell him to just watch the ball. I learned a lot from Pete." Carroll got the opportunity of a lifetime with an offer of a thirty-three-million-dollar NFL contract to become head coach of the Seattle Seahawks and left USC at the end the 2009 season. Dr. Bartner remembers the Carroll years as some of the most gratifying in his decades at USC, because of course, winning is fun! The band and the team have never been closer. Carroll was right when he said he knew that Coach Goux would be proud.

Carroll isn't the only Trojan football coach to write a book. So has Assistant Coach John Baxter, who coached the Trojans with Head Coach Clay Helton. Except for one year when he coached at Dr. Bartner's alma mater, University of Michigan, Coach Baxter was on staff at USC since the 2010 season, with nearly forty years coaching college athletes. Considered one of the best in the business, he earned the National Special Teams Coordinator of the Year in 2011. Not only is he a great motivator and skill instructor on the gridiron, Baxter also has a passion for education, and that is the crux of his 2013 book, *I Hate School: How a College Football Coach Has Inspired Students to Value Education and Become Lifelong Learners*. Dr. Bartner appreciated his message so much that he invited Coach Baxter to speak at the annual TMB Band Camp Leadership Retreat. "I think Coach Baxter is one of the most articulate, knowledgeable men I have ever met," said Dr. Bartner. "He's an unbelievable leader and motivator who plants seeds in kids about the importance of caring for one another. That is the key to building trust and respect. That's what he does for his football team, and that's what I want for this band. It's all about the Trojan Family."

Another Trojan football coach who held a similar belief for building family bonds was interim head coach Ed Orgeron, who filled the role for the remainder of the 2013 season after Lane Kiffin was dismissed and before Steve Sarkisian came on board in 2014. Dr. Bartner remembers how Orgeron would say, "The band and the team—we are ONE! The band is the heartbeat of the team." That was evidenced every time the team ran to meet the band after the game, win or lose. Even though "Coach O" had a rough end to the season losing to UCLA, and his interim spot didn't become permanent, Dr. Bartner said he did leave a permanent mark on the university by further uniting the team and the band.

## Pride of the Trojans

With the trail of tremendous coaches over the years, it's no wonder the University of Southern California Trojans football team is dreaded and admired for a reason: the players never quit! Even when they're down, they *Drive It!* and Fight On!—occasionally to the bitter end, and often to a magnificent last-second finish. The sound of the band playing "Tribute to Troy" fills their ears the whole time, to the chagrin of the opponents. As television coverage has expanded over the decades, football players are in the national spotlight more and more, and the Trojan Marching Band is right there with them. Whether it's an image of the drum major stabbing the field, the percussion line pounding its drums, or the entire band covering the field from end zone to end zone, the Spirit of Troy is instantly recognizable for its association with the USC Trojans. While the band has become famous, football players deserve the spotlight, too. USC coaches have trained many of the biggest names in the game who have won the highest award in the sport, the Heisman Trophy, not to mention dozens of others who have gone on to a professional career in the NFL. Dr. Bartner has been there in person to witness the history-making moments.

The first big star to shoot across Dr. Bartner's field was none other than Lynn Swann, the wide receiver who was first to auspiciously climb the ladder to conduct the band in the early 1970s. The team was coming off the practice field and walked by the band's practice field. Swann broke away from the team and ran over to the band and told Bartner, "I want to conduct the band!" So Dr. Bartner instructed them to play "Lone Ranger," and Swann held the sword and led the tune. It wasn't long before climbing the ladder with the sword to conduct the band for "Conquest" became a jock rally tradition. Swann was part of Coach McKay's team that won the 1972 national championship and two Rose Bowls. He reminisced with Bartner about his vivid memories of the band playing in dungeon-like locker rooms, recalling the original jock rallies with Coach Marv Goux. It was hot and sweaty and there was nothing like it anywhere but at USC. Swann went on to be the twenty-first pick in the first round of the 1974 draft by the Pittsburgh Steelers. While in the Steel City, Swann caught passes from Terry Bradshaw to help the team win four Super Bowls, including Super Bowl X, where he was named MVP. He was elected to the College Football Hall of Fame in 1993 and the Pro Football Hall of Fame in 2001. As a communications and journalism major at USC, Swann's post-football career took him to sports commentary for *ABC Sports* for some thirty years. He would often get to report from the sidelines of the fields on which he once played. During one postgame interview when USC had beaten Northwestern in the 1996 Rose Bowl, Swann was trying to ask Coach John Robinson some questions, and after acknowledging the team and fans for a great game, Robinson said, "Let's go to the band!" Aside from covering football games, Swann had the privilege of reporting for several Olympic Games, including the 1984 Summer Games in Los Angeles (for which, incidentally, Dr. Bartner directed the eight-hundred-member massed band for the Opening Ceremonies in the Coliseum). Swann took a spin in politics when in 2002 President George W. Bush appointed him as the chairman on the President's Council on Physical Fitness and Sports, a post he held for three years. He stepped down from that position to make an unsuccessful run for Pennsylvania governor. Swann's multi-faceted career landed him back where he started nearly five decades before: back at the University of Southern California, this time as athletic director. A new Trojan Marching Band tradition began with Swann's return to campus in 2016. Dr. Bartner presented Lynn Swann with an engraved replica drum major sword as a symbol of Trojan Spirit and pride. "He was the first guy to conduct the band with the sword, and the first to receive the honor of a commemorative sword," said Bartner. Swann worked closely with Dr. Bartner coordinating the band's performances for home games, as well as his athletic office contributing to the travel fund for the Spirit of Troy to attend away games. Swann and the football team and Dr. Bartner and the band had come full circle at a whole new level. Swann departed in 2019 to pursue other ventures.

Lynn Swann was not the first former USC football star to hold the athletic directorship. He took over the office after the departure of his teammate, former Trojan quarterback Pat Haden, who held the position for six years. He had taken the helm after the retirement of Mike Garrett, who in 1965 became USC's first-ever Heisman Trophy winner. In fact, Garrett was the first player from a California school to earn that award. The story goes that Coach John McKay told him before the season started that he was pushing him for the Heisman Trophy—and it worked. He earned the trophy and USC retired his number #20. The star tailback went on to be drafted by the Kansas City Chiefs (after a hoopla of alleged misdirection by the L.A. Rams and the Oakland Raiders)[3] and become the first Heisman winner to appear in a Super Bowl. In fact, it was the very first-ever Super Bowl in 1967, played where else than the Los Angeles Coliseum. Unfortunately, the Chiefs lost to the Green Bay Packers in that first AFL-NFL matchup. But Garrett was on the Chiefs team that won in Super Bowl IV, right before the American Football League and the National Football League merged. Garrett made a name for himself in the pros and then returned to college athletics to make a name again for the University of Southern California. Garrett brought back John Robinson for a second go-round that resulted in a few good years. And then, he scored big with his (at first controversial) hiring of Pete Carroll as head coach after Paul Hackett's term didn't turn out as well as he hoped. The Trojan Marching Band stepped into the limelight right along with the team as the football program rose to national prominence like it had when Garrett was a player. Garrett's time on the Trojan football team was before Dr. Bartner's time, but he experienced and witnessed the synergy while serving as athletic director. Garrett once shared how Marv Goux taught him the importance of the Trojan Marching Band and Dr. Arthur C. Bartner. He said their legacy is forever intertwined with the great heritage of the University of Southern California. That heritage, dedicated to Trojan sports history, is on display for the world to see at a special location on the USC campus, appropriately called Heritage Hall. As one more demonstration of the close connection between the band and the team, it is on the steps of this treasured building that Dr. Bartner assembles the Trojan Marching Band before every home game. It's as if the band absorbs the pride and energy of every team in Trojan history as it emanates from the trophies and awards held within Heritage Hall's walls.

The whole facility is like one giant two-story trophy case. Immediately inside the glass panel doors is the Hall of Champions, and taking center stage is a life-sized statue of a Trojan drum major stabbing the field. Surrounding the bronze is a single sloping-gradient pedestal holding the six Heisman Trophies awarded to USC Trojan football players: Mike Garrett (1965), O.J. Simpson (1968), Charles White (1979), Marcus Allen (1981), Carson Palmer (2002), and Matt Leinart (2004). Dr. Bartner remembers many of the key moments that these players faced as they drove it down the field. He was integrally involved with the campaigns for the last four honorees, with the Trojan Marching Band playing these young men on to victory, game after game, with refrain after refrain of "Tribute to Troy" and "Fight On!" "There's a reason the Trojan Marching Band drum major is the focal point of Heritage Hall," Dr. Bartner noted. "We are there for each other, always."

Even if their name isn't on a plaque or trophy somewhere, football players teem with praise and appreciation for Dr. Bartner and the band. Trojan running back who was second in the 1974 Heisman vote, Anthony Davis, recalled Dr. Bartner's energy being just like Coach McKay, running the band like a general.

Cornerback and safety in Robinson's 1978 national championship team, Ronnie Lott, compared Dr. Bartner to the great USC coaches, instilling greatness in players. Another Heisman runner-up, after his 1988 almost-undefeated senior season, was quarterback Rodney Peete. He got to hold the sword and conduct "Conquest" from atop the ladder to thank the band for helping the team come back from a 12-0 deficit against UCLA in 1987. "Sweet Peete" turned it around in the fourth quarter to win 17-13 and clinch the Rose Bowl berth. He said he got chills on the ladder and it's one of his favorite memories of all time. It was especially meaningful for him because, he had first seen the TMB when he was a ball-boy on the sidelines of the Arizona football team, where his father was a coach. Peete tells the story that he knew in that moment that one day he would play for USC, because he knew from the band's first note that the Wildcats weren't going to lose the game—because of the support of the band! Later season quarterbacks like Carson Palmer and Matt Leinart have shared a similar reaction to the honor of conducting the band from the ladder, noting there's nothing like being surrounded by a sea of Trojans, especially the Trojan Marching Band.

## Trojan Dreams Come True

The renovation of Heritage Hall to this configuration that includes the tribute to the Spirit of Troy was completed in 2014, providing a twenty-first century update for the offices of the USC Department of Intercollegiate Athletics. The layout of the contents may be different, but since it was first constructed in 1971, Heritage Hall has always been home to the realization of athletic dreams, achievements, and recognition of all USC student-athletes (and not just football!). The walls and halls are elegantly crowded with trophy after trophy, cup after cup, plaque after plaque, and medal after medal—all a reflection of the characteristics of a Trojan: Faithful, Scholarly, Skillful, Courageous, Ambitious.

Those attributes are especially fitting for a young man named Jake Olson. He may not have a trophy or a plaque in Heritage Hall, but he has the hearts of the Trojan family. When he and his twin sister were babies, his parents had concerns about his eyes. Doctors discovered he was afflicted with retinoblastoma, a rare cancer of the retina, so they removed his left eye. Jake grew up visually impaired but could see well enough to cheer on his family's favorite football team, the USC Trojans. Even with aggressive treatment all through childhood, by the time he turned twelve, his right eye had deteriorated and would need to be removed, too. With six weeks before the surgery that would leave him blind, all he wanted to do was to "see" the Trojans one last time. Then-coach Pete Carroll heard about the boy's wish and not only let Olson chill in the locker rooms and hang with the team for practices, but he also invited him to be on the sidelines for games—giving the young man memories to last a lifetime, including getting to see the TMB perform up close. But it didn't end there.

Fast-forward seven years, and Jake Olson had not let his disability affect his morale. Rather, he used it to propel himself academically and athletically so that he could get admitted to USC and be a walk-on player with the Trojan football team. He did just that in 2015. Olson moved into his dorm with his seeing eye dog, Quebec, and while getting settled in, he heard a familiar sound and exclaimed, "This is so sick: I can hear the band!" Jake's dad described the view from his dorm window, saying he could clearly see the grass of the practice football field, and right next to that, the Spirit of Troy was practicing the fight songs. For two years, Olson heard Dr. Bartner and the band from the sidelines, but his redshirt junior year, he got the opportunity of a lifetime. The only position a blind man could play on a football field was as a long snapper, something Olson had done successfully in high school. Now as a USC Trojan, in front of tens of thousands of fans, he would be the first blind man to play in a live college football game. He snapped the ball perfectly for the kicker to make the point after touchdown for USC to beat Western Michigan, 49-31. After the game, Olson thanked head coach Clay Helton and Assistant Coach John Baxter for believing in him and providing this opportunity, and then "To Coach Carroll," he wrote on Instagram, "None of this would have been possible without you. If you hadn't made me a member of the Trojan Family when I was 12, I don't know where my life would be." Pete Carroll said he "couldn't stop crying" when he heard about the play, praising Jake for his courage, character, and grit. Olson graduated in 2019 with a business degree and plans to become a motivational speaker. Jake's play made worldwide headlines after that 2017 game, but the real highlight was postgame with the Spirit of Troy and climbing that ladder with the sword for the second time in his life. "That was an incredibly special experience," Jake said. "The first time I did it was when I was going blind at age 12, and it was really emotional for me to be back on top of that ladder again. It really felt like my life had come full circle. I definitely did not ever think as a 12-year-old going blind that I would one day be leading the band as a player." [4]Dr. Bartner could only stand back in admiration and appreciation for this demonstration of what it means to truly be a Trojan.

At the time of this writing, USC has had one blind special teams player, thirty-eight different starting quarterbacks, ten head football coaches, and nine athletic directors since 1970—but only one marching band director. With the ebb and flow of wins and losses, one thing has remained constant: Dr. Arthur C. Bartner and the Spirit of Troy, the University of Southern California Trojan Marching Band—a.k.a. Hollywood's Band! Through the years, he and the band have become more than used to the national spotlight—they now expect and anticipate it! That's probably a good thing because Dr. Bartner had plenty more national attention coming his way.

## High Note: Be Loyal

It may not have started out that way, but with encouragement and influence from a few key people through the decades, the Spirit of Troy and the Trojan football team are a loyal family. From the moment Marv Goux embraced Dr. Bartner to the thoughtful role modeling of John Robinson, the travel companionship of Larry Smith, and the positive reinforcement of Pete Carroll, the team and the band built an unbreakable bond. The band drives it for the team, and the team drives it for the band. ***When you care as much about the success of others as you do about your own, your personal level of excellence inherently rises with the growth of mutual respect and admiration.*** The band director and the coaches devoted themselves to bringing out the best in their students. As part of the Trojan family, they want nothing more than for their students to succeed, because their success is the director's and coaches' reward. *Be loyal.*

# 12

# NATIONAL RECOGNITION

*Dr. Arthur C. Bartner instructs members of the Olympic Band preparing for Opening Ceremonies of the XXIII Olympiad.*
Courtesy: Tim Seno

# CHAPTER TWELVE

## NATIONAL RECOGNITION

While leading the three-hundred-member Trojan Marching Band for a football game at the Los Angeles Coliseum is pretty huge, it is by no means the largest band Dr. Bartner has ever conducted. During his tenure with the USC TMB, he became so in demand that he directed groups of hundreds for multiple other major events. In fact, by the 1980s, Dr. Bartner had become known as The Maestro of Massed Bands. The young trumpet player from New Jersey who went to college in Michigan and moved west to tackle unknown challenges had grown into the most sought-after name in the college marching band profession. Every time he turned around, he was receiving another request to take command of another ensemble, in addition to his regular responsibilities with USC's TMB and Disney's AACB. On one hand, Dr. Bartner loved it and couldn't believe his good fortune to be afforded such incredible opportunities! On the other hand, the crazy, busy schedule caused a strain in his life that was sometimes as stressful as completing his doctorate. Even so, the pressure was worth it for the rewards and national recognition that came his way and brought him further respect, and by association, further esteem for the University of Southern California and its Trojan Marching Band as well.

### Names of the Games

Within just a few years of his moving to Los Angeles, heavy hitters throughout Hollywood already knew the name Dr. Arthur

C. Bartner. With his success of several celebrity-filled Rose Bowl performances, dozens of television and movie appearances, and his entertainment prowess at Disneyland—including directing a 450-piece massed band at the 1982 Grand Opening of EPCOT Center in Disneyworld—it's no wonder that when the City of Angels was awarded the 1984 Olympic Games that the committee called Dr. Bartner. They wanted him to conduct a massed band for the Opening Ceremonies. The appointment was evidence that Dr. Bartner was traveling in high-level entertainment industry circles, as his colleagues on the Olympic entertainment committee were world-famous. His friend at Paramount, Hank Ehrlich, had introduced him to award-winning composer John Williams in 1976 when the Trojan Marching Band performed live on stage at the Academy Awards. Williams, already known for crafting some of the best loved movie scores, including *Star Wars,* was one of the composers to write original music for the Olympic ceremonies. Although he wasn't part of the official planning committee, the musical fanfare he created is still performed at the Games decades later. The director of the show was another familiar face, Tommy Walker, the former USC-football-player-slash-drum-major who became the head of Disney Entertainment and later opened his own event production company. Walker produced the opening and closing ceremonies for the 1960 Winter Olympics at Squaw Valley in Lake Tahoe, California and the 1980 Winter Olympics at Lake Placid, New York. Taking the reigns as the music director for the XXIII Olympiad was Jack Elliott. As a composer and arranger, Elliott wrote the music for popular television shows like *Barney Miller, Starsky and Hutch, Charlie's Angels,* and *The Love Boat,* just to name a few. He was also the orchestra director for the Grammy Awards for thirty-one years and later became the musical director of the

Henry Mancini Institute. (Yes, that's the same Henry Mancini who stood in the rain to conduct the Trojan Marching Band at Dr. Bartner's first Notre Dame home game at the Coliseum and was the catalyst to many more celebrity connections.) The show required plenty of complex movements on the field, so Emmy Award-winning director and choreographer, Ron Field, came on board. He choreographed routines for stars from Fred Astaire to Mikhail Baryshnikov to Michael Jackson, as well Broadway shows and as the stage performance for multiple Academy, Emmy, and Tony Award broadcasts. The executive producer of the entire Opening and Closing Ceremonies was David Wolper, a former USC Film School student and ground-breaking, award-winning producer who made television history several times. In fact, he was dubbed "Mr. Documentary" by *Time Magazine* for his Emmy Award-winning docuseries, *Roots* in the 1970s, *The Thorn Birds* and *North and South* in the 1980s, as well as pioneering nature shows on primetime television with *The Undersea World of Jacques Cousteau* and *National Geographic* specials. He also worked on several movies including the childhood classic *Willy Wonka and the Chocolate Factory*. Even with all this success, Wolper maintained that one of his greatest accomplishments was his volunteer work for the 1984 Olympics, saying it was "the biggest, most original, most tasteful, most emotionally evocative show ever done."[1] L.A. Mayor Tom Bradley appointed Wolper to the seven-person committee who successfully brought the games to Los Angeles. So, here was Dr. Bartner, the forty-something-year-old band director of the USC Trojan Marching Band, coordinating one of the most magnificent field shows ever produced, with the likes of Walker, Elliott, Field, and Wolper—and Dr. Bartner had proven he deserved to be at that table.

The dignified group of gentlemen gathered for multiple planning meetings in the months leading up to the '84 Games. Coordinating a cast of some nine thousand people plus seventy-eight hundred athletes was no small feat. Wolper was working with a budget of about five million dollars for a four-hour show that would culminate with the parade of countries. But before the athletes came out, he wanted to put on a dazzling display of American traditions to unite sports with culture and art. Wolper tells the story of describing his vision to Dr. Bartner of having the Opening Ceremonies be a salute to American music, and Dr. Bartner's response was immediate: "Let's have one of the biggest and best marching bands ever. How about eight hundred of the best musicians from universities in every state of the country? Can you imagine what that sound would be?" And Wolper said, "Let's do it!" And so, he did. Dr. Bartner put out the word to his band director colleagues across the United States that he was recruiting the best of the best to play a big band medley for the Opening Ceremonies on July 28, 1984. He received recommendations and requests for thousands of students and selected eight hundred of them in what became the largest massed band ever assembled to date. The musicians came from all fifty states to Los Angeles to practice together every day for two weeks before the Games. Wearing shorts and t-shirts on a dusty field at Pepperdine University, hundreds of students rehearsed from 8:30 in the morning until 10 at night, learning the music and field maneuvers. Then it was time for a run-through in the performance arena. It was a miraculous sight, especially since there were 125 marching band members from USC and 125 from UCLA on the field at the same time. "The first time I heard the eight hundred playing was at a rehearsal on the Coliseum floor," recalled Wolper. "As they started to march and play, every workman in the stands stopped and just watched in awe. I got goosebumps it was so powerful. I rushed down to the field, hugged Art and told him, 'You did it, by God, you did it!'"[2]

As Dr. Bartner and the musicians emerged through the Coliseum tunnels and aisles to take the field on that perfect-weather summer-day, ABC journalists Peter Jennings and Jim McKay announced the arrival of the Olympic All-American College Marching Band on their television coverage of the Opening Ceremonies. Within the moving arcs and shifting lines were ninety-six trombones, one-hundred-forty-four trumpets, forty tubas, and a percussion line sixty players strong. The shadow of the Goodyear blimp passed over the northern seats of the Coliseum as the ensemble stepped into formation. Marching in white uniforms with light blue capes on their backs and colorful Olympic rings on their chests, musicians played a lively medley of tunes from Duke Ellington, Glenn Miller, and Benny Goodman. Crisp notes and sharp shapes filled the field to the delight of more than ninety-two thousand people in the stadium and millions more watching on live television around the world. This was, after all, the first time the Olympics were broadcast in full color. In fact, during their planning process, Wolper and the design committee considered exactly where the cameras would be stationed in each venue during the Games. The best video angle was from below the media box on the south side of the stadium that, facing north, could get a wide shot of the entire Coliseum floor, so viewers could witness the mesmerizing kaleidoscope of patterns and sounds. Multiple cameras on ground level captured Silk twirlers smiling, trombone players sliding, and drummers pounding in sync, while Dr. Bartner, in his own white suit, conducted from his ladder at the fifty-yard line. The band was so big he had two assistants directing midway on either side, one of which was his former TMB student, Ken Dye. Another Trojan Band student, Barry Spanier, had helped Dr. Bartner during the Olympic practices for this performance. For the finale, the massed band formed an outline of the United States that filled the entire turf, and under L.A.'s spacious skies, they played a patriotic arrangement of "America the Beautiful." As the performance concluded and the broadcast went for a commercial break, Peter Jennings commented, "Great precision—and spirit, too!" Even though he didn't hear the announcer's compliment, Dr. Bartner could not have been more proud. "As the band boarded the buses after the opening ended, I walked alongside each bus, high-fiving these great kids as they leaned out of the windows," he said. "It was as if they had won gold medals. They knew they'd been a part of history—a great moment in front of the world." It was also a great moment for Dr. Bartner, who was becoming known as so much more than a college marching band director. While his main priority remained with USC and Hollywood's Band and his secondary role was as director of the Disneyland All-American College Band, he would take charge of many more bands in the years to come.

A few months after the very successful Olympic extravaganza, Dr. Bartner was on the field instead of the ladder during a football game halftime show. The USC School of Music honored him, David Wolper, and Tommy Walker for their contributions as part of the music school's 100th anniversary. Then, a month later, the date of November 24, 1984 was named "Dr. Arthur C. Bartner Day" in Los Angeles in recognition of his work at the XXIII Olympiad. "That was an honor for sure," said Dr. Bartner. "But the real privilege was being a part of the experience that all those hundreds of kids got to have, literally performing on a world stage. I look at it as a way of touching other people's lives, hopefully developing a love for music. That's why I love directing these massed bands because you can reach so many people." The most redemptive commendation Dr. Bartner received after the Olympics came from a very unexpected source in December 1984. Dr. Bartner was attending the CBDNA convention (College Band Directors National Association) in Chicago. "Guess who happened to be standing by the entryway when I walked in," marveled Dr. Bartner. "Of course, it was William D. Revelli! I hadn't seen him since I got my doctorate in 1979. He was surrounded by his entourage, and he came up to me and gave me the biggest hug you've ever seen. And he said, 'That Olympic band was the best marching band I've ever heard! I'm so proud that you're one of my boys.' Talk about a moment of vindication after all these years."

## Presidential Performance

The Maestro of Massed Bands would have many more occasions to provide young men and women around the nation with once-in-a-lifetime opportunities. The word was out that Dr. Bartner was the man to call if someone was looking for a professional who could organize and mobilize a massive group of musicians for a special occasion, and what could be more remarkable than the 50th Presidential Inauguration? President Ronald Reagan was re-elected in 1984 and his public swearing-in ceremony was held in Washington, D.C. on January 21, 1985. (His official oath was taken in private on January 20, as mandated by law.) The producer of the event, Bob Jani, asked Dr. Bartner to direct the All-American College Marching Band for the traditional parade on Inauguration Day. He and about three hundred eighty band members stayed at a military base in Virginia to rehearse for the week before the celebration. All systems were go for a wonderful performance, except for one thing: the weather. It was the coldest Inauguration Day on record, with temperatures hovering at zero and the wind chill up to -30 below. Reagan had to take the oath inside the Capitol building rather than on the back veranda as has been done for decades. More than one hundred forty thousand people were in the district, having purchased tickets to witness the occasion. Dr. Bartner and the band hoped for warmer temperatures for the parade, but the inauguration committee decided that public health and safety must prevail. The decision was reached overnight to cancel the procession. They would not be marching down Pennsylvania Avenue after all. The co-chairman of the Republican National Committee expressed her sincere regrets saying, "We don't want these kids to get sick, but I know this will disappoint them, and that breaks my heart. But it's better than freezing to death."[3] That went for Dr. Bartner's group and dozens of other high school and college bands who had traveled from around the country to participate.

All was not lost, however, because within hours, the Inaugural Committee had come up with a Plan B. They towed a giant American flag parade float into the Capital Centre in Landover, Maryland and set it up as the backdrop for a make-shift stage. Then, the morning when the parade would have been in motion, the bands instead filled the stands to join the president and first lady for a show by the All-American College Marching Band. Dr. Bartner's ensemble was the only band that would be on the floor to perform the patriotic songs it had planned for the parade. In the presence of the Commander in Chief and his wife, and the vice president and Mrs. George Bush, the emcee announced, "Ladies and Gentlemen, from colleges and universities across our nation, welcome the All-American College Marching Band, directed by Dr. Arthur C. Bartner." With giant grins, the Reagans watched as the men and women in bright white and royal blue filled the floor before them and started playing Yankee Doodle Dandy. With television cameras behind him, viewers at home watched Dr. Bartner as he stood upon an elevated platform directly across the arena from the president. He called the band about-face and conducted a medley of "The Music of America." At the final note, the executive office couples rose to their feet and gave Dr. Bartner and the college band a standing ovation. Nancy Reagan came to the podium and shared her gratitude and sympathies with the band members. "I know how hard you worked and how long you worked, and I wish it could have been different, but you wouldn't have liked frostbite. So, thank you for letting us come out and hear you and see you and tell you in person how sorry we are." As she sat back down next to Ronald Reagan, he whispered something to her, causing her eyes to blink wide open and her hands to rush to cover her mouth! With embarrassed laughter, she returned to the podium and said, "I forgot something! I was supposed to introduce my roommate, who happens to be my husband, the President of the United States." Taking it in stride, he said in jest, "How could you forget me?" President Reagan spoke for a few minutes. Noting that the parade organizers consulted professional medical advice as part of their decision-making process, Reagan told the disappointed band members how much he appreciated their hard work and talent. "I'm told that this is the coldest Inauguration Day in history, but looking out at all of you, I somehow feel there is a lot of warmth inside this building… I know you didn't get your chance to salute all of us, but I just want you to know how happy and how important it was for Nancy and myself, and the vice president and Mrs. Bush to come to salute all of you." [4]Before the All-American College Band departed, they gave the president one of the shako hats from the group's uniform, perhaps a foreshadowing of the Trojan Marching Band giving Reagan a helmet at the conclusion of his second term in office. Dr. Bartner couldn't have been more pleased with the performance. "Talk about turning something negative into something positive," he said. "It was an awesome memory, for me and for all those kids, for the President of the United States to speak directly to us. Plus, all kinds of Hollywood celebrities were there, too, like Frank Sinatra and Tom Selleck, who happened to play baseball at USC. I went up to Selleck to introduce myself because my wife loves him. And he starts gushing about how excited *he* was to meet *me*! Another awesome memory for me was that I had an all-access pass to all the Inaugural Balls with all the celebrities and politicians. I felt like an official government official who could go anywhere—it was incredible!" It was just the beginning of a banner year for Bartner and big marching bands.

## Patriotic Performances

Just two weeks before the inauguration, Dr. Bartner and the Trojan Marching Band were at their second home in Pasadena, California for the USC—Ohio State Rose Bowl matchup. Before the Trojans won the game, 20-17, Dr. Bartner conducted his very favorite halftime show of all time. "I can't believe it actually worked," said Dr. Bartner, speaking about a surprise highlight of the halftime performance. "We had a tough time with it at rehearsal, but when it mattered, it actually worked! And I LOVED this show! It's my favorite ever!" Televised on NBC, sportscasters Dick Enberg and Merlin Olsen introduced the band as it started playing "We're an American Band" to coordinate with the theme of the 1985 Rose Parade "The Spirit of America." Over the stadium speakers, the announcer described the performance. "Nowhere is the Spirit of America more eloquently stated than on the Statue of Liberty. Give me your tired, your poor, your huddled masses yearning to breathe free." Adding to the suspense of the show, Enberg said, "We understand there's a special surprise underneath the red, white, and blue curtain at centerfield." While the Spirit of Troy played the epic composition by Aaron Copeland, "Fanfare for the Common Man," prop assistants wheeled out a large container, and just in time for the crescendo, hot air filled the balloon-statue—and Lady Liberty stood proud and tall in the middle of the stadium. "OH! A chilling climax to these halftime festivities!" exclaimed Enberg. "The Southern California band and the tribute to the Great Lady and the refurbishing of that marvelous monument."[5]

Little did anyone know then that in only eighteen months, the actual Statue of Liberty on Ellis Island would be the backdrop for one of the most patriotic performances Dr. Bartner would ever conduct and that the nation would ever see. Dr. Bartner became the director of the Statue of Liberty All-American Marching Band during "Liberty Weekend" in honor of the rededication of Lady Liberty. The renovation of the statue in New York Harbor began in 1984 with a two-hundred-thirty-million-dollar fundraising campaign led by Chrysler chief Lee Iacocca with the goal that the restoration be complete in time for her centennial. After the triumphant collaboration on the Olympic Opening Ceremonies, entertainment producer David Wolper realized Dr. Bartner would be the perfect man for the job to create an exhibition fitting for the nation's greatest symbol of freedom. "Wolper wasn't sold on the idea at first, though," said Dr. Bartner. "I had to talk him into it, and we were both glad I did." Wolper had John Williams conduct the Liberty Orchestra and Tommy Walker produce the fireworks and other pieces of multiple shows during the event. This time, USC's Trojan Marching Band drumline and Silks would be a key element of the five- hundred-piece ensemble, drawn once again from all fifty states in the country. Dr. Bartner met the students in mid-June at William Paterson College in New Jersey, where they were paired up with roommates from colleges different than their own. He wanted them to have a cultural experience and make new friendships from coast to coast. Then came seventeen days of intense rehearsals, some of which were playing and marching from 8:30 a.m. until 10 p.m. The musicians had to learn complex maneuvers for a performance on a field that did not have the typical hash marks they were used to. Dr. Bartner encouraged them at a band meeting with the knowledge that the whole show had been choreographed with television producers, telling them, "You're going to get the greatest TV coverage that any band has ever gotten."[6] In preparation for that national recognition, Dr. Bartner held a practice for their entrance to the main stage, but rain delayed the rehearsal, and they didn't return to their dorms until three in the morning. "We didn't ask the kids to do that," said Dr. Bartner. "They wanted to rehearse because they love performing!"

The stage on Governors Island was a massive, multi-level masterpiece that held all five hundred band members for the opening ceremonies. Tommy Walker wanted to get some photos of that stage and the island from the top of the Statue of Liberty, and he invited Wolper, Dr. Bartner, and the band manager to join him. "I'm thinking we'd go inside and take the elevator or stairs up. But NO!" said Dr. Bartner. "He's taking the four of us up on the outside construction elevator, which is about as big as a closet! And it's all open on every side, so we're basically scaling the Statue of Liberty all the way up to the torch. I. Am. Petrified! I'm afraid of heights and I'm like, how tall is this statue? I'm outside with the torch. I am braced to the back of this 2x4 elevator, and I can't move or breathe. And to get his pictures, Tommy walks across this wooden plank, and all of a sudden, his hat blows off! And I'm watching it float... all the way down to the water. Thank God I survived that!"

"Liberty Weekend" was a four-day spectacular, filled with Hollywood celebrities, which was to be expected with Wolper as executive producer. All three major networks of the time covered portions of the event, but ABC television paid big bucks for exclusive rights to air more than the others, with hosts Peter Jennings and Barbara Walters bringing the festivities into millions of homes around the country. They broadcasted performances from stars like Neil Diamond, Elizabeth Taylor, Frank Sinatra, Liza Minelli, Willie Nelson, Shirley MacLaine, Lionel Richie, John Denver, Barry Manilow, and a young Whitney Houston, among many others. The event also had a dignified feel, with a special viewing box built specifically for President and Mrs. Reagan. They welcomed French President and Madame Francois Mitterrand to join them for the event honoring the statuesque gift from France a century prior. Once again, the First Family and guests had prime seating to view a marching band performance directed by Dr. Arthur C. Bartner. His first televised presentation with the Liberty Band was on July 3, 1986. President Reagan offered a few remarks and then pressed a button that beamed a laser across the harbor to signal the unveiling of the restored Statue of Liberty, which became aglow in red, white, and blue lights. After enjoying celebrity performances at Governor's Island, the Reagans returned to the stage and gave a cue: "With a prayer that this lamp will never be extinguished, I ask that you all join me in this symbolic act of faith, this lighting of Miss Liberty's torch." With the trumpet fanfare, Dr. Bartner stood up and signaled the band to play "Stars and Stripes Forever." And with the band's first notes, New York Harbor was dark no longer as Lady Liberty's torch lit up and so did the night sky with a nonstop five-minute explosive fireworks display. While the audience had their eyes on the statue, the band took the stage and played in perfect synchronization with the fireworks. It was a powerfully emotional moment for Dr. Bartner to realize the national patriotism that he and the band helped stir in the hearts of millions.

Another venue for pageantry was Liberty State Park, where John Williams conducted the Boston Pops orchestra, featuring the Liberty Band Fanfare Trumpets and other celebrity performers. Dr. Bartner even met John Denver there, and while he also saw Whitney Houston, he didn't meet her. True to his commitment to always give band members a bit of relaxation and fun amid their hard work, Dr. Bartner lobbied event organizers to allow the musicians to have a picnic and attend the Americana Concert and massive fireworks show on the 4th of July. No time off for the drumline, however, as they performed a special percussion arrangement synchronized to the bombs bursting in air over the harbor and across the entire New York City skyline, in what director Tommy Walker called "The Big Bang!" It was the largest fireworks display ever, exploding for thirty minutes straight with forty thousand projectiles, at the cost of about eight hundred thousand dollars. When the eruptions concluded, the band's thirteen buses couldn't get to the venue through the sea of some twenty-five thousand spectators. After a three-hour delay, Dr. Bartner worked some magic and finally connected the buses with all five hundred band members on board, but he accidentally got left behind. The buses left without him! Fortunately, he found a teaching assistant with a car and caught a ride to the dorms by about 5 in the morning. It's a good thing he and the band got to sleep in a little bit, with a later call-time than usual: 9 a.m. to board the buses for a day of practice at Giants Stadium in the Meadowlands.

Saturday, July 5 was all about perfecting every note, every turn, and every halt on the field of their ten-minute exhibition. After drilling it all day, then came dress rehearsal: full white uniform with a two-colored cape, red on the back, blue on the underside, which made for fascinating visuals as the players turned in unison. Some twelve thousand people watched the run-through while the band played as if it were the real deal. The main event was the next evening, produced by the one and only Don Mischer. He's the same man who produced the Emmy Awards, Academy Awards, Billboard Music Awards, Olympic Games Ceremonies, and shows for the likes of Barbara Streisand, Prince, and Paul McCartney. The evening of Sunday, July 6, was the grand finale, what Dr. Bartner and the band had poured their heart and soul into for seventeen days: the live television coverage of the Closing Ceremonies, with the tribute by the Statue of Liberty All-American Marching Band. For the second time in Dr. Bartner's career, the band under his direction was introduced by Elizabeth Taylor. "Remember. Rejoice. Renew. This is the theme of tonight's presentation," she spoke from the podium in a glowing white glitzy gown. "And this is the time to rejoice. We rejoice that we are living in the land of opportunity and that America imposed no restrictions on creative expression and creativity. We rejoice that America has always given these artists an atmosphere in which to grow, to flourish, and dare to be daring. We rejoice these artists always had a place to display their talents and an audience to appreciate their efforts. Tonight, some of these artists will have a chance to say thank you in a way they know best, with their music. To start our salute, ladies and gentlemen, the five hundred members of the Salute [sic] of Liberty All-American Marching Band."[7] Pouring in from multiple hidden entrances on both sides of the stadium, the musicians marched in under dimmed lights to join the diamond of percussion at centerfield, and when the spotlights came on, the whole band faced front, and the first notes blared. Straight lines snapped into squares, which melted into rotating circles, reversing direction, contracting, expanding, and transitioning into complicated swirls. The change of tune led to more geometric designs that morphed like magic for the eyes as the players took the shape of intricate flowers that spun like pinwheels. Aerial shots showed the perfection and precision of the spacing and lines as the band turned into the Rockettes, kicking and dancing instead of marching. It was truly a performance unlike anything ever seen before, with the audience on the edge of their seats waiting to see what show tune and shape would come next. Every member had memorized every note and hit every mark, and Dr. Bartner had every reason to be beaming with pride. He told them as much after the show when they got back to their dorm hall. "I am so proud of you guys and gals! One of your compatriots came up to me and said, 'We worked seventeen long, hard, miserable days for ten minutes.' And you know what my answer was? 'There were millions and millions of people who saw those ten minutes, and now there's going to be dance routines and red capes all over this country,'" and the band laughed and cheered. "You guys were terrific, and I congratulate each and every one of you." The Statue of Liberty All-American Marching Band had left a patriotic imprint on the hearts of each other, on Dr. Bartner, and on people around the nation.

## But Wait, There's More

The United States observed another important national anniversary in the 1980s, and of course Dr. Bartner was there for that, too. While parade officials in Washington D.C. may have cancelled the Inauguration Parade because of bone-chilling cold, the organizers of another patriotic procession in Philadelphia did NOT cancel it because of rain. No, Dr. Bartner and a one-hundred-twenty-piece band still marched in the downpour for the celebration of the 200th Anniversary of the signing of the United States Constitution on September 17, 1987. As part of the "We the People 200" celebration, Dr. Bartner took on the role of drum major and led the Official Fanfare Unit dressed in blue-and-white colonial-style uniforms from Independence Hall to the Philadelphia Museum of Art, where they also performed a concert. "Famous Christian singer Sandi Patty sang an amazing rendition of the National Anthem," said Dr. Bartner. "And Barry Manilow was there, too." The event was not quite as extravagant of a production as Liberty Weekend was, but it was still televised and billed as the largest parade in U.S. history, spanning four hours with some fifteen-thousand participants.

In the midst of these incredible patriotic shows, Dr. Bartner also conducted "The World's Largest Marching Band" of five thousand high school musicians from Illinois, Missouri, and Arkansas for the reopening of Union Station in St. Louis in late summer of 1985. "That band was so big, there was no way the front ranks could hear the back of the band," recalled Dr. Bartner. "To get them all to play just one note together was a thrill!" Then, in 1987, Dr. Bartner was the head of the massive one-thousand-piece band for the Opening Ceremonies of 10th Pan American Games in Indianapolis, Indiana—and this was indeed quite a production. In fact, organizers called it the largest outdoor live entertainment show ever. Dr. Bartner would agree, as he had to ride a moped to get from one end of the band to the other. Vice President George and Barbara Bush attended the ceremonies held on the straight-away of the Indianapolis Speedway. Walt Disney World produced the spectacle full of giant, colorful costumes, balloons, flags, dancers, parachuters, and even Mickey Mouse and friends. The Games hosted forty-three hundred athletes from thirty-eight countries for what was only the second time the United States had hosted the athletic competition. The Pan American Games are held every six years (instead of four years like the Olympics.)

Another sporting event that is no longer held is the Olympic Festival, but when it was in operation under Radio City Music Hall Productions, Dr. Bartner ran the band for those Opening Ceremonies, too, in 1986 in at the Astrodome in Houston, Texas (while wearing a cowboy hat and boots!), and in 1990 at the Metrodome in Minneapolis, Minnesota. Oh, and don't forget about the Goodwill Games held in Seattle just two weeks later, designed to generate good will between the U.S. and Russia. In the television coverage of those opening ceremonies, Dr. Bartner could be seen atop his ladder while a parachuter landed on the field next to the marching band. Then there was the World Cup Fanfare Unit for the international soccer tournament held at the Rose Bowl in 1994, comprised of the Trojan

Marching Band and Southern California high school band members.

As if that weren't enough, there were also several National Football League Super Bowls to boot. In 1987 for Super Bowl XXI, Dr. Bartner led the band for the halftime show: a Salute to Hollywood's 100th Anniversary, headlined by George Burns and Mickey Rooney. The following year, he directed the mid-game performance for Super Bowl XXII, featuring Chubby Checker and multiple pianos, reminiscent of the Kimball piano presentation of the 1984 Olympic Opening Ceremonies. In 1990, Dr. Bartner directed the massed band at Super Bowl XXIV at the Superdome in New Orleans, Louisiana. The focus of that show was the 40th Anniversary of the Peanuts Comic Strip. Then, in 1993 the TMB participated for Super Bowl XXVII, which featured Michael Jackson's "Heal the World" halftime show at the Pasadena Rose Bowl. In the 1980s, Dr. Bartner also served as band director two Japanese Bands for the Ricoh Japan Bowl in Yokohama. He was teaching them how to play tunes for the matchup of two All-Star American football teams. One band played for the east team, the other for the west. "My job was to coordinate so it looked like a normal American football game," said Dr. Bartner. "And these band guys played GREAT!" Amid all of the athletic stuff were massed bands for other big events, like closing day at the Democratic National Convention in Atlanta, Georgia in 1988 when Michael Dukakis was nominated, and again in 1992 when Bill Clinton was nominated at Madison Square Garden in New York. It's obvious why Dr. Bartner became known as "The Maestro of Massed Bands." He and the musicians he's directed have touched the lives of millions of people who watch these special events.

If it feels exhausting to read about all this, imagine living it.

While the 1980s were the glory days for Dr. Bartner and marching band halftime shows at major events, the decade was also overwhelming at times. His schedule was one thing right after another after another. He loved what he was doing, working with people he admired and trusted, conducting music he adored, and directing students he treasured. But it was grueling because he was simultaneously running the Disney Band in the summers and the Trojan Marching Band with a dozen football games every fall, multiple smaller events on the USC campus, conducting orchestra concerts in Los Angeles, and influencing the lives of hundreds of young musicians by hosting High School Band Days at the Coliseum. Plus, he missed his family. Over the years, the entertainment for Super Bowls and other national events, sporting or otherwise, have become more high-tech, high-dollar, high-falutin types of productions. Stepping away from much of the massed band hoopla, Dr. Bartner was able to turn his attention to other life-changing experiences —like traveling the world with the Trojan Marching Band. Dr. Bartner and Hollywood's Band were going global!

## High Note: Be Dedicated

With every success on the field and on screen, the national visibility of the TMB went to exponential new heights. Not only was the band more and more in demand, so was Dr. Bartner himself. His perseverance through the early years combined with his commitment to excellence through transparency, diversity, connection, passion, and loyalty generated more recognition than he ever could have imagined—including unexpected overdue validation from the man who once told him to "forget it." While driving it one major event to the next monumental celebration, Dr. Bartner could not have been more dedicated in his profession. He was ambitious and loved looking for that next best special guest appearance. ***Dedication is your visible expression of a commitment to excellence in an activity from beginning to end, and every step in between, driving it to success, no matter what.*** Dedication is fueled by determination which is ignited by passion. Put another way, if you're passionate, you'll be determined to succeed. When the time came for Dr. Bartner to shift directions, his dedication never wavered. His primary purpose and passion remained with providing his students with excellent opportunities. *Be dedicated.*

# POSTGAME

## CONFIDENCE

Courtesy: Ling Luo

# 13

# WORLD AMBASSADORS

*The University of Southern California Trojan Marching Band in 2006 after performing at its home away from home, the Colosseum in Rome, Italy.* Courtesy: Ben Chua

# CHAPTER THIRTEEN

## WORLD AMBASSADORS

Once Hollywood's Band mastered the national spotlight, it was time to conquer the world stage. Think of the most famous international landmarks around the globe and chances are pretty good that Dr. Bartner and the Trojan Marching Band have not only been there but performed a live concert there. Dr. Bartner's growing and glowing reputation has taken him and Hollywood's Band across the ocean many times over since their very first trip to the Orient with the football team for the Tokyo Mirage Bowl in 1985. A few years later, the TMB began taking biennial trips of its own as goodwill ambassadors, touring twenty countries (several more than once) on six continents over the next three decades. International delegations have invited Dr. Bartner to bring the band to help commemorate major world events, like the 50th Anniversary at Normandy, the fall of the Berlin Wall, and six World Expos. The marching band's unique sound has filled the ears of crowds at the Great Wall of China, the Blarney Castle in Ireland, the Eiffel Tower in France, the Sydney Opera House in Australia, and many other world-famous sites. The band never fails to make an impression while marching on foreign soil.

### Expanding Musical Horizons

The first-ever Spirit of Troy international summer adventure came about with an invitation stemming from Olympic connections. Former Trojan Marching Band trumpet player Barry

Spanier had assisted Dr. Bartner with the 1984 Olympic Opening Ceremonies. Spanier had developed a great working relationship with an Australian music director, Ric Birch, who aided show producer David Wolper with portions of the XXIII Olympiad. Birch invited Spanier to accompany him back to Australia to help him prepare for the 1988 World Expo in Brisbane. Birch wanted Spanier to bring the American marching band tradition down under. His job was to recruit, nurture, and work with local high schools [in Australia] to develop their own bands, who could then come out and perform at the Expo. He was also in charge of a sixty-four-piece band of college musicians from all over Australia, who performed five days a week during the six-month Expo. And it was that band that the USC Song Girls and eighty-eight members of the Trojan Marching Band met on center stage in the summer of 1988. Spanier organized a battle of the bands, Expo-style. "The Australians played 'Waltzing Matilda' and then we played back 'Stars and Stripes,' and it went back and forth," remembered Dr. Bartner. "They would play their hottest tune, and we'd play 'Sing, Sing, Sing.' It was a marriage of two cultures—Hollywood's Band and Australia's band. A great moment!" Of course, even greater than that, Dr. Bartner felt, was the cultural expressions that expanded band members' horizons while south of the equator. The USC band members stayed billet-style; that is, in homes with the Australian band members, which was a great way to experience the culture. Expo Exec Ric Birch hosted Dr. Bartner and his wife Barbara, serving them a BBQ at his home after a night on the town. When the Expo opened earlier in the year, a few months before the TMB arrived, Queen Elizabeth made the official welcome for the Expo that celebrated Australia's bicentennial and revitalized the city of Brisbane. The Exposition covered half a mile along the South Bank of the Brisbane River with exhibits, entertainment, and innovations from forty different countries, so the band enjoyed flavors from around the world in one stop. Aussieland was only the beginning of many cross-cultural excursions for Dr. Bartner and Hollywood's Band.

## A Piece of History

Most anyone who goes on vacation will pick up a souvenir or two, but during the Trojan Marching Band's second trip overseas, the band members had an opportunity to take home a genuine, tangible piece of history. In 1990, Dr. Bartner took sixty members of the Spirit of Troy for a nineteen-day, five-country concert tour through Europe. "It was like the 1940s road bands," said Dr. Bartner. "They get on a bus, play a one-nighter, get back on the bus, then play another city. It was a big band phenomenon to go around the country on a bus like that." Dr. Bartner, Barbara, the Cotlers, and the Song Girls with their instructor, Ann Bothwell, rode on the lower deck, and the rest of the band was on the upper deck. That trip was the most days and most nations for any single excursion the TMB has ever done—plenty of time to not only perform, but also to take in sights of cultural and historical importance within the cities they visited. The first stop was Amsterdam, home of canals, windmills, Anne Frank's House, and the Heineken brewery, all of which the Spirit of Troy toured. The Dutch applauded the band's performance in Dam Square. However, Dr. Bartner did not love the Amsterdam hotel accommodations as the property was below the canal water level. "You look out the windows and see water!" said Dr. Bartner. "Plus, every time a Song Girl had to blow dry her hair, she'd blow the fuse. The manager gave me the key because he was tired of restarting the electricity."

Throughout Europe, the band rode in that double-decker bus from city to city, country to country. It was only about two and a half hours to the next stop in Brussels, Belgium. There, the band had accommodations at a four-star Sheraton Hotel, with a finely appointed and gold-trimmed lobby and spacious rooms in a thirty-floor tower. Band members got settled into their double bunks and it was time to put on their uniforms for their second European performance. As they followed the USC Song Girls and solo baton twirler into the Grand Place, Dr. Bartner and the Spirit of Troy were surprised and very pleased at how enthusiastic the foreign crowd was: cheering, applauding, and mimicking the V-for-victory fingers, even though they likely didn't know what it meant. "The Belgians acted as if they had never seen or heard anything like it before, and they loved it!" said Dr. Bartner. "It was one of the most fun and memorable performances we had ever done." Following the show, Dr. Bartner took advantage of a grand double-sided staircase in the plaza to take a group photo. That evening and the next day were scheduled for free time, so some students took a day-long side-tour to nearby Brugge to pick up some Belgian chocolate and delicate handcrafted lace for which the community is known. The least favorite part of the trip was the long—really long—bus rides between destinations, like the eight-hour ride from Brussels to Berlin.

History buffs will know that a significant, world-changing event took place in Germany in the late 1980s. After World War II, the country was split into zones, with the eastern part going to the Soviet Union and the western part going to the Allied Forces, with a similar arrangement for the city of Berlin itself. As

Cold War tensions rose and basic resources shrunk in the Eastern Bloc, people began fleeing the communist German Democratic Republic for freedom in the West German Federal Republic. During the summer of 1961, some sixty-five thousand people defected, causing the Soviet government to halt the flood by, overnight, erecting an actual wall between East and West Berlin. In a matter of hours, families were permanently separated if they happened to be on opposite sides of the wall. It started as a barbed wire barrier, but became a concrete structure that easterners were forced to build around themselves. No one was allowed through, and in fact, at least one hundred seventy-one people were killed attempting it. But that changed in November 1989, when negotiations between the U.S. and Russia finally succeeded in "tearing down this wall."

The fall of the wall occurred only seven months before Dr. Bartner and the USC Trojan Marching Band were at a once-contentious Checkpoint Charlie, passing freely between West and East Berlin. Band members purchased communist memorabilia and became "wall woodpeckers" by using rented chisels and hammers to knock away chunks of the wall to bring home a tangible piece of world history. The reunification of east and west was not official until October of 1990, so the Spirit of Troy visited Germany when the city was technically still divided. "We had wonderful tour guides," said Dr. Bartner. "In West Berlin, we had a German WWII Lufthansa pilot lead the group, giving us the history from a German point of view. And in East Berlin, we were hosted by students, who wanted to know all about America and what American students do. The German students planned our visit months in advance so they could host the band for a big night out to a bowling alley. It was really something special." Ironically, the nicest meal the band had during the entire European tour was in East Berlin, in the restaurant at the top of the landmark spire television tower. Waiters served chicken cordon bleu and wine with a panoramic view of the city, which made the disparity between the zones painfully obvious—stark, plain block buildings in the east and ornate, embellished buildings in the west. Doubly-ironically, the worst accommodations during the entire trip were in West Berlin at a youth hostel, with four people and all their stuff crammed in a tiny room in which they could open the window to be eaten by mosquitos or keep it closed to sweat and suffocate. The hostel did not have laundry facilities, and it was too hot and humid to hand wash and hang dry clothing, so Dr. Bartner and his wife took it upon themselves to try and find a laundromat by walking the streets in Berlin in the middle of the night. "When we finally found a place, we couldn't figure out how to operate these things, because it was all in German," laughed Dr. Bartner. "We thought it was a washer, and it was actually the dryer. A German came to our rescue and explained it and put in coins for us. Highlight of the tour!" None of that mattered, though, when the band put on their uniforms to perform for both sides of the city.

The evidence of the devastation of wartime air raids is forever preserved with the historic Kaiser Wilhelm Memorial Church in West Berlin. The imperial cathedral, spire, and bell tower were badly damaged in World War II bombings, and the blackened remnants were one of the only structures still standing after the war. In sharp contrast, a new church of 1960s modern architecture was constructed adjacent to and in conjunction with the old relic. It was on the steps of this landmark that Dr. Bartner and the Trojan Marching Band delivered a new spirit of vitality to the people of the city in the form of music, the likes of which West Berliners had never seen. The reaction to the band on the other side of the wall was even more poignant. The only people East Berliners ever saw marching through their streets were threatening ranks of armed military, so it was a shock to see Song Girls and Silk twirlers smiling while dancing to the band's rousing, happy tunes. "We were the first college band to play in East Berlin after the wall was torn down," recalled Dr. Bartner. Many older spectators had tears in their eyes as they never expected to see anything like it in their lifetime of oppression and isolation. The emotion was palpable for Dr. Bartner and band members who didn't realize that a single performance could impact them as much as it did the observers who had only recently found freedom.

Millions of others never realized liberty, as they lost their lives at concentration camps like Dachau, just outside of Munich, which was the TMB's next stop. Band members had a somber, soul-stirring experience as they explored the grounds of the former internment facility. The message at the museum was "Never Again." "It was an eye-opening experience," said Dr. Bartner. "You never forget it. It was probably the quietest I've ever heard the band." Even once back on the bus, it took a while for the heaviness of the exposure to such sorrow to finally lift. Eventually, spirits raised, and everyone was once again enjoying the sights, sounds, pubs, carnivals, and performances in a new city. After a 10 p.m. jam-packed performance at the Glockenspiel in Munich, a white-water rafting excursion in the Bavarian Alps of a small border town in Northern Italy, a stop at Neuschwanstein Castle, a couple days in Innsbruck and Salzburg, Austria, and it was time for another long bus ride back to Amsterdam for the return flight home. The Trojan Marching Band's second-ever international excursion was a monumental success, and Dr. Bartner decided to make it a tradition every other year or so.

The next place he took the band in May of 1992 was to Spain, where the Trojan Marching Band was part of the United States National Day festivities of the World Expo in Seville. While there, the band stayed in Army barracks, and Dr. Bartner was afraid it would be worse than the hostel in Berlin. "I thought it was going to be miserable," said Dr. Bartner. "But turns out there was a pool, bowling, and billiards, and they had the best time!" Marilyn Quayle, wife of Vice President Dan Quayle, was President George Bush's representative at the event that celebrated American music and song, from ragtime to rock. Hollywood's Band was introduced by celebrities Barbara Eden and Tony Randall. Dr. Bartner and the band toured other cities in Spain, ahead of the 1992 Summer Olympics in Barcelona. The ensemble also caught a high-speed ferry from Spain's southern coast across the Strait of Gibraltar to Northern Africa for a tour of Morocco—checking off a fifth continent, for those keeping track. While the Expo was educational and entertaining, the next tour would take the Spirit of Troy back to Europe for another historic commemoration.

## Reliving History

Before the city of Berlin was reunited, before the wall was dismantled, and even before the country of Germany was divided into zones, the great war had to come to an end. One specific invasion is credited with triggering the resolution to the six-year, multi-continent conflict. Operation D-Day, June 6, 1944, was when the first wave of Allied Forces stormed the beaches at Normandy, France in the largest amphibious attack in world history. Supplemented by thousands of paratroopers diving from above, some one hundred fifty-six thousand soldiers from the United States, Canada, and Britain were part of the strategy that confused the Germans and turned the war in the Allies' favor. Thousands of young men violently lost their lives on those beaches, leaving those who managed to survive to live with dreadful memories of what they had seen on those shores. Dr. Bartner was just a little boy when all of this was going on, but he remembers the jubilation around him when the war ended. So, to be invited to bring the Spirit of Troy to the 50th Anniversary of the day that changed the world was an incredible honor.

The "D+50" commemoration activities at the D-Day Monument included a short speech by then-President Bill Clinton before an audience of aging World War II veterans. "Oh, they may walk with a little less spring in their step," said the president, "and their ranks are growing thinner. But let us never forget: When they were young, these men saved the world." [1]At the site of British observances at Arromanches, Queen Elizabeth and Prince Phillip stood in a modified jeep as it carried them along the wet beach to their viewing box for the ceremonies. Another location of the sixty-mile stretch of the liberation area had a reenactment of paratroopers jumping from C-130 airplanes to recognize their contribution to the invasion.

The band members were able to immerse themselves in the immense history in the areas surrounding Normandy's beaches. They meandered through a cemetery full of white crosses and an occasional Star of David marker, denoting grave sites for those who sacrificed their lives for world freedom. Nearby was Sainte Mere Eglise, the first town to be liberated after the invasion. One of the paratroopers in that mission accidentally landed on the church steeple and was stranded there for a time, pretending to be dead so that he may live. It was this church where Dr. Bartner and the Trojan Marching Band, in full uniform, stopped to perform. "When we started playing for them, there was such an outpouring of emotion," remembered Dr. Bartner. "Other people who had lived through World War II came out and embraced members of the band. We had played 'Stars and Stripes Forever,' and it was one of those great moving moments." In the middle of the concert, one gentleman introduced himself to Dr. Bartner and showed him a picture of himself when he was part of the resistance in 1944. The mutual gratitude was evident as the band and countrymen and women shared a meaningful connection that day. Some members of the band felt a more warm-hearted interaction with the people in the French countryside than they had experienced when they toured Paris earlier in the week. They performed beneath the Eiffel Tower and then set up for a photo-op with the monument as the backdrop. Very few ensembles are fortunate enough to have such an up-close-and-personal connection with history as these band members did. Berlin in 1990 and Normandy in 1994 were two unforgettable trips, and Dr. Bartner couldn't wait to see what he could come up with next to give the band another once-in-a-lifetime experience.

The rest of the 1990s saw Hollywood's Band visit Juarez, Mexico for a bull fight after a bowl game in El Paso, Texas, and then tour four more European countries. In '96, the band visited London, England to perform in the rain and fog beneath a gazebo in Hyde Park. Dr. Bartner conducted a concert outside of Clifton Cathedral, but when they got to Edinburgh Castle in Scotland, the weather was so bad, they allowed the band to play inside. "How many marching bands get to perform inside a historic castle?!" exclaimed Dr. Bartner. Then, in '98, the Spirit of Troy was invited to yet another World Expo, this time in Lisbon, Portugal. While on the Iberian Peninsula, the band visited Spain again, too. With fourteen countries and five continents under its belt in only a decade, Dr. Bartner and Hollywood's Band were getting to be world-famous, too.

## Friends Around the World

The first international tour of the new millennium was back down under. The 2000 Olympic Summer Games were to be held in Sydney that year, so in advance of the festivities, Dr. Bartner took the Trojan Marching Band to Australia, since any other member who went on the first trip for the Brisbane Expo had long since graduated. It just so happened that the U.S. Ambassador to Australia, Genta Holmes, was a USC alumna. Dr. Bartner's wife, Barbara, accompanied him on this tour, and the couple invited the ambassador to join them for a concert. "We were performing in front of the Sydney Opera House, so we asked Genta to join us in a special guest box we had created," recalled Dr. Bartner. "When the concert was over, she took the entire band on a dinner cruise of Sydney Harbor. What a great way for the band members to get a personal tour of this special city. We even had the ten-piece perform in the ferry boat. Can you imagine how loud that was?" The Spirit of Troy also performed on the historic (built in 1882) Sydney Cricket Grounds for an Australian Rules Football match. "Aussie Rules," as the sport is called, is nothing like traditional American football, but fun to watch all the same. After the game, the entire crowd stayed to watch the band perform a concert. "All the pubs thought there was an accident or something," recalled Dr. Bartner. "Because no one went to the pubs that night. They were all watching the band! The team invited me to their victory party and gave me a Brisbane Bears jersey." Dr. Bartner and the band were interviewed for not one but two shows on Sydney television before heading north to tour Cairns and the Great Barrier Reef to conclude that excursion. "That was some way to end that trip," said Dr. Bartner. "Every one of us got seasick. I was as green as could be. Someone told me the remedy was to jump into the water, so I did, and I about froze to death. So, my choices were freeze or be sick. Then someone said it would help to go below deck and watch the fish. The fish were beautiful, but it made me worse! It was so claustrophobic. It was the most miserable I've ever been on any trip. I couldn't wait to get my feet on the ground."

Barbara Bartner received the honor of meeting another foreign ambassador—and an even higher-level government official—two years later when she again accompanied the band on its international journey. In 2002, the TMB traveled to Hungary, Austria and the Czech Republic. After seeing the sights and performing in the capital cities of Budapest and Vienna, the band and Barbara Bartner went on to Prague, but without Dr. Bartner. He had a speaking commitment at a worldwide entertainment conference in China. He was to give a lecture on entertainment and education at the college level to industry leaders in China. "I was treated like royalty, flown first class, limousine rides everywhere. But my wife wound up getting the real royal treatment!" Dr. Bartner put his wife and associate directors in charge for the rest of the European trip. The Spirit of Troy donned full uniform and marched down a side street on its way to perform in Prague's Old Town Square. Somewhere nearby, a U.S. Secret Service agent recognized the sound of the Trojan Marching Band. It turns out that First Lady Laura Bush was in town and staying at the residence of U.S. Ambassador Craig Stapleton. The ambassador's wife, Dorothy, happened to be a Trojan fan, so they invited the TMB to perform at a reception the next day in honor of Laura Bush. "So, the band and my wife got to go out to the ambassador's house, get a tour, and take a photo with Laura Bush, and I'm not even there," Dr. Bartner jokingly complained. "I'm in Nanchang, China where my presentation is getting censored because we offer student scholarships and they don't—and my wife is hanging out with the first lady. What are the odds?" It goes to show that Hollywood's Band is, in fact, known around the world.

Believe it or not, something similar happened in Hong Kong the next year. The plan was to go international every other year, but Dr. Bartner couldn't pass up a 2003 invitation to become the first American marching band to ever perform in the Cathay Pacific International New Year's Parade. (The only other American group to attend was the Dallas Cowboy Cheerleaders!) Fortunately, the celebration is held on the 4th of February, so it didn't conflict with the Trojan football team's first appearance in the Orange Bowl. Turns out, a USC Trustee and alumnus lived in Hong Kong and heard the Trojan Marching Band was in town. Billionaire real estate developer and philanthropist Ronnie Chan invited Dr. Bartner and the band to join him on his private yacht after their parade performance to watch the New Year's fireworks from the harbor. "Ronnie made that trip really special for the band. It was breathtaking! The Trojan Family really is worldwide," said Dr. Bartner.

The Spirit of Troy made a good enough impression in Hong Kong that the band was invited for a repeat performance at the 2004 Hong Kong International New Year's Parade. Later that summer, the band made its first trip to Mainland China, to tour and perform in Beijing. "Security was very, VERY heavy. We had the Chinese Army escorting us on both sides of the band," Dr. Bartner remembered. "They weren't worried about the band. They were afraid their people would get too excited, and they didn't want an incident." Everything went smoothly, though, and then they went to the home of the Terracotta Warriors, Xi'an. "The band received a good deal of press, appearing on the front page of the China Times in Beijing and the local Xi'an papers, too," said Dr. Bartner. "Because it was the first time that an American marching band ever was given a key to the city. The only other person up to that time to receive a key was President Bill Clinton. At their presentation ceremony, they put on a show, like they did for the president, and the costumes and drums were fabulous. It was an amazing show." Later, in Shanghai, all of the shops closed on the famous Nanjing Street for the band to perform, but the highlight, especially for the band members, was playing "Conquest" on the Great Wall of China. "Once again, it's about the experience for these kids," said Dr. Bartner. "Every time we go someplace, I look for a way to give them a memory, something that no one else they know has ever done or will ever do. That's why I love international travel."

## But Who's Counting?

Asia beckoned Dr. Bartner and the band again in 2005, this time for the World Expo in Aichi, Japan. After performing there, the Spirit of Troy held shows in Nagoya, Kyoto, and Tokyo. In fact, the TMB became the first marching band to perform at DisneySea Park in Japan, as well as at a Nippon Professional Baseball game. A friend of USC's former baseball coach Rod Dedeaux made the ball game arrangements and Dr. Bartner's friend from Disney, Larry Billman, coordinated the theme park performance. Billman was brought to Tokyo to put together a Broadway show and arranged for the TMB to be the marching band to perform for it. "The Japanese didn't know what to make of this thing," recalled Dr. Bartner. DisneySea allowed the band members to enter the park at no charge, but they would not comp the chaperones. "I don't think they understood that the chaperones were part of the band's entourage," remembered Dr. Bartner, so he bought their tickets. One of the highlights of that 2005 trip was getting to see how band instruments are made at the Yamaha Corporation in Osaka. "It was fascinating," said Dr. Bartner. "Everyone in the plant is also a musician. They played the horns they made before they would ship them. It was cool to see!"

The next decade brought several more firsts for Dr. Bartner and the band. For example, the TMB had played hundreds of times at the Coliseum in Los Angeles, but never at the original Colosseum in Rome, Italy. That changed in 2006! An American touring inside the Roman relic suddenly heard a familiar drum cadence and loud trumpets. He grabbed his video camera, turned it on, ran to the nearest balcony, and wriggled his way to the front to capture the band marching around the Colosseum playing "Tribute to Troy!"[2] Hundreds of people gathered to watch and listen as the Spirit of Troy performed for the very first time at its home away from home. "Definitely a poignant highlight of our trip to Italy," said Dr. Bartner. The Colosseum was the culmination of a tour that began in Venice, went to Bologna, then through Tuscany to Florence, where they performed in front of Michelangelo's statue of David. Dr. Bartner conducted the band in the Piazza della Signoria, the site of the fiery cultural desecration of thousands of books and works of art in the mid-

1400s, which was also the location where the bonfire perpetrator, Savonarola, was burned at stake. "This is the plaza where all that happened, and the band learned about that history." The ensemble would return to Italy for a third time in 2015 for the Milan World Expo to open the USA Pavilion's National Day and do a private performance for the Consulate General of the United States. While in Milan, the Spirit of Troy performed at the castle Sforza, now a museum that houses works of art, including a Michelangelo self-portrait. "The band got special permission to see the exhibit," said Dr. Bartner. "They left their horns outside to walk around the sculpture and then go back outside. The Plaza Square is absolutely famous, and now these kids had seen it first-hand." The TMB would also catch a few days in Switzerland on that 2015 trip.

The Trojan Marching Band made it to its sixth continent in 2008, for anyone who may have lost count. The trip to Rio de Janeiro, Brazil was the band's first time to South America. Reminiscent of the television coverage in Sydney eight years earlier, a Brazilian news reporter speaking Portuguese did a live report from the steps of Rio's City Hall, where hundreds watched the band play "William Tell Overture." The band also performed at a Brazilian club soccer game, "where until you've been to an authentic soccer game, you don't know how exciting it is," and a show on the famous Ipanema Beach, "which was so crowded and dense it was suffocating," said Dr. Bartner. "Then we took the band out of town to an orphanage, and we played for kids who had probably never heard a band or met an American before. I taught them about the instruments, here's a flute, and here's a clarinet, and had a band member play a few notes. The musicians shook hands with the little kids, and it was just the most rewarding event ever."

Then it was back to China for the 2010 World Expo in Shanghai, where the Trojan Band closed the show with famous jazz legend and singer, Harry Connick, Jr. "Yes, I was starstruck, like I usually am," said Dr. Bartner. "Especially because you know I love jazz! That's my foundation!" Connick Jr. spent several minutes hanging out with the band and introducing them to the musicians of his band before they took the stage. "It was a touch of Hollywood, even across the ocean!" Members of the Trojan Marching Band made it back to China twice more—once in 2014 when the drumline played for the grand opening of the first-ever Old Navy store in China, and then again in 2016 for the by-invitation-only Hong Kong Chinese New Year Parade in Macao, featuring the Year of the Monkey. A twenty-piece TMB stepped off the night-time parade of lights that was televised back in the states, too. While the band waited for it to begin, a crazy thing happened. "We were playing our tunes, warming up, and a bunch of other groups surrounded us, and we started trading tunes," said Dr. Bartner. "You couldn't plan this. They were dancing to our music, we high-fived to theirs. It was spontaneous, all these international groups celebrating music together. It was just awesome." That makes six total trips to China during Dr. Bartner's time leading the band on international tours.

Finally, Dr. Bartner and the band crossed the pond to the U.K. in 2012, for a pre-London Olympics affair, playing a huge concert in Trafalgar Square on the entry steps to the National Gallery. "You'd have thought we were Elton John, that crowd was so huge," remembered Dr. Bartner. Afterwards, the USC alumni who lived there took Dr. Bartner and his wife to high tea in a venue overlooking London. "Barbara and I have never eaten so much, scones with whipped cream, sandwiches, it was amazing. They call it tea; I call it dinner!" Then, in 2018, the band took its first-ever tour of Ireland. "The band has been to six continents and all over Europe, and this is the one country we hadn't been to yet," said Dr. Bartner before the journey. "We'd like to share our marching band culture with the Irish people. We're excited to give performances at two of its most famous castles." And they did just that, playing for crowds at Dublin Castle and Blarney Castle—followed by band members kissing that Blarney Stone! And after an incredible run of worldwide performances, that was the last international concert tour Dr. Bartner made before his retirement in 2020.

"It has been an honor all these years to represent the University of Southern California, the state of California, and the United States of America for all of these events and international appearances," said Dr. Bartner. "Sometimes I can't believe I actually went to all of those places. We always had a purpose for these trips. Yes, the idea was to be on vacation and have fun while we were there, but I wanted these kids to have a life-changing experience, open their eyes to other cultures, other worlds. Music can take people places, whether you're playing it or listening to it. And I wanted to influence these kids' lives musically, culturally, professionally, and emotionally. We're a famous band from a famous university, and time and again, things just seemed to happen that enhanced the band's experience. I've loved every trip I've been on with the Trojan Marching Band, and I hope they all did, too."

## High Note: Be Memorable

Dr. Bartner and the TMB didn't just drive it down the field, drive it through town, or drive it across country. Dr. Bartner had students driving it around the globe! His commitment to unique musical experiences for his students led to a tradition of international travel. Performing in a foreign country created an interesting dynamic in that the shows were memorable for both the audience and the performers. When marching band members shared their talent and American culture, it built their confidence to see spectators enjoyed their performance. Creating memories involves evoking an emotional response, a sentimental connection, or a poignant moment. ***The greater confidence you have in your talents, skills, and abilities, the more memorable an impact you can make in another's life experience, which contributes to developing even more confidence.*** The talent the Trojan musicians possessed was clear to Dr. Bartner as he watched the emotional and cultural exchanges that took place on six of seven continents. His own confidence grew, too, with the evidence of the excellence he was helping to instill in young musicians. As much as the students were creating memories with performances on foreign soil, Dr. Bartner was realizing the reminiscing he would get to recall one day as well. *Be memorable.*

# 14

# DISNEYLAND BAND

*In between shows as the director of the Disneyland All-American College Band in California, Dr. Bartner holds the son of a TMB alumni couple, 1997.* Courtesy: Cheryl Cox

# CHAPTER FOURTEEN

## DISNEYLAND BAND

Globe-trotting around the world was only part of what Dr. Bartner did during the summers. He also spent plenty of time at the Happiest Place on Earth! Anyone who has ever been to Disneyland knows there's much more to the theme park than Mickey Mouse and friends, princesses and villains, thrilling roller coaster rides, and spinning teacups. The merriment goes beyond the character-filled parades, helium-filled balloons, spinning lights, funnel cakes, and soft serve ice cream. Throughout the amusement park, guests find multiple entertainment venues where bands play rousing tunes that add to the gleeful atmosphere. For eleven weeks of the summer months, one such group of musicians is the All-American College Band. Somehow, in the middle of everything else Dr. Bartner was doing, he was also the director of the AACB. The fact is, the platinum albums, the movie and television appearances, the Olympic shows, the massed bands for national events, and even the international journeys may not ever have happened if it weren't for the AACB. Truthfully, Hollywood's Band itself wouldn't be what it is if it weren't for what Dr. Bartner learned through directing the All-American College Band at Disneyland. And the crazy thing is, the Disneyland Band almost didn't happen either!

### Adventurous Offers

From early on, when he realized that becoming a professional basketball player was not in the sheet music, Dr. Bartner was content to be a good old-fashioned college marching band director. He enjoyed the athleticism of it, and the discipline of it. He loved the music. He was inspired by the kids he taught. He wanted to build a great band with a great reputation and play great tunes for a great football team at a great school. Dr. Bartner would have been happy with that, but fate had more in mind for him. He had no idea he was being watched while he was conducting the Trojan Marching Band in front of Sleeping Beauty Castle as part of the 1974 Rose Bowl week festivities. It never crossed his mind that he would get a phone call from Disneyland's Director of Entertainment and be offered an opportunity of a lifetime. He would never have thought he would take on a second major job in addition to the already-demanding vocation as the marching band director for the University of Southern California. But he did. And, besides marrying his school-days sweetheart, it was the best decision he ever made. Everything that followed in his career is a direct result of choosing Disney over Mexico.

When Disney execs called Dr. Bartner, the band director already had another opportunity in the hopper. As arranged in the spring of 1974, Dr. Bartner was scheduled to spend that summer south of the border. A government official in the capital city of the State of Mexico was a USC alum who loved the Trojan Marching Band. He wanted to bring that level of musicianship to his community in Toluca. So he invited the band director to create a brand-new marching band program—a skill at which Dr. Bartner is quite adept, building something from the ground up. Dr. Bartner had been to Mexico a few times, done all the curriculum planning, met the kids, and it was all organized. Then Jim Christensen from Disney called, and suddenly, Dr. Bartner had two options on the table. It reminded him of a few years prior when he was entertaining the West Virginia University opportunity, and then USC called. "I had known about the All-American College Band and the prestige of working for Disney," said Dr. Bartner. "This was a major step for me in my career. I couldn't turn down Disney's offer, so I took the job." At the same time, he couldn't leave the Toluca band in a lurch, so he recommended Ken Dye take over, and he happily accepted the challenge. That marching band in Mexico still operates decades later.

## Making Music in the Magic Kingdom

So, instead of central Mexico, Dr. Bartner and his young family spent the summer of '74 in the Sunshine State. The All-American College Band in Anaheim, California was operated by another director, so Dr. Bartner filled the position at Disney World in Orlando, Florida. In late winter/early spring, he and the Anaheim director held auditions in several cities around the country, seeking the best players to fill the band. Hundreds of college musicians applied for only twenty spots: four trumpets, four trombones, four percussionists, four saxophones, two mellophones, and two tubas, plus a pair of dancers. Each part would also double on another instrument, depending on the tune, so these are seriously talented musicians. Not only did they have to be technically good on their instrument, but they also had to have a performer's personality. Dr. Bartner listened for notes, but he also watched their character. Audiences respond to exuberant, high spirits, so no matter which instrument they played, they had to be engaging, encouraging, and full of energy to make music in the Magic Kingdom for eight hours a day, five days a week. Plus, these musicians would be inseparable the whole time, so they had to get along, or it could become a wearisome summer—and not just for the students!

That first season held a learning curve for everyone, including Dr. Bartner. This gig wasn't just a let's-play-music-around-the-park once-in-a-while type deal. The All-American College Band was a very structured, production-centric music industry intensive. While the students were already skilled upon arrival, Dr. Bartner's goal was to have them depart as professional performers. He wanted the students to know this wasn't just a summer job, even though it was a paid internship. It was a career advancement move, and the schedule proved it. The first two weeks were rehearse, rehearse, rehearse, rehearse—and rehearse some more. From 9 a.m. to 5 p.m., the band learned music and corresponding choreography. Then that evening, students had to memorize their parts so they were prepared for rehearsal again the next morning. There would be no lyres and no hiding behind other players, so they had to know their stuff! Finally, it was time for dress rehearsal. Naturally, that could not happen during the day, when the park was full of thousands of guests, so Dr. Bartner and the Disney Band pulled an all-nighter. They had four hours—from one to five in the morning—to visit every venue and run through every show. There were about twenty numbers total, with different themes for the different lands: Patriotic tunes in Town Square, Dixieland tunes in Frontierland, Contemporary Pop Rock in Tomorrowland, and between venues, they'd march through the park—all while blowing full-out, beaming smiles, and bouncing exuberantly. During dress rehearsal, even though only Dr. Bartner was watching, they pretended they had an audience. The band members acted "as if" because they wanted their enthusiasm to be contagious in the crowd, especially with children. They hoped to inspire youths' interest in playing an instrument someday—and at the very least distract them from the long, hot lines for a few minutes for grateful parents. By the end of the late-night/early-morning practice session, the college students were ready for a day off to do nothing but rest their chops. Exhausted would be an understatement, as would be, "Well, that was fun." And it was just the beginning.

The next nine weeks would be jam-packed with clinics taught by professional musicians, including drummer Gregg Field, trumpet pro Wayne Bergeron, trombonist Jake "Jiggs" Wigham, saxophonist Sal Lazano, and many others. Dr. Bartner tried to bring in a specialist for each instrument, along with producers, composers, arrangers, agents, and all manner of music and entertainment industry experts. They instructed the AACB members in specific techniques while instilling increased passion for music and learning the business of Show Business. Dr. Bartner loved it! So did the college musicians, and so did thousands of people who were entertained through the years. Following the three-hour clinics, the All-American College Band players put on uniforms for their daily lineup of five different shows over five hours. Dr. Bartner led them from venue to venue, emceeing the performance—which he absolutely adored. "I really built my entertainment skills at Disney," said Dr. Bartner. "I learned how to read a crowd, how to sense when the enthusiasm was waning and figure out what I could do or say to get the show back on track. I am a firm believer in growth, musically and in maturity, and that's what Disney did for me, and that's what I hope the band did for these kids."

Dr. Bartner wrote the script, so to speak, for the performers to engage with the crowd through the tunes, which were either in alignment with the theme of the land, or perhaps a newly released movie, depending on the year. It was always about connecting with the audience, playing music that would cause kids and grown-ups alike to tap their toes and even dance. Introducing each student in each section gave the band members an opportunity to show off their personality. Sometimes they played a solo to a specific person in the audience, often a small child, because the youngster loved the attention and the parents appreciated the memory. The biggest crowds were when the AACB did their last performance of the night, playing for the audience who lined Main Street waiting for the Disney Parade. A favorite moment for Dr. Bartner and the AACB, was the retreat of the American flag in Town Square at the end of a busy day of performances. Crowds gathered as Disney personnel saluted the flag while the band played patriotic tunes. Then, as the red, white, and blue ensign was hoisted down and respectfully folded, Dr. Bartner directed "The Star-Spangled Banner." From the "National Anthem" to rearranged rock songs to classical to jazz, from slower melodies to music that gets one up and hopping, the students in the Disney All-American College Band played it all. It was Dr. Bartner's goal that by the time they finished the eleven-week program, the band members grew from amateurs to professionals who could hold their own in any performance opportunity. "It's pretty great when I run into a former Disney Band student and they tell me it was the best summer of their lives," said Dr. Bartner. "Many of them have gone on to become professional musicians or conductors or band directors themselves. It's an honor to have played even a small part in their success."

Dr. Bartner led the AACB at Walt Disney World for a couple of years before getting the position full-time in California, under the management of Disney Band Manager Bob Raddock. "He was my manager, who took care of me during my AACB days at Disney," said Dr. Bartner. "He was a really good guy." As Dr. Bartner's alliance with the wonderful world of Disney evolved, so did his career opportunities.

## Big Dreams Do Come True

"This is the realization of Walt Disney's dream to create a permanent showcase of technology and world culture," said the announcer, comedian Danny Kaye. "It's a living monument to past achievements and a testament to the hopes of the future."[1] Kaye stood on a balcony overlooking an esplanade alive with the first public guests to ever visit the "Experimental Prototype Community of Tomorrow," better known as EPCOT Center, near Orlando, Florida. Kaye and seven-year-old Drew Barrymore hosted the Disney television special, guiding viewers on a virtual tour through the three-hundred-acre theme park. Grand opening day was October 1, 1982—exactly eleven years after the grand opening of Walt Disney World and three years after the groundbreaking ceremony that began construction. The celebrity-filled TV show was taped to air later that month, as part of several celebrations at Disney's third theme park. Among the festivities was, of course, the AACB Band Director, Dr. Arthur C. Bartner—and not just the twenty-piece band from his old marching grounds. Rather, he convened students from one hundred forty-six universities across all fifty states in what would be the debut of his virtuosity for directing a national massed band.

The EPCOT Center All-American College Marching Band would be the biggest band Dr. Bartner had assembled up to that point in his career—even bigger than the (at that time) two-hundred-fifty-member Trojan Marching Band in Southern California, which he left under the capable supervision of his associate director, Tony Fox. Dr. Bartner missed two USC football games to lead the Disney ensemble, not something he would ordinarily do if he could help it, but the exposure and education of this event was worth it. (He started the never-miss-a-game-streak five years later.) Dr. Bartner was exhilarated for the challenge of mustering four hundred fifty musicians into one cohesive unit, especially considering the enormity of this EPCOT event. The park had been open for two weeks by the time he arrived in Orlando for planning meetings with organizers and section leaders on Thursday, October 14, 1982. Students started arriving on Sunday, October 17, for a week of prep for multiple performances. They basically took over the Holiday Inn on International Drive. The band filled the entire ballroom when practicing their music, which they did every night for about three hours. The band filled every hotel room for sleeping, which they tried to do for a few hours each night, if they weren't too excited or out late performing. Each morning, the massive massed band bussed to a nearby high school to learn their marching ranks and maneuvers. Midway through rehearsal, on Wednesday afternoon, band members got a free afternoon and free admission to EPCOT. The new friends explored the park, where in a few days they would be stars of the show.

Dr. Bartner and the All-American College Marching Band were a main feature of the official dedication ceremonies for the "World Showcase." When the park opened in 1982, the culture, heritage, landmarks, and flavors of nine countries were represented in replica around the shore of the round-ish lagoon at the center of the park—four nations to the left, four to the right. Directly across the lagoon from the entrance is the centerpiece of the World Showcase: The American Adventure. A Monticelloesque colonial estate invited visitors to be immersed in the heritage and rich history of the United States. Getting to know the landscape and layout of the path was important for the band's upcoming performance. Upon entrance from "Future World," the first nation to the right is Canada, with maple trees and a miniature Victoria Gardens welcoming visitors to the Great White North. Moving around the lagoon, visitors found cobblestone streets of the United Kingdom, with pubs and promenades reminiscent of the British Empire. A one-tenth replica of the Eiffel Tower signified the next country on the lagoon, with bakeries and chateaus for which France is known. The ornate architecture and austere landscapes of the Japanese cannot be mistaken as visitors move up the walkway. Next stop is America. Then, back at the entrance and going left instead, visitors saw the marquee of Mexico, a replica of a Mesoamerican pyramid and the Fountain of Life. Further up the left side of the lagoon is the mystery and serenity of the People's Republic of China, highlighted by its ornamental gardens. Rounding the bend of the lagoon, the Old-World ambiance of Germany mixed with its Oktoberfest Biergartens. Finally, just before the American Adventure, visitors encountered the art and science revolution of Italy, complete with Venetian canals and Neptune's Fountain. (Interestingly, except for Canada, Dr. Bartner and the TMB traveled to the real international destination for each of these EPCOT countries.) The World Showcase Plaza and promenade would soon be filled with music from the All-American College Marching Band.

Before the live performances scheduled for the weekend, the band did a television recording with Danny Kaye on Thursday and a dress rehearsal on Friday, leading up to the big show on Saturday. EPCOT closed early to the public that day, October 23, so the park could set up for the dedication ceremonies. All proudly dressed in the uniform representing their home university, band members gathered for their first performance at the American Adventure auditorium. The band played patriotic tunes for guests at the welcoming ceremony. Organizers introduced and thanked participants and the Honorary Chairperson of the World Showcase Festival Program, Mrs. Leonore Annenberg. (Incidentally, this is the same Mrs. Annenberg of the Annenberg Foundation who gifted philanthropically to and served on the founding governing board of the Annenberg School for Communication and Journalism at the University of Southern California.) Following the short presentation, Dr. Bartner conducted a final song to end part one of the day's festivities. Band members stored their instruments for a few hours of free time to enjoy the sights, sounds, and foods of the World Showcase Festival, as long as they were back at the American Adventure in time for the big show. "That Gala evening was my fondest memory of the event," said Dr. Bartner. "They gave me an all-access pass to every venue, so I got to go to every stage and hear every big band, all of my idols growing up. My first idol, Harry James. Then Lionel Hampton was there, and Bob Crosby and the Bobcats, even Buddy Rich. I went from one big band to another big band to another—I was like a kid in a candy store!"

Then came the 10 p.m. step-off for the finale performance. To unify the multi-colored look of different university uniforms, Disney provided each band member with a white shako hat and an overlay with a golden Disney "D" on the front. Once everyone had their uniform ready, it was show time. "This is why knowing the lay of the land was so important," said Dr. Bartner. "As we left the American Adventure, we split the band into two groups, half marching down the right side of the lagoon, and the other half going down the left side, with the goal of meeting in the middle at the same time, at the center of the World Showcase Plaza. Miraculously, it worked!" The band passing by each international pavilion was the signal for other performers and guests to join the parade and follow it to the front of the park for optimal viewing of the premier of "Le Carnaval Lumiere"—a light and fireworks show over the lagoon. "It was really an awesome way to end the night—except for the drizzling rain. But we were in Florida, so..."

Yes, it rained on Disney's parade that night, and Dr. Bartner and the All-American College Marching Band got soaked, but being the consummate professional he is, Dr. Bartner insisted the show must go on for the ten thousand guests. Somehow the uniforms and overlays managed to dry overnight, in the few hours they had before call-time for the final day of EPCOT dedication ceremonies. This time, Dr. Bartner and the band performed in "Future World," which is anchored by the giant geosphere known as "Spaceship Earth." Just behind that, in the central plaza is the "CommuniCore Fountain." It was here that Donn Tatum, the chairman of the executive committee for the festival, paid tribute to the late Walt Disney. "I only wish Walt were here to share this moment," he said. The man who "imagineered" all the magic had passed away only five years before EPCOT was completed. His wife, Lillian, represented the Disney family at the ceremonies. "Now it gives me great pleasure to introduce you to an extraordinary assemblage of talented young musicians," continued Tatum. "Each one of these musicians was nominated by his or her band director, so it is with great honor that they appear here today."[2] The All-American College Marching Band made a grand entrance on the rooftops of the buildings surrounding the fountain. It was an impressive sight, with one hundred eight trumpets, seventy-six trombones, and forty-two tubas, along with saxophones, mellophones, and a large, loud percussion line. After the band played a welcoming tune, the chairman asked everyone to rise for the National Anthem. Dr. Bartner conducted the band while the crowd paid tribute to the flying American flag that had been presented especially for that occasion by President and Mrs. Reagan. The band stood at attention for the remainder of the dedication, and finally, with the other twenty-three international performance groups, played a tune composed specifically for the event, "We've Only Just Begun to Dream." A flyover of Air National Guard jets and a short fireworks display, and Dr. Bartner's first massive massed band program was complete, having made dreams come true for four hundred fifty college musicians. This Disney EPCOT experience really whet Dr. Bartner's whistle for conducting massed bands. Not only did he love it, but he was also really good at it, which is why he'd only just begun to direct for Disney.

## The Disney Domino Effect

Dr. Bartner was so grateful for his good fortune. With the tremendous success of the EPCOT massed band and his continued mastery of artistry with the Disneyland All-American College Band, Dr. Bartner became Disney's go-to guy for any large-scale event. He had cultivated a close relationship with the powers that be in the organization, especially Robert Jani. "Bob was truly a creative genius with unbelievable showbiz instincts," said Dr. Bartner. "I count him as one of my most important mentors." It was Jani who "discovered" Dr. Bartner only four years into his college career, having seen the band director conduct the Spirit of Troy with such high energy at Disneyland during the 1974 Rose Bowl festivities. It was Jani who a few months later instructed Jim Christensen to hire Dr. Bartner for the AACB. It was Jani who believed Dr. Bartner would be the perfect person to direct the 1982 massed band for EPCOT. It was Jani who created the original plan for the 1984 Olympic Opening Ceremonies and recommended Dr. Bartner conduct that band (even after the event management was transferred from Disney to a private administration under David Wolper.) It was Jani who made the connections that opened the floodgates of opportunities for Dr. Bartner. Once word got out, even other production companies were inviting and hiring Dr. Bartner to help with major events. The 1985 Presidential Inauguration Parade, the 1986 Liberty Band, the 1987 We the People Constitutional Band, Pan American Games, Olympic Festivals, Good Will Games, Super Bowls, and on and on. What Dr. Bartner learned from Disney and these other massed band extravaganzas, he was able to bring back to the University of Southern California Trojan Marching Band and build on its showmanship and entertainment prowess. The domino effect is what contributed to the prestige of Hollywood's Band, opening more doors for the TMB as well. Each band made the next even better, and Dr. Bartner's reputation grew. Of course, he had to do his part and live up to the expectations and bring in top notch musicians who put on stellar shows. It was part of why the band director is such a perfectionist and is so intense if the band didn't perform up to par. He wanted the bands under his direction to always give maximum effort, not just to make Dr. Bartner look good, not just to make Disney (or whatever production company) look good, but so the performers themselves look good and know the feeling of being professional musicians who can entertain and engage any crowd at any type of event. What Dr. Bartner did for band members, he did to help them always be the best they could be. He accepted nothing less. And that is why Jani and other event organizers called on Dr. Bartner any time a major event needed a band. "I was at the top of my game," said Dr. Bartner. "Disney was making history, developing parks, and producing events all over the world, and I got to be part of it—and the best part is, so did thousands of kids."

## Disney Overseas

No sooner did Dr. Bartner get home from the EPCOT grand opening, and it was on to preparing for the next event, and then another, and another, one right after the other. The 1980s were a magical, high-pitched, musical blur of activity as Dr. Bartner's schedule was one long full-note that never seemed to hit a rest. By the turn of the decade, he realized he had to kick it down an octave or two if he (and his family relationships) were going to survive. Dr. Bartner became more selective in the opportunities he would accept. One to which he had to say yes was the grand opening of EuroDisney, near Paris, France in spring of 1992. As it had been doing successfully for years, Disney produced a star-studded television special and epic live production at the park to celebrate the beginning of a new era—and new continent—for family entertainment. Naturally, Dr. Bartner was put in charge of the All-American Marching Band, raising the bar once again. This time, it was six hundred fifty musicians, not from colleges, but from high schools around the U.S. At the band welcome meeting, surrounded by his USC band staff as assistants, Dr. Bartner set his expectations for the students as they prepared for this worldwide media event. "The only way this works is if you mentally [focus] for the next four days," Dr. Bartner said from atop a platform in a temporary shelter built for the band. "I mean, folks, this is a four-day season. This is not a season that starts in July or August and goes for four months. This is four DAYS!"

The sections got to work immediately, setting up ranks shoulder to shoulder, practicing the gliding march across the parking lot. (By the way, only the USC TMB marched with the chair.) After the first day, Dr. Bartner saw progress. "I'm very impressed. So far, it's going great. It's a little shaky, but you have to remember, this is the first time that they've actually moved and played at the same time," he said. "But there's a lot of talent out there, and by the time Sunday rolls around, it's going to be awesome."[3]

True to form, Dr. Bartner made sure it wasn't all work and no play. The high school band students got to be tourists in Paris, visiting the Arc de Triomphe, the golden statue of Joan of Arc, the Louvre, the Cathedral of Notre Dame, and of course, the Eiffel Tower. Dress rehearsal was the next day, and then Sunday, April 12, 1992, was opening day. Similar to what Disney did for the EPCOT band, musicians wore matching shakos and overlays, with the addition of a long red cape. Playing the tune "Be Our Guest" from Disney's latest movie, *Beauty and the Beast,* the band emerged from the main entrance tunnel to the waiting crowd, where Disney executives welcomed guests and invited them to follow the band into park. Later, the six hundred fifty musicians marched a parade down the Paris version of Main Street, which mimics the original in California but with French flair. That evening, at the finale concert by Temptations and the Four Tops, the band entered from both sides of the stage, and the crowd jumped to its feet in applause. Dr. Bartner and the band even made the television coverage hosted by Don Johnson and Melanie Griffith. "Backing up the Temps and the Pops was the 650-piece All-American Marching Band, featuring the best student musicians from each of the fifty states," said Griffith. "These kids raised their own travel expenses so they could travel to Paris just for tonight's grand opening."[4] Finally, Dr. Bartner and the band stood ready with all the famous Disney characters while then-CEO Michael Eisner officially cut the ribbon in front of Sleeping Beauty Castle. Mickey Mouse appeared through the castle doors, waving and welcoming everyone to join him for an evening in the park. Band members all rushed in to enjoy their final moments at what is now called Disneyland Paris before heading back to the tent for their own band celebration, where even Dr. Bartner got in on the dancing! He was proud of this group and pleased with yet another successful event. Coincidentally, as a side note, years later, Dr. Bartner and Hollywood's Band were invited to play at Eisner's birthday party. "One of the neighbors called the cops on the band for violating a noise ordinance," said Dr. Bartner. "We didn't realize it, because by the time the police arrived, we had finished playing and had the horns put away. That was a crazy way to meet Michael Eisner!"

## Disney Days Gone By

Four years after opening EuroDisney, Dr. Bartner was back in Orlando for the 25th Anniversary of Walt Disney World. "I remember having this huge group of high school band kids and we had to rehearse at night because the park was full during the day," recalled Dr. Bartner. "We were rehearsing that night in the back lot, and there happened to be an eclipse of the moon, and we all got to see it from Disney World!" Four years after that was the 45th Anniversary of Disneyland. Five years later, he took the Trojan Marching Band to Tokyo DisneySea Park in Japan to become the first American marching band to perform there. Of course, the Trojan Marching Band had been performing at Disneyland every so often when USC would earn a spot in the Rose Bowl, so Dr. Bartner was in the Magic Kingdom a lot throughout the years. He never did get to meet Walt Disney himself, but at Disneyland's 50th Anniversary celebration in 2005, Dr. Bartner met Disney's daughter, Diane Disney Miller, who had married former USC football player Ron Miller. She was the guest speaker at the 50th anniversary ceremonies, along with then-California Governor Arnold Schwarzenegger.

By then, Dr. Bartner had decided his time had come to step away from the AACB. After multiple massed bands across the Disney properties and other related performances, and after twenty-eight years leading the Disneyland All-American College Band, Dr. Bartner recognized that someone else should have a turn directing these great students at the Happiest Place on Earth. He finally retired as lead conductor, but he stayed on as a consultant to provide continuity for a new director. Fortunately, that was an easy position to fill. Another professor and professional musician from USC was happy to take over. As a jazz studies professor at the USC Thornton School of Music, Ron McCurdy had the skills, knowledge, and background. In fact, he was in Dr. Bartner's first AACB in Florida in 1974, when he was a student at Florida A&M, so he had additional perspective to offer. "Pretty cool that I brought him into the business, and then he took my place," said Dr. Bartner. When the All-American College Band celebrated its 45th Anniversary in 2015, McCurdy invited Dr. Bartner back to guest conduct. "That was a great flashback," said Dr. Bartner. "It brought back some really great memories. To this day, there is no greater thrill for me than to march down Main Street. I've done it with the USC band, with the AACB, and with massed bands at Disney parks all over the world. It doesn't matter which band or what size. It's a thrill for me. There's just something about getting all these guests excited about music and entertainment. I just love that kind of thing. Getting this job all those years ago really changed my life. It made my career. I loved every minute, and I am forever thankful."

Dr. Bartner remains especially grateful to his mentor and friend, Bob Jani, who passed away in 1989 at the age of fifty-five after a three-year struggle with Lou Gehrig's disease. "Bob taught me more about showmanship and entertainment and audience engagement than I ever learned in school. He helped me develop my instincts and made me a better conductor, teacher, and person. I hope I've been a good steward of his knowledge and passed it along to every student I've had the honor to teach because of the opportunities that Bob provided. I wouldn't be where I am today if it weren't for Bob." Dr. Bartner also gives a lot of credit to Jani's influence and inspiration for the Trojan Marching Band earning its solid reputation as Hollywood's Band, and all that it has accomplished around the world, the nation, and at home in Los Angeles.

## High Note: Be Impressive

By the time he became director of the All-American College Band for Disney, Dr. Bartner had seen and heard hundreds of kids play just about every kind of instrument. He had an ear and an eye for selecting young men and women who could play—and live—in harmony together. The applicants for the Disneyland Band not only had to be excellent musicians, but they also had to be fantastic performers. It was highly competitive, something Dr. Bartner appreciated being both athlete and musician. The players who made the greatest impression with their personality and ability to bring spirit to the music and energetic interaction with the audience—those are the ones who were selected. ***Consistently performing at the highest levels develops excellence. Success drives more success, and that builds confidence to perform again.*** The experience and expertise to which these band students were exposed was top-notch. Dr. Bartner's goal was that every AACB member who invested their summer performing with the world of Disney would depart with the confidence required to succeed in competitive the world of music—and that starts with knowing how to leave a great impression. *Be impressive.*

# 15

# L.A.'S BAND

*The Trojan Marching Band under the direction of Dr. Bartner entertains fans at Los Angeles Dodger Stadium before the first pitch on Opening Day, 2014.* Courtesy: Benjamin Chua

# CHAPTER FIFTEEN

## L.A.'S BAND

While Dr. Bartner and the Trojan Marching Band have performed for tens of thousands of people around the world, they are, of course, most often seen in Southern California. It's not unusual for Hollywood's Band to be invited to welcome dignitaries visiting Los Angeles, including U.S. Presidents and even the Pope. The band has been on hand to congratulate Hollywood celebrities, like Liza Minelli and Jerry Buss, for receiving a star on the Hollywood Walk of Fame. The band played for crowds at movie premieres, like *King Kong* and *Grease*, surrounded by blockbuster superstars and their screaming fans. Music videos, rock concerts, national television shows, international athletic competitions, and professional sports teams with the Lakers, Dodgers, Rams, and Raiders—living in Los Angeles, the second largest city in the country, definitely has its privileges. By the mid-2000s, Hollywood's Band was a well-oiled machine, performing at some three hundred fifty different gigs in a three-hundred-sixty-five-day period, not counting athletic events. That means a portion of the band, whether a ten-piece, twenty-piece, forty-piece, or even eighty-piece band, played somewhere nearly every day of the year—sometimes multiple times per day! Of course, there was no physical way Dr. Bartner himself could be at every single one of those gigs. This level of activity and visibility is only possible because of the foundation and staff he built over the decades.

## Team Players

If cloning oneself were a real thing, Dr. Bartner might have done it, because there was a period when he wanted to be in several places at one time, simply because he was passionate about all of it. He recognized, though, that delegating and sharing the responsibility was beneficial to developing leadership in the program. About the same time the Trojan Marching Band was hitting the airwaves with "Tusk" and Fleetwood Mac, the band was also hitting the court at the Fabulous Forum as the new basketball band for the Los Angeles Lakers. Dr. Gerald "Jerry" Buss had acquired ownership of the team in 1979 in what was, at the time, one of the largest ever sports team takeovers in history. At age forty-six, Buss bought the Lakers, Kings, the Forum, and a ranch in the Sierra Nevada Mountains for $67.5 million. He built a fortune in real estate after earning his doctorate in physical chemistry at USC by age twenty-four. As a huge Trojan fan, Dr. Buss approached Dr. Bartner with the idea of having the band perform at tennis matches for Buss' other pro team, the Los Angeles Strings. That didn't really resonate with Dr. Bartner, but when Buss suggested playing for the Lakers, that was an idea he could buy into. He was a former varsity player, after all! Buss had a vision of transforming pro basketball games into a new era of sports entertainment, and Hollywood's Band would be a big part of that innovation.

Dr. Bartner took a twenty-piece band to the Forum for the first time on October 16, 1979. Buss and the fans loved it, and it became a regular part of "Showtime!" on the court. "I've always gotten great enjoyment from the intensity of the atmosphere at college football and basketball games," said Dr. Buss. "All that energy, I thought, was missing at Laker and all NBA games. The band, the cheerleaders, rooting for your team was an environment that I wanted to create at our games, for our fans, and for our players. I thank Art Bartner... for his part in making the band a part of the Laker dynamic."[1] Dr. Bartner and the band were jamming in the stands while million-dollar marquee players Magic Johnson and Kareem Abdul-Jabbar were running, dribbling, and slam-dunking, with famous faces like Jack Nicholson cheering courtside. It wasn't long before the Forum became the place to see and be seen, with Hollywood celebrities flocking to the games. Hollywood's Band was a natural fit.

The Laker Band was a highlight for Dr. Bartner, who directed as many games as he could for several years. However, in the '80s, when he was auditioning musicians for the AACB and planning drills for the Trojans, the Olympics, EPCOT, and other events, it simply became too much. He often delegated the Laker Band responsibility to other team players in Trojan Band Family, not only giving them another glimpse of the glitz and glamour of Hollywood, but also providing them with additional experience as professional performers and conductors. Dr. Bartner had teaching assistants like trumpet player Barry Spanier sub for him at the Laker games. Spanier became very involved in many of the events that Dr. Bartner directed, including the '84 Olympics and the '88 World Expo. Spanier later coordinated the two-thousand-piece band for the 2000 Olympics in Sydney. After several years as a freelance music director and getting his masters at New York University, Spanier found his place as the director of the Tulane University Marching Band, which hadn't had a band in thirty years. He built it from scratch, starting in 2005. "That's what I learned at USC, what role a band program can and should play at a university," said Spanier. Another Trojan Band member who frequently helped Dr. Bartner with the Laker Band was trombone player Mark Laycock. Laycock credits Dr. Bartner for how that experience conducting the basketball band contributed to his passion for directing his own orchestra at Wichita State University. "As a freshman [in 1982], I had no idea [of Dr. Bartner's expertise]. You're scared of the man and hope he doesn't learn your name," recalled Laycock. "He's obviously inspired me, given me career advice, and helped me with those first conducting opportunities. A lot of people don't know the great amount of knowledge he has about music. Dr. Bartner is pigeonholed into this coach kind of thing, he does that really well, but he needs to be credited for the vast amount of knowledge he has about music in general."[2] Laycock and Dr. Bartner meet for lunch whenever they can.

Then there's Rick Cox. He joined the USC TMB as a trumpet player in 1981, and as a big basketball fan, tried out for the Laker Band his freshman year. Cox went on to become the trumpet section leader, and then in 1986, Dr. Bartner had him take over as Director of the Laker Band. As an Assistant Director for the Trojan Marching Band, Cox has been conducting the basketball ensemble ever since. Each year, he holds auditions for TMB members who want one of the twenty spots. They have to be the best of the best, because it's high-visibility performing. "We add a live dimension," said Cox in an ESPN interview. "With live music, people can relate to that. It's kind of a nice link between the superhuman feats they're seeing on the court and this regular real, live kind of jazz music that they're hearing us play."[3] Like what Dr. Bartner did at football games, Cox organized all the tunes to coordinate with the basketball games. The performance opened with the theme from *Rocky* and then they'd play other rock charts for time outs and halftime, complete with dancing by the USC Song Girls, who were the first "Laker

Girls"—originally known as "Golden Girls." When the Laker Band was first created, the band was close to the action on the court, and Cox remembers Abdul-Jabar giving him music requests. Later, the band got moved up next to "Jerry's Box" in the Forum. Dr. Buss showed his appreciation for the band's contribution with occasional refreshments, along with ten dollars per musician per game and an extra free ticket to the matchup. At the end of each Showtime, the Laker Band would reciprocate by playing Dr. Buss's favorite tune, "Just a Gigolo." That tradition continued when the pro basketball team moved to the Staples Center in downtown Los Angeles. The players were set up high up in section 308 with high-tech microphones to blast their sound through the one-million-square-foot arena, but they sound so good, the crowd often mistakes them for recorded music. "The view of the game is great," said Cox. When the Lakers were on their national championship streak, the band went along for the ride for a couple of the celebratory parades through downtown Los Angeles. A quarter of a million fans lined the streets to congratulate their favorite team as they rode by atop fire trucks.

The Laker Band exemplifies the symbiotic relationship between the USC TMB and the Los Angeles community, to which Rick Cox has committed himself his whole life. "Rick has been awesome with the Laker Band all these years," said Dr. Bartner. "He's another great, loyal Trojan that I can really trust. He's been around almost as long as I have!" It was on the TMB's 1990 European tour that Rick got to know a Silk named Cheryl, who would become his wife at a ceremony attended by Dr. Bartner himself. "If it weren't for being in the band, I may never have gotten married," said Rick. They raised their three children, a son and two daughters, in L.A., going to many... many...

basketball and football games. Like father, like son, their oldest, Jake, joined the Trojan Marching Band in the 2010s and became the trumpet section leader—and a member of the Laker Band, playing alongside his dad. "That's the real definition of the Trojan Family," said Dr. Bartner. "That's why I do what I do, to be an influence in the lives of these band guys, to keep the love of real music alive for generations."

## More than a Marching Band

Besides raising the roof at a basketball arena or igniting fans at a football field, music can also bring a gratifyingly sophisticated, yet moving, ambiance to an audience—something Dr. Bartner has been doing for decades with the USC Concert Band. While some Trojan Marching Band members take the second semester off after the frenetic football season, many musicians prefer to keep the music going and join the concert ensemble. In the '70s, it was a group of music majors from the Thornton School of Music, but the department ended the program in 1981. Dr. Bartner refused to let the ensemble die, so he brought it back, building it with members of the Trojan Marching Band. One of their first performances was held in April of 1983, called "Pops at Pickfair." Before its demolition in 1990, Pickfair was a famous Beverly Hills mansion, so called by combining the names of its original owners, silent film stars Mary Pickford and Douglas Fairbanks, who regularly hosted parties in the 1920s and 1930s for celebrities like Charlie Chaplin, Clark Gable, Joan Crawford, and even Albert Einstein, Amelia Earhart, Henry Ford, and Babe Ruth. In 1983, the forty-two-room estate belonged to L.A. Lakers' owner Jerry Buss. He welcomed hundreds of guests to the sprawling grounds for the first-ever fundraiser for the new

Spirit of Troy band support group. USC President and Mrs. James H. Zumberge and Women's Athletics Director Barbara Hedges were on hand to encourage attendees to contribute to a new scholarship fund for the Trojan Marching Band. Dr. Bartner coordinated chamber music, Dixieland, and a jazz combo down by the pool while fans mingled. This al fresco benefit concert continued in several different venues over the next few years. The USC Concert Band performed for "Pops at Paramount" in spring 1989 and "Pops at the Police Academy" in 1990, which also celebrated Dr. Bartner's 20th Anniversary. Dr. Bartner's protege, Ken Dye, guest-conducted that ensemble, at which President Zumberge again promoted fundraising to support the Band Grant Endowment. "These concerts are not only fun to do, but they also help fund the necessities for the band," said Dr. Bartner. "The band requires several hundred thousand dollars each year to be able to have band members travel to away football games, not to mention having the staff to organize it all. We pay for uniforms and helmets, instruments, and all that, so there is no cost to the students. And we now offer stipends and band grants, too. That's why I really appreciate every contribution that comes into this office for the endowments. It's what allows us to continue to be Hollywood's Band."

The Pops spring concerts were held in other seasons at the Nixon and Reagan Presidential Libraries and at the Tournament of Roses House in Pasadena, as well as the USC President's residence bequeathed by Seely Mudd, but Dr. Bartner wanted to find an indoor venue where the acoustics were better, and he could conduct a more proper, elegant performance to highlight the talent of the student musicians. A place where, instead of wearing cardinal and gold capes, they could wear traditional concert black attire. The concert band found a semi-permanent home with the help of USC alum Doug Padelford and his wife Anita. In 1997, Doug Padelford was President of the Friends of the Cerritos Center for the Performing Arts, and he generously invited the USC Concert Band to perform at the state-of-the-art facility. The stage was set for dozens of premier conductors, composers, and performers to guest star with Dr. Bartner and the concert musicians, bringing another level of Hollywood flair to Hollywood's Band. Among the first to have the honor was acclaimed music producer David Foster, who produced the music for the film *Bodyguard,* starring Kevin Costner and Whitney Houston, who sang "I Will Always Love You" in that movie. Foster was also producer for musicians including Michael Jackson, Kenny Loggins, Kenny Rogers, Jennifer Lopez, Madonna, the group Chicago, and dozens more. Dr. Bartner presented Foster with a Trojan helmet for his artistry with the Spirit of Troy Concert Band.

Over the next thirteen years, the who's who of guest conductors for the Pops at Cerritos concerts became a mind-blowing list of incredible talent and achievement. "I wanted to give these students an opportunity to be mentored by and conducted by world-famous, award-winning composers," said Dr. Bartner. "And these concerts did just that. It's an honor to have collaborated with these men and women who have dedicated their lives to making incredible music." The following year, celebrity guests included drummer Louie Bellson (who also performed live with the TMB at the 1972 USC-Notre Dame football game) and premier violinist Charlie Bisharat. Guest conducting the Spirit of Troy Concert Band in 1998 was Michael Arnold Kamen, who composed the scores for *Mr. Holland's Opus, Robin Hood: Prince of Thieves, Die Hard,* and more than forty-five others. The composer of the theme for *Ghostbusters, Magnificent Seven,* and *The Ten*

*Commandments* was Elmer Bernstein, and he conducted for the 1999 event.

The Pops at Cerritos concert of 2000 was an extra special occasion, because it honored the composer of "Conquest"—USC's battle cry fight song to which the white stallion mascot charges around the field after the Trojans score a touchdown at football games. Considered one of the godfathers of Hollywood film scores, Alfred Newman wrote the "Conquest" arrangement for the movie *Captain from Castile*, and then in 1950 gifted the arrangement to USC to use in perpetuity. To mark the 50th anniversary of that bequest, Dr. Bartner invited Newman's family to be a part of the salute to their father, who won nine Oscars with forty-three nominations. He was the most Oscar-nominated composer in history, until John Williams of *Star Wars* fame broke that record in 2011. (In fact, John Williams got his start playing piano for Newman!) In attendance were two of Newman's five children, Maria and Thomas, who are accomplished musicians in their own right, making the Newmans the most award-nominated family in history, with ninety-two nominations. Maria is a decorated violinist and classical composer, and Thomas has scored more than seventy-five films, including *Finding Nemo*, *The Green Mile*, and *Shawshank Redemption*. They appreciated the tribute to their father's musical legacy at the concert, which crescendoed with a rousing version of "Conquest," of course. "What a great gift Alfred Newman gave to USC," said Dr. Bartner. "It's really the most powerful battle cry of any university in the country. We play it after every victory!"

Pops at Cerritos 2001 featured guest conductors Richard and Robert Sherman of Disney's Sherman Brothers, who composed music for, among many others, *Mary Poppins*, *Bedknobs and Broomsticks*, and *Chitty Chitty Bang Bang* (which, by the way, was filmed at Neuschwanstein Castle where Dr. Bartner took the band in 1990.) Their most famous tune is the world's most performed song of all time, "It's a Small World." Dr. Bartner made the brothers honorary band members, recognition which the Sherman family appreciated. Subsequent Pops events featured the St. Charles Borromeo Choir conducted by Paul Salamunovich, trumpet player Wayne Bergeron, pianist Shelly Berg, jazz and blues singer Barbara Morrison, songbook singer Patti Austin, actress Sharon Gless, and Dale Kristien of *Phantom of the Opera* fame. The year 2004 was a tribute by Monica Mancini to her father Henry Mancini for the tenth anniversary of his passing. The master of ceremonies for the 2006 Pops event was the Fonz, Henry Winkler, who was also made an honorary band member with a Trojan helmet.

Eventually, to help manage costs and personnel, the spring concerts were moved back to campus, where Dr. Bartner would invite celebrity guests to perform with the USC Concert Band at Bovard Auditorium. Dr. Bartner conducted thirty-seven Pops concerts during his tenure, in addition to everything else he did. "Dr. Art Bartner is a joy to watch as he conducts his musical aggregations," said Richard Sherman. "His expertise, precision, and demand for excellence, is only surpassed by the inspiration and encouragement he imparts to his youthful musicians. It's no wonder that the USC band has been rated one of the finest musical organizations in the nation."[4] Dr. Bartner felt that was high praise coming from one of the greatest composers in the world. "That's what this is all about," said Dr. Bartner. "Making music that makes memories, for the students performing, the conductors conducting, and the audience listening. It's just been outstanding for these kids to be exposed to this level and variety of professionals in the industry through these concerts. Besides,

I LOVE to conduct. With the marching band, I'm directing, but with the concert band, I'm conducting. I get my baton, use my left hand to cut and get dynamics. It's how I keep my conducting chops as a legitimate conductor. I was trained to do this, and I LOVE doing this."

## Hollywood's Band at the Hollywood Bowl

Many master conductors have stood before the USC Concert Band, and the Trojan Marching Band, for that matter. But none is as easily recognizable as the one who waved the baton during Dr. Bartner's first-ever performance at the famed Hollywood Bowl, the 17,500-seat venue within eyeshot of the world-renowned hillside Hollywood sign. On the Fourth of July in 1982, the band played a medley of patriotic songs for a Family Fireworks Picnic Concert, under the direction of Big Bird. Yes, the eight-foot-two yellow anthropomorphic canary from *Sesame Street*, portrayed by Carroll Spinney, guest-conducted the band during the family-friendly holiday performance. Spinney was the puppeteer for Big Bird and Oscar the Grouch since their inception in 1969 until a few years before his passing in 2018. "Talk about a career," said Dr. Bartner. "Having Big Bird lead the band was a fun twist. And it got the concert band noticed and invited back to the Hollywood Bowl." In fact, the USC ensemble became a regular at the venue for Independence Day festivities.

For several years, one of Dr. Bartner's favorite shows was when the band-minus-percussion took the stage to synchronize with the fireworks for the finale of the Los Angeles Philharmonic performance of Tchaikovsky's *1812 Overture*. The orchestra was led by famed conductor Gustavo Dudamel, who Dr. Bartner calls his classical idol. "I've learned more during rehearsal following him for 1812 than I've ever learned about conducting. He's that marvelous," said Dr. Bartner. "Performing at the same time the fireworks are going off is just awesome. We have to try and play louder than the explosions! The string players didn't want to ruin their instruments trying to do that."

Many other artists have had sections of the band join them at the famous amphitheater to amplify their show, like when the drummers joined the Go-Go's on stage to play "We Got the Beat" in celebration of their induction into the Hollywood Bowl Hall of Fame. The TMB was also there when John Williams was inducted, as well as when the Hollywood Bowl paid tribute to Jerry Herman's Broadway. The Herman show was a PBS special that aired over and over again, giving the band years of visibility. Another summertime two-night performance featured an eighty-piece band playing the movie score it recorded for the hit film, *Croods*. The opening scene of the movie needed a fast-paced, strong drums and horns, "Tusk"-inspired tune for the characters to play pseudo-football with a dinosaur egg. Composer Alan Silvestri knew just where to find that sound, so he got with Dr. Bartner at Bovard Auditorium in January 2013 to have the band record the music. Combining the percussion and brass with the orchestra recording he made in London the year before, Silvestri had his number, "Smash and Grab." When DreamWorks Animation celebrated its 20th anniversary at the Hollywood Bowl, it only made sense to have the USC band play its portion of the soundtrack—live—as part of the concert. Silvestri even held up his hand to say "Fight On" after he conducted the performance. "The Trojan Marching Band is known as Hollywood's Band," said Dr. Bartner. "You can't get any bigger than performing at the Hollywood Bowl during the summer. It's a very prestigious place to play."

## City Celebrations

The list of prestigious events for which Hollywood's Band has performed goes on and on and on, so it's a good thing Dr. Bartner had the assistance of his assistants. After years of doing it on his own, he was relieved to have band managers who keep track of all the invitations and commitments, because every time he turned around, Hollywood's Band was asked to perform any time the city had an opening or anniversary. In 1989, Dr. Bartner and the Trojan Marching Band were part of a huge celebration for the 25th anniversary of the Los Angeles Music Center, in a special event emceed by Charleton Heston and Carol Channing. The country's first freeway, the Pasadena Arroyo Seco (the 110, in L.A-speak) turned fifty in 1990; the 200th anniversary of the Bill of Rights was observed at L.A. City Hall in 1991; The Los Angeles Central Library reopened in October 1993; then-Governor Pete Wilson cut the ribbon for the city's newest freeway, the 105, two weeks later; the L.A. Convention Center South Hall opened a month after that; Pershing Square was rededicated in early 1994; Los Angeles City Hall was rededicated on its 74th Anniversary in 2002; and there were several other commemorations sprinkled in between. Sometimes those performances become unexpected surprises, as with a gig at the Los Angeles International Airport. United contributed sixty-nine million dollars to renovation efforts for the venue to become the United Airlines Field at the Los Angeles Memorial Coliseum in 2019. Travelers and United employees were surprised when the TMB marched into their lobby for an impromptu concert to celebrate the announcement.

As Dr. Bartner's career advanced into multiple decades, many gigs—like an anniversary for a burger joint or college student day at the L.A. County Fair—were events that he need not attend, as the ten-piece or twenty-piece band manager handled it on their own. However, there were significant city celebrations that Dr. Bartner would never want to miss, especially when dignitaries were involved; for example, when the Chinese President Jiang Zemin was honored at the Beverly Hills Hotel, or when then-Vice President Al Gore was on hand for the grand opening of the California Science Center, or when Three Tenors were performing a concert at Dodgers Stadium in 1994. "To this day, I remember who was in the front row when the band marched in," recalled Dr. Bartner. "Frank Sinatra, Gene Kelly, the who's who of the entertainment business. But then, the concert itself with Placido Domingo, Luciano Pavarotti, and Jose Carerras, and Zubin Mehta conducting and Lalo Schifrin guest conducting. We played our tunes at intermission, but the band got to stay for the concert. It was amazing for all of us to be part of this cultural event of the year."

After decades of doing everything, it was only fair for Dr. Bartner to be more selective in which events he directed, even if sometimes the occasions required a more somber performance. That was the case in 2013, when Dr. Bartner and a ten-piece-minus-percussion played at a memorial service for a lifelong Trojan supporter. USC alum and billionaire Los Angeles Lakers owner Dr. Gerald "Jerry" Buss passed away at the age of eighty after a long battle with cancer. At his memorial service, Dr. Bartner conducted a moving rendition of "Amazing Grace" before a celebrity-filled congregation, and he remembers seeing Buss's daughter, Jeanie, with tears streaming down her face. Among the trumpet players in full uniform, grateful to be wearing the standard dark sunglasses, was the long-time Laker Band director Rick Cox. "Dr. Buss was one of a kind," said Dr. Bartner. "I was honored to call him my friend. He made a huge impact on this band and this city."

## City of Sports

If the city of Los Angeles hosted any sort of sporting event, it's a sure bet that Dr. Bartner and the Trojan Marching Band were there. Of course, there was that big deal in 1984—the Los Angeles Olympics at the Coliseum. That was followed by the Olympic Festival in 1991, and L.A.'s participation in the Olympic Torch ceremonies for the 1996 Atlanta Summer Games and the 2002 Salt Lake City Winter Games. There were other international invitationals where the TMB performed, too, like the World Cup Soccer Tournament in 1994 and the Davis Cup Tennis Tournament in 2000. The city of L.A. even hosted its own sports competition with the Los Angeles Inner-City Games in 1992. In the 80s and 90s, the Trojan Marching Band was occasionally asked to perform before an NFL Game for the Los Angeles Rams or Raiders. Dr. Bartner's involvement in city athletics actually goes back to the 1970s, when he assembled a massed band to kick off Major League Baseball Opening Day at Dodger Stadium, a tradition that lasted some twenty years. Several times, when the Blue made it to the World Series, the TMB performed at those games as well. In fact, Dr. Bartner garnered such a reputation with the Dodger organization that in 2009, when the band director celebrated the start of his fortieth year at USC, he received a special honor. Wearing a baseball jersey customized with the number 40, he got to throw out the first pitch of the game! "That was a thrill," said Dr. Bartner. "I hadn't thrown a baseball since my little league days, but I'm sure I threw a perfect strike. Not sure how, because I just closed my eyes and threw it!" The team named September 14, 2009 as USC Night at Dodger Stadium, and the band performed the National Anthem before the game and "God Bless America" during the seventh inning stretch.

## Music Lovers

Be it fifty thousand people at a baseball stadium, seventeen thousand at a basketball court, ninety thousand at a football field, thousands along a parade route or concert, or a couple dozen at a ribbon-cutting, the sound of music unites the participants. The love of music draws people together, whether that means performing it or dancing to it—or both! The sounds of the Trojan Marching Band under the direction of Dr. Arthur C. Bartner have been bonding people together for decades in all variety of venues. Sometimes the band does the inviting, and other times it is the invitee. In the late 1990s to early 2000s, Hollywood's Band was invited three times to lead the Hollywood Christmas Parade off a literal red carpet and down Hollywood Boulevard in a star-studded event held the Sunday after Thanksgiving. The three-and-a-half-mile route featured famous actors and actresses, popular singers, balloons, floats, and marching bands, all playing holiday-themed tunes to ring in the holiday spirit. One year, Leeza Gibbons and Bob Eubanks emceed a special live television broadcast in which the band was the featured entertainer at the start of the show, performing a concert before leading the parade through Hollywood.

From lighter holiday music to heavier rock songs, the Trojan Marching Band can play it all, because the TMB was also invited three times to perform with big names at the fast-growing Coachella Valley Music and Arts Festival, a couple hours south of Los Angeles. The collection of rising and reuniting music groups of various genres filled multiple tents with music lovers. The first time the TMB joined professional musicians on stage was in 2010, when thirty players crushed it on the main stage with progressive rock band, Coheed and Cambria. TMB students had selected that group's song "Welcome Home" to perform during the UCLA game halftime show in November of 2009. The rock group saw a video of the performance and retweeted it on Twitter in January 2010, and when they committed to perform at Coachella that April, having the TMB rock the stage with them for that song was a no-brainer. After the show, the rock group came to the TMB buses and personally greeted every member of the band, and they even thanked the Trojan Marching Band on their Facebook page, calling the band's performance "Epicness." "It's pretty amazing how these rock stars like to hang with the band," said Dr. Bartner. Five years later, the electronic pop duo, Odesza, wanted to add some drama to their show and invited members of the TMB percussion line to collaborate on a new tune. They performed "IPlayYouListen" at the Gobi tent for both weekends of the 2015 music festival. The following year, to capture the performance from a unique perspective, one TMB drummer put a portable "point of view" camera on his snare so everyone could see the crowd of a thousand people when the percussionists took the stage with electronic dance music trio, Major Lazer. "It just goes to show you, music crosses generations," said Dr. Bartner. "The flashing lights and loud, crowded audiences may not be my thing, but the band guys love it, and it's great that they get the opportunity to experience that."

Inspiring a new generation of music lovers is why, for decades, Dr. Bartner continued the tradition of High School Band Days. For many secondary school students, their high school marching band is their first experience playing an instrument. About every other year, Dr. Bartner invited a dozen or so Los Angeles area schools to learn music and perform it with the Trojan Marching Band during halftime of a USC football game at the Coliseum. Often, he also invited a guest conductor to lead the massed band of a thousand or more musicians. Dr. Bartner believes that exposing young musicians to composers and conductors like Bruce Broughton (*Silverado*), Alan Silvestri (*Forrest Gump*), and Michael Kamen (*Robin Hood, Mr. Holland's Opus*), to name a few, is important because youth get to experience the power of music to move an audience, and hopefully encourage them to pursue a career in the music industry. The crowd especially loved it when comedian Danny Kaye was the High School Band Days guest conductor. "I had met him at the grand opening of EPCOT, and I kept in touch with him and invited him to come direct the band," said Dr. Bartner. "He had me over to his house for breakfast to go over the music with him. He can't read a note of music, but he can memorize and conduct, and really work a crowd. He got the biggest audience response. He's the only guest who has ever gone into the rooting section to give high fives all the way up the aisle."

High School Band Days is also a way to involve young students in landmark city moments. In 2017, the city of Los Angeles learned that it would once again host the Olympic Games in 2028. To commemorate that, as well as the recent opening of USC's new University Village, Dr. Bartner invited a prominent figure who played an important role in both of those achievements. The invited guest conductor was Los Angeles Mayor Eric Garcetti, who stood atop the ladder directing fourteen hundred students as they played "I Love L.A." That also happened to be the tune that the TMB played at Garcetti's second inauguration earlier that same year, filling the steps of Los Angeles City Hall for the finale of the evening celebration. "Politics aside, Mayor Garcetti did a great job conducting," said Dr. Bartner. "I'm sure it helped that he knows about music, since he played jazz piano. I think the bands all did great, too."

Whether it involved high schools, music festivals, local or international sports competitions, concerts, parades, fundraisers, grand openings, anniversaries, or good old-fashioned football games, Dr. Bartner and the Trojan Marching Band were there to rouse the crowd and celebrate the cause. In fact, anytime there's a celebration, music adds an unparalleled electric energy to the atmosphere. It's no wonder Hollywood's Band is so famous and respected around the world, the nation, the city, and the university itself.

## High Note: Be Professional

Music has the power both to move people and make people move. When the marching band plays a rock chart, the beat causes people to clap their hands and dance to the music. When the concert band plays a ballad, the melody can bring people to tears. Whether it is stirring hearts or tapping toes, Dr. Bartner endeavors to conduct musicians so their sound evokes emotion in the audience. Inviting world-class musicians, including composers like David Foster and Alan Silvestri and conductors like Michael Kamen and Elmer Bernstein, is one more way Dr. Bartner exposed his students to masters in the music industry. ***When you maintain your commitment to excellence, you have the confidence to surround yourself with consummate professionals who display great talent and integrity, because you know you have earned your place among them.*** As a professional, you earn the trust of your colleagues. When the ten-piece or twenty-piece band performed, Dr. Bartner trusted them to behave and perform their best, because he could no longer be at every event. He appreciated musical innovation opportunities for the professional development of his students, like the celebrity-filled Pops concerts and Jerry Buss' Laker Basketball Band. Invitations such as these come when you are at the top of your game. *Be professional.*

# 16

# CELEBRATION BAND

*Just a few of the scores of USC athletes who have earned medals at the Olympic Games throughout the five decades that Dr. Bartner has been directing the Trojan Marching Band, 2016.*
Courtesy: Benjamin Chua

# CHAPTER SIXTEEN

## CELEBRATION BAND

The University of Southern California is a powerhouse private school with some of the most prominent research and education programs, decorated athletes, championship teams, and most accomplished alumni in the country—and of course, it also has a world-famous marching band to celebrate all of those achievements. While the assumption may be that the band is on hand only for athletic pursuits, the Trojan Marching Band is also very visible on campus for academic and student life-related events, including new student orientations, award banquets, and graduations, for example. Besides all the Hollywood big and small screen appearances, the TMB is well known around the alumni community for celebrating life's milestones, like weddings, anniversaries, and even fond farewells. As band director for five decades, Dr. Bartner has just about seen and done it all. When he decided in the 1960s to pursue a career in music education, he couldn't have imagined all the ways in which his band program would touch people's lives. His dedication to reaching people through music is definitely cause for celebration.

### Welcome to Campus & SCend Off

The number of students applying for admission to USC has grown immensely over the five decades that Dr. Bartner has been on campus, while at the same time the percentage accepted has gotten smaller. (In 2019, sixty-six thousand applied, and just under three thousand were admitted.) The university has become more and more competitive with the enrollment of an ever-higher caliber of students. Getting that acceptance notification is a "Welcome to the Family" letter. By the time new students arrive on campus, they have had multiple exposures to The Greatest Marching Band in the History of the Universe. Each fall, the admissions office offers the "Discover USC Open House," specifically for high school juniors and seniors who are considering an application to USC. The TMB does a fifteen-minute concert at the end of that campus tour, and in fact, sometimes the band gets credit for being the student's deciding factor to apply to USC. "After all, this is the band that's been in so many movies and television shows," said Dr. Bartner. "Of course kids want to be associated with Hollywood's Band!" Then, each spring, the admissions office holds several "Explore USC" events for admitted students who get to tour campus, meet professors, and experience school spirit—and hopefully decide to attend the university! Of course, the TMB is part of that campus event as well, performing a pep rally with cheers, chants, and fight songs. Finally, during summer, after applying, being accepted, and deciding to enroll at USC, students attend orientation, a giant welcome party that shows them everything there is to know about campus life. During the band's performance toward the end of orientation, the TMB recruitment manager shares what it's like to be in the band, and hopefully some students like what they hear enough to join the band!

For incoming students who aren't close to California, alumni associations across the country and around the world invite them to an official "SCend Off." The reception gives the new students (and their parents) a chance to ask questions and get advice from alumni and current students and get a feel for their upcoming USC experience. Many associations also award scholarships. A handful of clubs get a guest appearance from the Trojan Marching Band. The TMB has been a big part of one club's annual tradition since the 1980s. Each summer, a contingent of the TMB has taken a road trip to Lake Tahoe for the Northern Nevada Alumni Association SCend Off. "It's been one of the band's favorite trips for years," said Dr. Bartner. A busload of band members makes its way north to stay with alumni who host them in their homes. Skipping the uniforms, the band wears 'SC t-shirts, ball caps, and sunglasses to perform rock charts and fight songs under the pine trees with feet in the sand. That is, until they run down to the beach and play "Tusk" IN the lake! The band sure knows how to share the fun-loving spirit of the Trojan family.

While the TMB obviously can't get to every SCend Off around the world, new students experienced the spirit of the band sometime during their first few days on campus. A highlight of move-in day was when the band hosted a rally at day's end, celebrating the dorms and apartments being set up. Gathered around Tommy Trojan, Dr. Bartner gave incoming freshmen a bit of an education on what it means to be a Trojan and how to hold up their fingers in the victory sign. He'd also teach them how to do a SoCal Spell-out. "I love seeing the new faces of students coming to campus and experiencing the band, many for the first time," said Dr. Bartner. "They light up and really get into the music and feel the spirit of this university. I want them to feel like, 'Welcome Home' and know they are now part of this Trojan Family. OH—and I want to get them geared up and ready for the first football game, too!" The band paraded the new students across campus to the Residential College Cup, where food, fun activities, and friendly competition gave them a chance to make new friends and help them transition into their new home away from home.

## University Activities

USC offers about a thousand different ways to get involved on campus, and no doubt the band has been part of an event for many of them. Between the time the Trojan Marching Band plays "Conquest" as the students walk in with pomp and circumstance during their convocation ceremony to the moment the TMB serenades graduates at their commencement ceremony, USC students likely have scores of encounters with the Spirit of Troy, and not just at football games! When a club or honor society has an awards banquet, they can request the band send a ten-piece to play the fight songs. When the university's alumni association holds its annual celebration, the band is there to recognize honorees. "We are the most visible spirit organization on campus," said Dr. Bartner. "It's our job to pay tribute to every group we can fit into our schedule."

One event that has been on Dr. Bartner's and the band's calendar for four decades is "Swim With Mike." USC All-American swimmer Mike Nyeholt helped the Trojan team win three national championships during his college career in the 1970s. In fact, 1976 Olympic Gold Medalist John Naber credited Nyeholt with helping him train to win his four golds and one silver medal. After graduation, Nyeholt became paralyzed from the chest down in a motorcycle accident that left him with hefty hospital bills. His friends, Naber and Ron Orr, created a charity event, Swim FOR Mike, to help raise funds to pay his medical debts. During the event, Nyeholt came to the pool in a wheelchair with apparatus holding his head and neck steady to thank everyone for their support, and to tell them that he couldn't swim with them this time, but if they'd do the event again the following year, he would. And he did! They changed the name to Swim WITH Mike. The very first fundraiser was more successful than expected, so they set up the Physically Challenged Athletes Scholarship Fund and decided to make it an annual event. The event was held off campus for the first two years, and when it moved to the new Olympic pool on campus for its third year, Dr. Bartner brought the band to support the event. The TMB played "Tribute to Troy," "Fight On!" and other tunes as students jumped in the pool (some wearing intentionally silly costumes) to swim as long and hard as they could to collect pledges to fund the scholarship. Dr. Bartner even swam one time. "I swam against USC's Janet Evans, the Olympic gold medalist. I'm a terrible swimmer, and nearly drowned, but I did one lap! Needless to say, she did about ten laps to my one." To date, more than twenty-three million dollars in scholarships have been awarded to two hundred fifty-four students to help them overcome their tragedies, attend college, and realize their full potential. That includes a former USC band member. Mike Hoover played trumpet in the band in the late 1980s, and a sudden aneurysm stole his speech and left him paralyzed and bound to a wheelchair. "Mike marched the Rose Bowl with the band and then after his accident, couldn't play trumpet anymore, or be a music major anymore. Through the generosity of Swim With Mike, he was able to continue his education. It's a wonderful story." Now one hundred thirty-four other universities hold Swim With Mike fundraisers, too, and it all started with USC and the TMB. At the 40th anniversary of the Swim With Mike event in 2020, the charity recognized Dr. Bartner with a Volunteer Service award for his decades of commitment to the organization.

The USC swim team is not the only campus sports team to win national championships and produce Olympic athletes. In fact, USC men's and women's NCAA teams have a combined one hundred thirty national team titles, from football, baseball, basketball, and track to water polo, swimming, golf, tennis, volleyball, soccer, and gymnastics. An unprecedented number of those Trojan athletes are also Olympians. USC has produced four hundred thirty-five Olympic athletes, who have won one hundred thirty-five gold medals, eighty-eight silver, and sixty-five bronze—more than any other university in the United States. (That's not counting the 2020/2021 Olympics delayed by the COVID-19 pandemic.) Some of those athletes attended more than one Olympiad. More than once, the Spirit of Troy paid tribute to these athletes during a football game halftime show—including two hundred Trojan Olympians at the 1983 homecoming game, in advance of the upcoming 1984 Olympics. "We also do a halftime show honoring the athletes each football season following an Olympic Games," said Dr. Bartner. "We play John Williams' fanfare and recognize students who represented USC and their home countries, including many international students."

More than once, a delegation of band members followed an 'SC team to championship matchups around the nation. They were there to help the men's volleyball team defend their national title in 1981. In 1983, a contingent of the band accompanied the Women's Basketball team to Virginia where they played courtside cheering on the Women of Troy to their very first national championship. (They won their second title the following year.) The TMB regularly played for Trojan men's basketball games, and whenever the team made it to the "Big Dance," the band went, too, like they did in 2001 and 2006. The men's and women's water polo teams won multiple national championships, with the sounds of Tribute to Troy in the background. The Spirit of Troy followed the Women of Troy to their volleyball victory in 2002, the women's soccer championship in 2007, and the women's tennis team making it to the semi-finals in 2012. Fight songs were played when the Trojan men's tennis team won its record 21st national championship in 2014, which also marked the university's 100th national title in all sports. Baseball games, track meets, no matter what the sport, the Spirit of Troy performed beyond the gridiron for more than seventy-five competitions every year. "If any USC athletic team needs the Trojan Marching Band anywhere, any time, the Spirit of Troy will answer the call," said Dr. Bartner. "We are a football band, we are Hollywood's Band, and we are the university's band, no matter when, no matter where, no matter what."

## Happy Holidays

The loyalty of the Trojan Family is also evidenced by traditions that start out when an alum gets an idea, and then it sticks for decades. That's exactly what happened with the Fourth of July Parade on Santa Catalina Island. USC dental school alumnus Dr. Jack Wall, '51, and his wife, Hollywood actress Nita Bieber Wall, retired to the seventy-six-square mile isle about twenty miles off the California shore. The community of Avalon had celebrated Independence Day with a parade, but it was mostly golf carts scooting down the road, occasionally joined by the Army Band. Dr. Wall thought it could be something much more special, so as a Trojan fan who had been the dentist to many USC football players and coaches, he thought of the Trojan Marching Band. He reached out to Dr. Bartner and invited the band to come stay on the island for the Fourth. After a few meetings, and after Dr. Wall did all the fundraising to help pay for the ferry, food, and other expenses for the band, Dr. Bartner agreed. Unfortunately, that first year, 1990, Dr. Bartner was in Minneapolis preparing the massed band for the U.S. Olympic Festival, but he had Associate Band Director Tony Fox run the show on Catalina. The Spirit of Troy wore their uniforms to step off at noon for a patriotic parade through the little beach town, and then the musicians took a break for a couple of hours to enjoy a bit of the holiday on the beach. The entertainment was so well received and the band had so much fun that they agreed to do it again the following summer, and the next, and the next, and it grew into a more elaborate annual tradition as the years went by. Instead of sleeping on the floor of the high school gymnasium, fundraising covered hotel rooms for band members. Instead of just a short parade, the American flag-waving crowd followed the band to the town plaza, where the band performed a concert. In later years, the band did another concert at a benefit auction, where one lucky bidder could win the chance to conduct the band playing "Lone Ranger."

Dr. Bartner's favorite part about the Avalon gigs was getting to play at the famous Catalina Casino. "The ballroom there is where all of my idols from the big bands of the 1940s performed. Benny Goodman, Lionel Hampton, all those guys. And I'd feature Dr. Blair playing the famous 1920s Al Jolson jazz tune 'Avalon.' Those were good times." Dr. Bartner was referring to another USC dental school and TMB alum, Dr. Frank Blair, '42, who also helped make the band's Catalina visit possible. "He would meet us at the dock and play the fight song on his saxophone or clarinet as we got off the boat," recalled Dr. Bartner. "Then he'd follow us during the parade, too. But the most special thing he did was give each band member $50 to spend on snorkeling, mopeds, meals, whatever they wanted, because he remembered the challenge of being a college musician." The Blair family was a huge supporter of and donor to the TMB for decades. Dr. Bartner remembered visiting Frank at an assisted living home when he was nearing the end of his life. "We would sit in the lobby and Frank would play his saxophone for anybody who would listen. That's the power of music," said Dr. Bartner. "Here's a guy living his last days, and he starts playing tunes and it takes him back to fifty years ago. It was very touching." Dr. Blair passed away in 2011 at the age of ninety-two. Dr. Bartner still visits with the Blair family and enjoys sitting with them whenever they attend a USC event together. Dr. Wall passed away in 2005 at the age of fifty-four. With gratitude to both these men and their families, Dr. Bartner did attend several of the Catalina parades. Of course, that's when he wasn't traveling the globe for a World Expo or conducting the band at the Hollywood Bowl. "We almost always have something to do on the holidays, whether it's Fourth of July or Christmas or New Year's or another holiday," said Dr. Bartner. "This band is in demand for special occasions."

## Milestone Moments

The Trojan Marching Band, a.k.a. Hollywood's Band, receives upwards of six hundred invitations every year to perform somewhere for some momentous occasion. Of course, it's not possible to accept every one of them. The requests are typically for the ten-piece band to put on a show for a milestone moment in someone's life. Consisting of four trumpet players, three trombonists, one tuba, a snare drummer, and bass drummer, this small band still makes a loud sound! Wherever they go, guests go wild with the musicians' athletic antics and crazy dance moves. "The band loves to be part of happy occasions," said Dr. Bartner. "Their performance takes the party to another level!" Sometimes the audience knows the band is coming and waits in anticipation, and other times, it's a complete surprise. A common strategy is for a bride or groom to pull a fast one on their newlywed with a band performance at the reception. When the nuptials were for a couple who met in the band, it's especially fun. The family would hide the instrument until the band marches in playing "Tribute to Troy" and then whether it's a trumpet, trombone, tuba, or drum, the bride or groom (or both!) pick it up to join the show, in wedding gown or tuxedo and all. "In fact, it all started with my daughter Debbie's wedding," shared Dr. Bartner. "She was a Song Girl, and all the other Song Girls were either in the bridal party or invited guests. And we had a busload of the band come to the reception. The Song Girls did their routines, including Debbie in her wedding gown. It was a bummer when they danced 'All Right Now' and Debbie ripped her dress."

The band usually performed at the reception, but one time, it was actually part of the ceremony. Actress Holly Robinson was marrying former USC quarterback Rodney Peete in 1995. "She called me up and said she wants as many band members as I can get and she doesn't want Rodney to know about it," said Dr. Bartner. "So, right after Reverend Jesse Jackson pronounced them man and wife, now you can kiss the bride, in marches the band right down the aisle! We go straight up to the altar and Rodney loves the band, and he's just freaking out! He didn't have a clue! We then led the bride and groom out of the church to the courtyard and did a concert while all the guests came outside. It was crazy. But it's all about the Trojan Family."

The TMB also shows up unexpectedly-on-purpose for birthday and retirement parties, wedding anniversaries, corporate events, bar mitzvahs, and more! Wherever the band goes, it's a celebration. The band even performed for families who held a celebration of life for their loved one, including football players or donors who passed away. Roger Williams was a USC grad and huge Trojan fan. He had been released from his hospice care facility when there was no further treatment for his terminal illness. At the request of his family, the Spirit of Troy came to play "Fight on!" and "Conquest" to honor his dying wish. The family gathered around him as he lay in his hospital bed, holding up victory fingers, in what was one of the most sentimental performances the band has ever done. Whatever size band, whatever size event, the Trojan Marching Band is always full of spirit and puts on a great show to leave a memorable impression.

## Spirit of Support

In the beginning, when Dr. Bartner was still Mr. Bartner, he was a one-man-band, doing everything for the TMB all by himself. From arranging music, designing field shows, and recruiting new students to managing logistics, making photocopies, and fundraising, it was all on the band director. As the Spirit of Troy grew in numbers and reputation, he just had to get help, period. Besides, he also wasn't thirty years young anymore. When most band directors of his era were hanging up their whistles and folding up their ladders, Dr. Bartner was still climbing up and calling the plays and leading celebrations across town and around campus. By the 1990s and into the turn of the millennium, Dr. Bartner had reached a level of stature and financial stability through fundraising that he could hire more assistant band directors to share the load and responsibility. Dr. Bartner expanded the number of teaching assistants, so each section had its own to monitor and manage the specific requirements for its role on the field and at gigs, at home, and away. He has had some exceptionally loyal people assisting the development of Hollywood's Band over the years, some of whom have been with him for decades, because they, too, shared Dr. Bartner's vision of creating "The Greatest Marching Band in the History of the Universe." The band would not be able to perform at so many celebrations without their support.

During any performance, the two most visible elements of a marching band are the percussion line and the Silks. Both sections require additional practice every week with their own expert teachers. The Trojan Marching Band drumline has been trained by Tad Carpenter since the early 1980s. "Tad has contributed to the reputation of this band in ways I can't even describe," said Dr. Bartner. "His raw talent, experience, and ability to hear and teach a beat are remarkable. With every cadence he creates and instructs, he solidifies the drummers as the heartbeat of the band." Carpenter started playing drums when he was only eleven years old. His natural talent led him to a lifelong career developing skills for thousands of students at all levels. He assisted Dr. Bartner with the percussion line for the 1984 Olympic band and the 1994 World Cup ceremonies, just to name a few of their collaborations. Carpenter was also the percussion director for the Tournament of Roses Honor Band and Disney's All-American College Band.

Dr. Bartner also needed help with the other auxiliary group, the Silks. "There's obviously no way I could twirl a flag," said Dr. Bartner. "So, when I brought women into the band, I had to find a Silk instructor. I've had some great ones over the years, but Lee Carlson has been loyal to USC for decades." Dr. Bartner first met Carlson when he coached the flag twirlers for the 1984 Olympics, and he was so good, Dr. Bartner invited him to join the TMB staff. After coordinating the USC Silks for about twenty-five years, Carlson transitioned into designing field shows for the band, something he helped with for years anyway. "I don't create drills anymore," said Dr. Bartner. "It's all computerized now. Lee writes it and then it goes to our associate directors. They format it and get it to the section and squad leaders. Each band member has a number, and that's how they learn their place on the field." After four decades in the drum and bugle corps business, Carlson became the director of Drum Corps International, a non-profit organization that develops, standardizes, and enforces adjudication rules for sanctioned drum and bugle corps competitions in the U.S. and Canada. "Lee is a pro! We have been fortunate to have him doing our shows," said Dr. Bartner. "Back in the 70s, I used to do everything. Now we're 21st century and I delegate it. Even the printer we have now is fancy. It copies and staples everything. I think it can even make you lunch." Carpenter and Carlson are only two of the many talented and committed individuals who contributed to the growth, prestige, and success of Hollywood's Band. "I could never have done all this alone," said Dr. Bartner. "I could write another whole book about all the people who helped build this band. These guys, and other associate directors, assistant directors, band managers, teaching assistants—they all kept this band moving and shaking. I'm grateful to them all for their dedication to the Trojan Family."

## Always in the Band

"Once you're in the band, you're always in the band family," said Dr. Bartner. "We practice and perform together so often that the students really bond and build lifelong relationships. Even if they have very little else in common, the band brings them together." During his five-decade tenure as the band director of the University of Southern California, Dr. Bartner led thousands of students in the Trojan Marching Band. The diversity among their ranks is impressive. Only five percent of them are music majors, and close to twenty-five percent of them are engineering majors, ranging from aerospace to electrical. Pretty much every other major at the university has been represented by someone in the TMB throughout his fifty years. Several band members have gone on to have a career in the music industry, either as a professional musician, a conductor, a band director, or executives in instrument companies. Others became NASA scientists, lawyers, journalists, doctors—name a profession and a band member probably fills it. It's not just the miscellany of careers, it's the variety of personalities, nationalities, beliefs, and abilities as well. "We have an open, inclusive, diversified, transparent band. That's what I believe in," said Dr. Bartner. "This band is ALL-inclusive. We accept EVERYBODY! They just have to prove they bleed cardinal and gold and love USC. It helps if they have some musical talent, but if not, we can teach them, or we have a place for them in support positions, like prop crew or the band office. We're all Trojans!"

The diversity in the program is something for which Dr. Bartner is especially proud, because these young people marched in step for one purpose. Each year since 1976, he invited a section or two to return to campus and perform on the field with the current band for the homecoming game halftime show. Some years it's Silks and woodwinds, other years it's trumpets, another year percussion, or whichever section was up next in the rotation. But for his 25th anniversary in 1995, the TMB welcomed back any member from any section who could get to Los Angeles for the homecoming game. More than seven hundred fifty band alumni took the field with the two-hundred-fifty-member current band to form the largest Trojan Marching Band ever assembled. The one-thousand strong ensemble made the biggest USC block letters that the Coliseum crowd had ever seen. Even the Song Girls and the Yell Leaders returned for the event. It was a similar scene fifteen years later for Dr. Bartner's 40th anniversary, when five hundred members returned. The musicians (who may not all still play their instruments regularly) practiced the music to somewhat rebuild their chops, and the Silks watched videos to remember the flag twirling routines, and they all took the field for halftime and postgame. If fans thought the band was blaring loud on a normal basis, these alumni homecoming bands amplified the sound intensely. "It's always fun for them to see each other at our homecoming reunions," said Dr. Bartner. "It's like the years melt away and they're back in college again. I may not remember everyone's names and faces—because I've seen a lot of kids come through this program—but it's been a privilege to direct them in this band. Some students made me scream and yell and made me crazy, but they still showed up for this band and this team and this university. And that's what makes me proud."

Everything Dr. Bartner ever did was for the benefit of the students in the Trojan Marching Band. He lived his entire professional life devoted to building the TMB, the Spirit of Troy, Hollywood's Band, into "The Greatest Marching Band in the History of the Universe." Finally, after fifty years of hard work, late nights, early mornings, and relentless dedication to excellence, Dr. Bartner retired. With everything he accomplished, leaving a legacy like no other band director in the history of college marching bands, one thing's for sure: a part of Dr. Arthur C. Bartner will always be in the band, one way or another.

## High Note: Be Proud

Whether it was welcoming new students arriving to campus or bidding farewell to graduates departing—and many occasions in between—the Spirit of Troy loved to perform in celebration and encouragement. The musical salutes followed USC athletes to their championship games, students to their club banquets, Trojan family members to their weddings, and alumni for just about any other tradition they created. Not only were Dr. Bartner and the band proud to perform for these special occasions, but the event organizers were also proud to host them. ***Demonstrating pride in your work by showing up and playing full-out for any occasion, big or small, is a sign of confidence worthy of celebration. Learn to believe in yourself and know that you can do anything you decide to do.*** By the time Dr. Bartner neared retirement, the TMB performed somewhere nearly every day of the year, having turned down hundreds of other requests. Dr. Bartner could not have been more proud of that fact—or more proud of the band—considering where it began decades earlier. The band would not have become Hollywood's Band without the students' involvement and pride in their organization. *Be proud.*

# 17

# LEGENDARY LEGACY

*Arthur C. Bartner still loves playing trumpet at age eighty.*
Courtesy: Barbara Bartner

# CHAPTER SEVENTEEN

## LEGENDARY LEGACY

Dr. Arthur C. Bartner and the Spirit of Troy have forever made a mark on the entertainment world, earning the title Hollywood's Band for good reason. Movie and television credits aside, the impact he made in people's lives will endure in memories for ages to come. There are countless priceless images of him and the band performing all over the world, and as many as are found in this book, there are likely millions more than that he will never even see. From old negatives and 3x5 photos lost in shoe boxes to gigabytes of digital snapshots hidden on tiny SD cards, to random smartphone videos posted in the depths of YouTube, Insta, Flickr, FB, etc., there are five decades worth of reminiscence floating around. The transition from film to cyber-space is only one example of how much the world has changed in since Dr. Bartner first became band director at the University of Southern California.

Putting it in perspective, tuition at USC in 1970 was $2,004 per year. In 2019-2020, it was $57,256 per year. In 1970, a meat-packing plant operated across the street from campus and was turned into a University Village with a grocery store, bookstore, and other small shops. Nearly fifty years later, Dr. Bartner and the band played at the grand opening of a new seven-hundred-million-dollar high-tech University Village development with high-end retail stores and student apartments. In 1970, USC had an eighty-man band that no one noticed or respected. Five decades later, the band counted about half-and-half male-and-female, and for the first time ever, the members elected a young woman as drum major. *USA Today* twice named the three-hundred-member Spirit of Troy as the #1 College Marching Band in the nation, and the band and Dr. Bartner are now revered on campus and everywhere they go. Dr. Bartner's dream is that the band he built and led for fifty years *DRIVES IT!* and FIGHTS ON! for decades to come—so that it can inspire future generations of the Trojan family with a love of music and marching.

## Halls of Fame

For Dr. Bartner, it was never about fame or fortune, nor about accolades for himself. It has always been about recognition for the students and the hard work they put in memorizing music and field maneuvers, and putting on an entertaining, energizing show for an audience. Nonetheless, with the success the band has found under his direction, he has been honored with multiple awards. Perhaps one of the most sentimental commemorations came from his hometown where it all started, Columbia High School in Maplewood, New Jersey. Back when he struggled to decide between playing trumpet or basketball, he couldn't have known what lie in store with Hollywood's Band: Platinum Albums, Olympics, World Expos, and so forth. All he knew was that he loved playing both the instrument and the game. Some thirty years after high school graduation and eighteen years after starting at USC, Dr. Bartner was invited home to Maplewood to be inducted into the Columbia High School Hall of Fame. The honorees "have been role models while they, themselves, were students at CHS," reads the selection committee criteria. "And they should be distinguished in their current fields of endeavor, be leaders in their profession, have dedications toward the betterment of society... and be at the peak of their careers."[1]

That perfectly described Dr. Bartner in 1988, as by that time, "Tusk" was a thing, the Olympics were under his belt, the Disneyland Band was going strong, and he was leading the band on global excursions. "I combined my two passions, music and sports, with the marching band," recalled Dr. Bartner. "I loved the physicality of the marching band. I love the spirit. I love the discipline. And I love the entertainment value." At the induction ceremony, Dr. Bartner was given a plaque, and a duplicate hangs in a place of distinction at the school library, alongside other honorees, including Olympic track athlete Joetta Clark Diggs, late-night musician Max Weinberg, and Oscar-nominated actor Roy Scheider. Even in the recognition he has received, Dr. Bartner is surrounded by Hollywood celebrities.

Perhaps even more meaningful than the Hall of Fame recognition is an honor that came to Dr. Bartner from the National Association for Music Education in 2005. Each year, the NAfME designates a group of Lowell Mason Fellows, which is a prestigious distinction conferred upon individuals for their contributions in the field of music education. "This is a big deal," said Dr. Bartner. "The whole point of what I do is to educate students, raise their level of musicianship, and help them learn to entertain while playing great music. It's why I became a band director all those years ago. So, to have those efforts recognized is a true honor." What made this selection so special is that the nomination was made by the Walt Disney World Performing Arts Programs the year that Dr. Bartner retired from directing the Disney All-American College Band after twenty-eight years.

The legendary band director received another well-deserved Hall of Fame honor in 2012. After forty-two years conducting the band and not missing a single football game since 1987, the USC Athletics Hall of Fame inducted Dr. Bartner. "Many of tonight's inductees are individuals who never shrank from the challenges of competition but rose to the occasion when it counted most," said then-President Max Nikias at the black-tie gala. "Their extraordinary talents and astonishing records of achievement have fueled the fire of the competitive spirit and helped forge USC's glorious athletic identity." The description more than fit Dr. Bartner's career, developing a band from nothing big into something grand. His name now stands alongside many of the same players and coaches to whom the band director played "Tribute" and "Conquest" for decades. "This is a great honor," said Dr. Bartner. "But there are a lot of people who have played a major role [in building this band.] Marv Goux, John Robinson, Neil Pings... Pete Carroll, John Baxter..." Dr. Bartner took the opportunity to thank these mentors and others who helped him learn what it means to be a teacher, a mentor, a coach, and a Trojan! The irony is that Dr. Bartner had conducted the TMB at each of the induction ceremonies, and this time, the playing of "Conquest" was a tribute to him.

Trojan athletics also honored Dr. Bartner with the Marv Goux Spirit Award for his outstanding support of the football program, putting the band director's name on his mentor's memorial, Goux's Gate. A few years later, the USC coaches and student-athletes presented Dr. Bartner with yet another laudation. The "Legend of Troy" is awarded to an individual who has made a significant impact on Trojan athletics. Given that Dr. Bartner had been conducting the Spirit of Troy since the time he was playing football, it was serendipitous that during the 2019 student-athlete commencement ceremonies, then-Athletic Director Lynn Swann presented the award to the band director in recognition of his five decades of contributions to the spirit of the Trojan athletics.

As Dr. Bartner approached the end of his career, he received the most impressive and noteworthy distinction of his professional life. He had earned his undergraduate degree, master's, and doctorate from the University of Michigan in the 1970s, and finally, in 2019, Dr. Bartner received an Honorary Doctor of Music from the University of Southern California, the institution to which he dedicated his entire career. Noted as a "music icon" for his accomplishments, the university decorated Dr. Bartner with the highest distinction possible for his years setting the national standard for collegiate marching bands. "I was absolutely thrilled," said Dr. Bartner. "This was completely unexpected because band directors just don't get honorary degrees, so this was an anomaly." When he graduated with his Michigan credentials, Dr. Bartner never walked the processional to receive his degrees, because he was either playing trumpet or conducting. That changed on May 10, 2019, when as part of the platform party, he walked the pomp and circumstance for the first time. After all the other school graduation candidates were introduced, he joined the other honorary degree recipients and university dignitaries and processed from Bovard Auditorium, around the Youth Triumphant Fountain, to the stage on the steps of Doheny Library for the commencement ceremony. In cardinal and gold cap and gown, Dr. Bartner had reached the pinnacle of his career, seated on stage among the University Trustees and top administrators. Then-interim-President Wanda Austin welcomed the honorary doctorate degree recipients, referring lastly to "the renowned conductor of the Spirit of Troy, The Greatest Marching Band in the History of the Universe." The audience went wild, and Dr. Bartner grinned from ear to ear and modestly waved "Fight On!" When it was his turn to receive his honorary degree, he moved across the platform, and the students' hurrahs continued for many moments until he lowered his hand conductor style, as if to slow and quiet the music. “Dr. Bartner has been the heart and soul of our Trojan Marching Band for almost half a century,” said Dr. Austin as Dr. Bartner stood proudly. “He embodies the Trojan Spirit, inspiring our community with his showmanship, his dedication, and his tireless efforts to educate and uplift our students. His bold vision transformed our band into the renowned Spirit of Troy, while making its energetic performances an essential part of USC’s storied athletic tradition. Generations of USC students have thrived under his guidance as he has illustrated the importance of commitment, preparation, and teamwork in their daily lives. The USC community is especially proud to honor Dr. Bartner’s musical creativity, his outstanding mentorship, and his enduring legacy as he prepares to celebrate his 50th anniversary as the director of our Trojan Marching Band. By the authority vested in me by the USC Board of Trustees, I hereby confer upon Arthur C. Bartner the degree of Doctor of Music honoris causa. Please accept our warmest congratulations.”[2] As a trustee placed the velvet banner over his shoulders, Dr. Bartner smiled his appreciation and the crowd hollered once again. “I’ve had many memorable moments in my life,” said Dr. Bartner. “But this was by far the proudest moment ever. I wish to thank the University of Southern California for the opportunity, the support, and the freedom to build a band we can all be proud of.”

## What’s in a Name?

It’s one thing to receive recognition for a job well done, and it’s another entirely to have an award created with one’s own name on it. “I never would have thought that one day my name would be the name of an award. That's pretty cool," said Dr. Bartner. Even though the Trojan Marching Band is more associated with the gridiron than the diamond, the band has supported the Trojan baseball team through the years as well. In 2009, the Trojan Baseball Alumni Association initiated the Dr. Arthur C. Bartner Trojan Service Award. Since then, the TBAA has presented this award yearly to a deserving athlete who exemplifies dedicated service in the Trojan family and community. A few years later, the USC football team did the same thing, renaming its Trojan Commitment Award to be called the Dr. Arthur C. Bartner Trojan Commitment Award. The head coach bestows that honor on a Trojan football player who demonstrates dedication and commitment to the USC football program, just as Dr. Bartner has dedicated his life to supporting the team.

It was in recognition of that enduring allegiance to his profession and his students, that after nearly five decades at USC, Dr. Bartner finally received the greatest honor that can ever be bestowed upon anyone at any university, even more acclaimed than an honorary degree: a building with his name on it. The TMB practices on Cromwell Field, named after track coach Dean Cromwell, who led the USC track and field team to ten national championships from 1909 through 1948; he was also the Olympic track head coach at the 1948 Games. Across the street, the football team practices on Howard Jones Field, so called for USC's head football coach whose teams won four national championships and five Rose Bowls in the 1930s. The baseball field on campus is known as Dedeaux Field, in honor of Trojan baseball legend Rod Dedeaux, who led USC to eleven College World Series titles and twenty-eight conference titles. Other buildings are named for previous university presidents and other major contributors. Now, on the northwest corner of campus, the Spirit of Troy has its own facility, dubbed in 2018 as the Dr. Arthur C. Bartner Band Pavilion—honoring his support of more athletic and university events than most other campus coaches combined.

The seven-thousand square foot space was something Dr. Bartner had desired for decades. "This is a dream come true," Bartner said. "I've been trying to find a dedicated space for our students since I came to USC. I'm so happy this can happen before I leave the university, and I'm humbled that Steve and Rosemarie would honor me by naming the pavilion after me." Dr. Bartner was referring to Stephen and Rosemarie Johnson, both USC alumni, who made the lead financial gift to transform the second-floor work-out club of the Lyon Center into a full-service center for everything TMB related. The band members can store instruments, uniforms, helmets, and accessories in designated lockers with room to spare. The facility boasts an open-floor area with acoustic sound protection for music rehearsal. There is even a student lounge, where band members can socialize and/or study in between practices. Larger-than-life-size decal murals of Dr. Bartner and the band cover the walls, making it obvious who is housed behind the triple double-doors. Just inside is a lobby and front desk, where teaching assistants and student leaders get real-world work experience. That part of the office honors Jerry Buss, thanks to a contribution from the Laker Organization, now run by his daughter, Jeanie. The band director and staff have offices across the plaza in nearby King Hall. For his last couple years on campus, Dr. Bartner finally had an office with windows, for the first time in his career.

Not only was a band pavilion Dr. Bartner's lifelong vision, but it was also something band students had hoped for as well, and two of them took the initiative to make it happen. In 2016, saxophone player Corey Dennis and trumpet player Emily Moneymaker met with then-University President Max Nikias to demonstrate the band's needs. Nikias toured the cramped fifteen-hundred-square-foot space in the basement of Stonier Hall, which housed the band since 1994. That was the band's first central location, instead of being spread out in multiple "extra rooms" across campus. It had been named for the principal donor and long-time TMB and football team supporter Juliette "Julie" Kohl. The office was better than the room Dr. Bartner had when he first came to campus, but President Nikias agreed that the Spirit of Troy had outgrown that space and was deserving of its own bigger basecamp. He found the space, and it opened after only six months of renovations. The students, the Johnsons, and President and Mrs. Nikias joined Dr. and Barbara Bartner at the ribbon-cutting that officially opened the new home and new future for Hollywood's Band.

## Coming Full Circle

As the marching band of choice for so many movies, television shows, and rock stars, it's clear that Trojan Marching Band musicians are talented. "We are the soundtrack of the University of Southern California," said Dr. Bartner. It makes sense that the TMB would have its own albums, tapes, CDs, or digital collections, depending on the generation. The first professional album under the direction of Dr. Arthur C. Bartner came out in 1975, titled simply *The Spirit of Troy*, featuring the band's modern sound with current rock charts of the decade. Every few years, Dr. Bartner commissioned another new record, often in conjunction with a special occasion, like the centennial of the Trojan Marching Band in 1980, the 1984 Olympic Games, Dr. Bartner's

Silver Celebration in 1994, and even his 40th Anniversary in 2009. All total, Dr. Bartner and the multiple generations of band members have made more than a dozen music collections featuring the most popular tunes of the time. Music recording has come full circle, as when the Spirit of Troy's latest release in 2019 came out not only in digital download, but also on gold vinyl. In honor of Dr. Bartner's 50th anniversary, the album was titled *The Gold Standards* and was accompanied by a booklet of the top fifty musical moments in his TMB career. The evolution of multimedia has moved far beyond the original Fleetwood Mac music video that they recorded in the Dodger dugout. Several documentaries and podcasts feature interviews with Dr. Bartner about his life and times with Hollywood's Band. No doubt, he will go down in history as one of the most recorded and famed college marching band directors ever. After five decades of showmanship and spotlights, Dr. Bartner has become a celebrity in his own right—proven by the fact that there is even a Lego figurine and Bobblehead in his likeness!

## Family Harmony

Through all the crescendos and diminuendos of his marching band career, from his early days in chilly Michigan to the heartwarming dedication of the building in his name, there has been one constant for Dr. Bartner: his wife, Barbara. He readily admits that there were some sour notes when he was intensely occupied with multiple events and was not as attentive at home as he could have, or maybe should have been, especially through what he called the crazy eighties. "But she was always there, through it all," said Dr. Bartner. "We have been together since middle school, and I turned eighty in 2020, so that's a long time to put up with me. Barbara is a saint." The couple shared some incredible experiences together all around the world. There was the time in Xi'an, China when, during the Key to the City dinner, tradition was that the dignitaries wouldn't drink their wine until the lady at the table, in this case Barbara, had her first sip. She doesn't drink, so they waited a long time until an interpreter finally clued them in. Barbara met the first lady and multiple U.S. ambassadors in various countries, sat in a fifty-yard-line box for the 1984 Olympic Opening Ceremonies, and rubbed shoulders with untold Hollywood celebrities in the front row at the Oscars and the Grammys, all while her husband conducted the band. As the First Lady of the Spirit of Troy, Barbara shared her husband with Hollywood and the world for five decades, as have their children, Steven and Debbie. "That is my greatest regret," sighed Dr. Bartner. "I wish I had spent more time with my children, but I'm making up for it by spending more time with my seven grandchildren. I love and appreciate my family very much. I could never have done all that I've done without them." It was bittersweet when in April 2019, Barbara and their daughter Debbie sat in USC's Bovard Auditorium, as they had many, many times before. That evening was for Dr. Bartner's "Final Curtain," his last spring concert. The show featured several favorite stars who returned to musically bid him farewell. "It was a bit like a family reunion," said Dr. Bartner. "I have done many concerts, but this 'Final Curtain' was special, and I really took it in, because I knew it would be my last."

All the fun, all the challenges, all the victories, all the losses, all the life experiences—Dr. Bartner knows that none of it would have been possible without the students' dedication and the support of the Trojan fans. Their success is his success, and it didn't always come easy. While at times it seemed that good fortune simply shined its light upon Dr. Bartner and that opportunities easily fell into his lap, there was plenty of rain on his parade as well. (Seriously, he marched in rain a lot in his career, for rehearsals and performances!) He may have known how to play and conduct music like a pro, but as a young college marching band director, Dr. Bartner had a sudden steep learning curve when it came to student discipline, campus bureaucracy, and program fundraising. Fortunately, he was blessed with some amazing mentors to guide the way and show him how to take charge, maneuver, and finesse at just the right time for the greatest impact.

After fifty years of dedication to perseverance, excellence, and confidence, Dr. Bartner put down the baton and whistle in 2020. He spent a lifetime "driving it" and "fighting on" to build The Greatest Marching Band in the History of the Universe. "I want the traditions and drive to stay alive because that's what built this band," he said. "I want the band to keep the bond with the football team and all athletics because that's what created the Spirit of Troy. I want the band to stay in demand of rock stars and celebrities, because that's what made us Hollywood's Band." Dr. Bartner paused to take a breath. "I want former band members to keep coming back every chance they get, even when I'm gone, because that's how this became the Trojan Band Family. Every single person who played any part in the band, no matter how big or how small, whether performing or observing, is part of the Trojan Band Family." This is a family that spans multiple generations around the globe.

"My greatest reward," said Dr. Bartner, "is when an alumnus comes back five, ten, fifteen years later, and says the best part of their college experience was being a member of the Trojan Marching Band. Now they come back with their families and give back to the band and the university. That's why I've done this for fifty years. And that's why I hope the traditions live on long after I'm gone." The enduring loyalty of the Trojan Band Family is perhaps Dr. Arthur C. Bartner's greatest legacy. Fight On Forever!

## High Note: Be Willing to Grow... and Go

From the time Dr. Bartner (Mr. Bartner at the time) took the job as the director of the USC Trojan Marching Band until he retired fifty years later, the band nearly quadrupled in size. Its reputation also grew exponentially, from a band nobody cared about to the most recognized college marching band in the country. Dr. Bartner realized he had a lot to learn when he moved out west, but he was ambitious and determined to succeed. That meant he was also willing to take risks, and he was willing to keep learning and growing as a musician, as a leader, as a mentor, and as a person. Both Dr. Bartner himself and the TMB experienced some growing pains in the process, but it was worth it. ***Building anything worthwhile requires a willingness to grow—personally, professionally, foundationally, and literally—so that when the time comes to depart the organization, you can have confidence that it will go on successfully without you.*** In his last few years leading the band, Dr. Bartner was recognized with many awards and commendations, from his home high school hall of fame to the USC hall of fame to a band building bearing his name. But his greatest reward remains the same: instilling a spirit of perseverance, excellence, and confidence—the *Drive It!* tradition—in his students to inspire a love of music and marching for generations to come. *Be willing to grow... and go.*

## A Final High Note from Dr. Arthur C. Bartner

*Be Grateful*

I've been described as the most determined person you'll ever meet. I had to be to direct this band for fifty years. I'm talking about determination! This is a very important life lesson. Just like Christy was determined to publish this book, despite obstacles like a pandemic, she wasn't giving up. That's a trait I wanted to instill in the band: if you're passionate, you'll be determined to succeed. In the entertainment business, book writing, art, or whatever industry, you'll face a lot of rejection—and it's about perseverance and determination to never give up. That's why we say *Drive It!*

It was so important to set a structure of discipline and direction for students because they had none of that when I arrived. The band I inherited had no team leaders to push the band forward. So I got the students involved. I don't listen to the same contemporary music as these kids do, and I want them to perform what they love. Sometimes it meant taking a risk, especially when we brought mega stars to the field. You're putting it on the line and taking the risk to succeed. That's one of the secrets of success in life—being able to take risks. That's why we say *Drive It!*

I talk a lot about sharing your talent. When you do a celebration gig for a birthday or an anniversary, you're sharing your talent with alumni, the same as when you perform in a foreign country; you're sharing your talent with the world. When you share your talent at a game, you're making the fan experience more enjoyable and getting them involved in the game. It's about work ethic and energy and personality and enthusiasm. That's why we say *Drive It!*

We have done so many performances for athletics and TV shows and movies, but there's also community service projects we helped with, too, like cancer support, blood drives, marathons, Swim With Mike, and other community-related events. These band members also have classes, projects, papers, midterms, and eight to ten hours of band practice per week, not even counting game days. One of the most important life lessons you learn from being in the band is time management. If you have a lot of passions, like I do, you have to manage your time to be successful. That's why we say *Drive It!*

None of this would have been possible without the students. The students made this band. It was their determination and involvement, their talent and service, and their investment of time that made this The Greatest Marching Band in the History of the Universe. I am grateful to them. I couldn't do this alone. It's never been a one-man show. I am grateful to my family, my wife and partner for sixty years, my children and grandchildren, who all cared for me and this band and uplifted me when I needed it. I am grateful to the band staff, assistants, T.A.s, section and squad leaders for their hard work. It's all about the Trojan family. That's why we say *Drive It!*

I am also grateful to the USC Athletic Department for their support through the years. They made band trips possible, and the coaches have been great mentors throughout my fifty years. And I'm grateful to the University of Southern California because they gave me the opportunity. If they don't hire me and dig me out of Michigan, none of this would have ever happened. Everything we've talked about was only possible because I heard

"You're hired!" They said, "Here's this band that needs to be fixed. Fix it." They gave me the freedom to create Hollywood's Band, the Spirit of Troy, the University of Southern California Trojan Marching Band. When it's all said and done, we're all here, and you're reading this book, because of USC. I am so grateful. That's why we say *Drive It! and be grateful.*

## HIGH NOTES: DRIVE IT! TRADITION

**PERSEVERANCE**

Be decisive

Be supportive

Be disciplined

Be collaborative

Be prepared

**EXCELLENCE**

Be visible

Be transparent

Be diverse

Be connected

Be passionate

Be loyal

Be dedicated

**CONFIDENCE**

Be memorable

Be impressive

Be professional

Be proud

Be willing to grow… and go

**BE GRATEFUL**

# ACKNOWLEDGEMENTS

I guess I have my daughters to thank for inspiring this whole project—because I've gone all-out for their birthday celebrations since they were born. For her tenth birthday, Rylee wanted to celebrate with a party theme of rainbows and unicorns. So, we did. Rainbow balloons and streamers, seven-layer rainbow birthday cake, even the food was displayed in an array of colors. My daughter wore a rainbow dress and a unicorn headband, and the party favors were rainbow-striped, unicorn-horn-shaped lollipops and unicorn keychains. Then, as any respectable mother would do, I posted the precious party pictures on Facebook. Later that evening, when (most of) the mess was cleaned up, I collapsed on the couch. That's when I received a message from an old college friend. We hadn't spoken in two decades or more but we're "Friends on Facebook" and watch each other's lives from afar with occasional likes and wows. In fact, this was our first ever message. She had sent me a link to one of her favorite happy songs that came to mind when she saw my daughter's party pix: "Sunshine, Lollipops, and Rainbows" by Lesley Gore from 1965. I happened to see the message and we chatted.

Our alma mater had just lost a football game and we were lamenting the long flight home from Chicago that the team and the band were about to endure. A 6 a.m. flight is gross on a normal day, but after a spanking from a rival, it's even worse. Cheryl Cox and I were in the band together as Silks, which is a fancy name for tall flags, so we know that postgame pain personally. This time, her son, as a junior in the band, was about to make the trip home with a couple hundred of his closest friends. Cheryl and I reminisced, and I asked about the band director, marveling that he is STILL leading the band. He was old when WE were in the band twenty-five years ago. I asked her, "Isn't he supposed to be retiring soon?" And she said, "Yes, he's planning to in 2020." And I asked, "Has anyone written his biography yet? Maybe I should pitch it to him." And Cheryl's reply was, "You totally should! What a great idea! You'd be perfect for that! His ego would love that!" We LOL'd, and I had serious giddiness about the idea. I told Cheryl, "I was so happy to chat with you… and now look what happened!" She replied, "And it's all because of rainbows and unicorns! They really are magical!!" (This is word for word our conversation—complete with a magical unicorn sticker!) So, I guess I really have Cheryl Cox to thank, too.

Truly, Cheryl and her husband, Rick Cox, have been beyond supportive throughout this process. Anytime I was blurry-eyed and stressed out while researching, writing, and finding photos (oh, the photos!)—I could message Cheryl, and her kind heart would cheer me up and cheer me on—and remind me to Fight On! and keep on Drivin' It, especially in the fourth quarter two-minute drill! Then, since Rick is still active with band leadership, if I ever needed a connection or information confirmation, he was willing to help. Thank you, Rick! (He also took my daughters with him to a Laker game while I attended the Band Banquet as part of research for the book. Rylee and Tylar say "Thank you!") Rick and Cheryl, I remember seeing you two getting together in Europe. What a trip! And what a perfect example of the Trojan family legacy. (I'm sorry that Rickaerobics didn't make the manuscript, though. There was only so much space for Band Camp drills!)

I also must thank another fellow Silk and my college roommate, Leigh Phifer. How awesome that we can live a thousand miles apart and still chill like roommates even after months (or years) between visits. When I came to L.A. for research, that airbed with the USC blanket in your dining room was better than any hotel I could ever afford. Thank you for your repeated hospitality at le Hotel & Café de Phifer. (Wonder if you ever found that last sticky note? Because you never found my sunhat at band camp even though it survived a nineteen-day European tour!)

Now I offer a field-show-sized, heart-felt thank you to Dr. Bartner. (I still can't call you by anything else! It was hard for me to call you "Art" in these pages.) You are the reason I have these wonderful lifelong friends I acknowledged above—which is exactly what we talked about so often while developing this book. It really is all about the Trojan family. I am so grateful you kept fighting on through your career, even when it looked bleak downfield. Without your commitment to *Drive It!* with perseverance, excellence, and confidence, the band wouldn't be what it is today. I don't even know if I could count the hours we invested in this project, but it doesn't matter, because I loved getting to know you and getting to hear these crazy stories. If I had to choose a favorite, it would be a tie between two, each involving a visit to the Statue of Liberty. I couldn't stop laughing when you told me about your harrowing trip to the top of the Statue—OMG, that hat! And then my heart melted when I learned about your personal contribution that day so band members could tour the monument—you didn't have to do that, and you did. If I saw you walking down the street, I would run across traffic to see you. It has been my honor to share your story with the world. Thank you for sharing it with me. And thank you, Barbara, for sharing your husband, and Steven and Debbie for sharing your dad, with the Trojan family all these years. He really couldn't have survived it without you by his side. Your dedication to him is the reason he could commit himself to his passion. Thank you!

Backing up to within twenty-four hours of the rainbow connection conversation, I called another Silk alum and college friend, Maria Jordan, who was the band alumni coordinator at the time. Thanks for helping with my first outreach to Dr. Bartner. Appreciation also to Brett Padelford, Cynthia Wiese, and other band staff who looked after me when I came to campus for research (especially Jessica Belch, because: parking passes!) You all do a lot of juggling in that office, and it's appreciated!

In one of life's amazing synchronicities, just as I was stepping off with this project, a brilliant publishing expert reappeared in my world. I had been following Kathy Ver Eeck on Facebook for a couple years, and she was creating a brand-new group to support authors with writing their pitch, finding an agent, and getting their book published. I joined as a founding member, and her motivating hot seats and hilarious sense of humor kept me in the game when I had no more timeouts left. Thank you,

Kathy, and all the P2Peeps. Even when I'm not posting, I'm watching and cheering from the sideline.

I believe everything happens for a reason, so getting to travel internationally and arrive home literally a week before the pandemic shut down the world was not an accident. One of my best bus buddies on the journey was Karie Cassell. I am so happy and grateful we stayed in touch because, well, she's fun, but also because I happened to see her post about her book launch. Since COVID derailed my original publishing plans, I was looking for an alternative, and Karie made the best referral. Thank you, Karie, for your introduction to Juliet Clark and thank you, Juliet, for your introduction to Kristen Johnson. The three of you helped me kick it into gear and *Drive It!* into the endzone. If it weren't for you, this book might still be in a three-ring binder.

I faced a few pivots while marching through this project, and I want to thank Paddy and Scott for their extraordinary kindness at each turn. Much love and appreciation also to my brave friend Katie, who reminded me that a greater intelligence is always at work when things don't go the way we thought they would. It's clear that a computer and Google weren't the only tools I utilized to bring this project to fruition.

That final lap was a doozie, though, with some last-minute surprises (not related to Juliet or Kris.) But when it looked like fourth down and short, two more fellow Trojan band alumni stepped up! I could not be more grateful to Ling Luo (another former Silk), who has taken some of the most creative and spectacular photos I've ever seen, and then Benjamin Chua (no, NOT another former silk, but clarinet player—bchua@usc.edu), who has probably taken more pictures than anyone I've ever known. Thank you both! Without your talent and generosity, these stories wouldn't have visual memories to accompany them. Fight On, Trojan family! Thank you to the band for being the band and the team for being the team. Thanks to all the alumni who posted stories, answered questions, and shared photos. Even if I didn't get to include your specifics, I truly appreciate your contribution—not only to the book, but to the TMB and the Trojan family as a whole. I hope this endeavor gave you a chance to enjoy the memories and recognize how fortunate we are to have been part of The Greatest Marching Band in the History of the Universe.

I do realize how blessed I am to have these memories and WHY I had these opportunities in the first place. It was because of the sacrifices my parents made so that I could attend USC. I'm sure I'll never know the full extent, but I do know I'm extremely grateful. I still choke up when I think about discovering the beautiful hibiscus bloom that my mom covertly placed on my coffee table after helping me move in to my on-campus apartment. (Cell phones and texting didn't exist yet, so I don't know how my mom did it!) I was alone without roommates, having arrived a week early for band camp. Not gonna lie: those first few days were kinda tough. But it got better. I had no idea of all the amazing friends I would make and trips I would take—including that nineteen-day performance trek through Europe. And now look, Mom, three decades later, I've written a book about it all. Thank you for all the papers and speeches you helped me perfect that supported my passion for words and stories. (You are given a glass of water…) Much love to my mom and dad, Charlayne and Jeff Coburn, for this dream I didn't even know I had at the time.

Even with my personal experience of being in the TMB, I knew from the beginning that writing Dr. Bartner's biography was going to be a monumental task. Trying to compress eighty years of life and fifty years of band history into a few hundred pages was not going to be easy. There are so many more stories, experiences, adventures, and lessons that this book could be a thousand pages. (Maybe I'll come back and write more of those another time.) But now that this project is complete, it's time to relax and enjoy evenings and weekends with my family again… and maybe sleep past 4 a.m. for a change. I am proud of my daughters for getting themselves up and ready for school while I worked on the book. I am grateful for my husband, who fed himself and the kids dinner more evenings than he should have while I worked on the book. I appreciate the understanding of dear friends and extended family whose invitations for weekend fun I passed on while I worked on the book. Tyler, Tylar, and Rylee—I love you soooooooo much. Thank you for your patience, love, and belief in me. Your encouragement during late nights and early mornings (especially surprise coffee and water refills on my desk) mean the world to me. You are why I *Drive It!*

Finally, to future generations of Trojans, including my older daughter Tylar, class of 2024—Fight On! Fingers crossed that Rylee also chooses USC five years from now—may you be deeply thankful for opportunities that come your way because you get to attend this university. And may you realize that a big part of why this place is as prestigious as it is… is because Dr. Arthur C. Bartner never quit. He built a bond that put USC on the map, directing both the band and the team to *Drive It!* down the field. So, whenever you hear the fight songs echoing from the center of campus, may the sound of Hollywood's Band, the Spirit of Troy, the University of Southern California Trojan Marching Band encourage YOU to *Drive It!* with perseverance, excellence, and confidence. FIGHT ON!

# ENDNOTES

## 4. Finding Funding

1. USC's Nickname: "Trojans" https://usctrojans.-com/sports/2018/7/25/usc-history-traditions-nickname-trojans.aspx

## 5. Scoring Big Time

1. Keith H. Walker and Robert W. Jensen, *The Man on the Ladder.* (Los Angeles: Figueroa Press, 2010), 183.
2. Embo-Vision, "1973 Rose Bowl – Feat. D. Ross," YouTube Video, 9:11, February 11, 2019. https://www.youtube.com/watch?v=Y70PH9p_qjM
3. Jim Baird, "Looking back at Ohio State and USC's 3-year 'War of the Roses,' December 11, 2017, https://www.landgrantholyland.-com/2017/12/11/16755514/ohio-state-usc-bowl-game-history-rose-cotton

## 6. Shining Reputation

1. Debi Jocelyn, "1973 #6 USC at #8 Notre Dame 1 of 1," YouTube video, 5:21:58. December 22, 2016, https://www.youtube.com/watch?v=zX3L-coZvBoQ
2. Debi Jocelyn, "1973 #9 USC vs #8 UCLA 1 of 1," YouTube video, 4:19:18, December 21, 2016. https://www.youtube.com/watch?v=SBnDCoshUu0
3. Haunted Song, "Fleetwood Mac ~ "Tusk" outtake footage," YouTube video, 4:21, November 10, 2009, https://www.youtube.com/watch?v=r43auXFDin0&t=77s
4. Haunted Song, "Fleetwood Mac ~ "Tusk" outtake footage."

## 7. Pivot Points

1. Rob Felton, "Trojan Hoarse," *Los Angeles Times*, October 29, 2000, https://www.latimes.com/archives/la-xpm-2000-oct-29-tm-43663-story.html
2. Rob Felton, "Trojan Hoarse."

## 8. Putting on a Show

1. Bruce Anderson, "Give Him Credit for the Charge, Tommy Walker Converted Six Notes into a Famous Fanfare," *Vault*, November 12, 1990. https://vault.si.com/vault/1990/11/12/give-him-credit-for-the-charge-tommy-walker-converted-six-notes-into-a-famous-fanfare
2. USC Trojan Marching Band 2018 Press Pack, "Halftime Heroics," 2018.
3. John Hall, "The Sideshow," *Los Angeles Times*, November 7, 1977, https://latimes.newspapers.com/image/383623394
4. Keith H. Walker and Robert W. Jensen, *The Man on the Ladder,* 188.
5. Keith H. Walker and Robert W. Jensen, *The Man on the Ladder,* 189.

## 10. On the Road Again

1. Kristi Dosh, "College Football Playoff Payouts By Conference For 2017-2018," *Forbes*, December 30, 2017, https://www.forbes.com/sites/kristi-dosh/2017/12/30/college-football-playoff-payouts-by-conference-for-2017-2018/?sh=635325a52704
2. Mal Florence, "Mirage Bowl Trip Not All It Appeared to the Teams," Los Angeles Times, November 28, 1985, https://www.latimes.-com/archives/la-xpm-1985-11-28-sp-9162-story.html

## 11. Heartbeat of the Team

1. TrojanWarrior1, "An Ode to Marv Goux leading up to the Notre Dame game," USCfootball.com, October 14, 2011, https://247sports.com/college/usc/Board/29/Contents/An-Ode-to-Marv-Goux-leading-up-to-the-Notre-Dame-game-5878585/
2. Keith H. Walker and Robert W. Jensen, *The Man on the Ladder*, 6.

3. Larry Burnett, "VICE Sports Q&A: Mike Garrett," vice.com, February 10, 2016, https://www.vice.com/en/article/9apwqa/vice-sports-qa-mike-garrett-football-legend-and-polarizing-figure-at-usc
4. Eric Lindberg, "Get to Know USC Football's Inspiring and Surprising Jake Olson," USC Trojan Family, Spring 2008, https://news.usc.edu/trojan-family/qa-meet-jake-olson-business-major-uscs-blind-long-snapper/

## 12. National Recognition

1. Keith H. Walker and Robert W. Jensen, *The Man on the Ladder*, 36.
2. Keith H. Walker and Robert W. Jensen, *The Man on the Ladder*, 36.
3. Raymond Coffey and Storer Rowley, "Inaugural Parade Stopped Cold," *Chicago Tribune*, January 21, 1985, https://www.chicagotribune.-com/news/ct-xpm-1985-01-21-8501040861-story.html
4. Reagan Library, "President Reagan's Remarks at the Inaugural Festivities and Band Concert on January 21, 1985," YouTube video, 43:20, September 12, 2016 https://www.youtube.com/watch?v=KAbz4OVYeu0&list=PLEL2J-7BrhestuvkvJyoahl0WASMrc0MO&index=8
5. Danny Maley, "USC Trojan Band Rose Bowl 1985 American Band-Fanfare for Common Man," YouTube video, 3:42, July 3, 2006, https://www.y-outube.com/watch?v=0W2IcLMo4WM
6. Tom Finigan, "1986 Statue of Liberty All American Marching Band," YouTube video, 1:38:26, July 22, 2012, https://www.youtube.com/watch?v=Ki95FGbypiY&t=188s
7. Jeff Callaway, "Statue of Liberty Band: Broadway Show introduced by Elizabeth Taylor (1 of 2)," YouTube video, 11:26, April 29, 2012, https://www.youtube.com/watch?v=kGunnggutUQ&t=97s

## 13. World Ambassadors

1. Eric Liu, "The Message of D-Day," The Atlantic.com, June 5, 2014, https://www.theatlantic.com/politics/archive/2014/06/d-dayforever/371993/
2. Andiamoveloceyovic, "USC Marching Trojans at the Roman 'Coliseum,'" YouTube video, 1:17, https://www.youtube.com/watch?v=9PaOXLMthSg

## 14. Disneyland Band

1. DisneyParkVideos, "EPCOT Center – The Opening Celebration," YouTube video, 48:59, https://www.youtube.com/watch?v=rSchZRcE_eg
2. "EPCOT Grand Opening Master Script," disneydocs.net/epcot, item 21 part 1, page 62, October 1982, https://www.disneydocs.net/epcot
3. Mydaughtersara, "EuroDisney Grand Opening – Part 1 of 4," YouTube video, 14:57, https://www.youtube.com/watch?v=Y2YepTc-WieU&list=PLPHiCzyrg1lg8guNq8ntEHiSB8FDYD6LC&t=297s
4. OnstageDisney, "1992 The Grand Opening of Euro Disney," YouTube video, 1:33:12, https://www.youtube.com/watch?v=GC6UwPLNioI

## 15. L.A.'s Band

1. Keith H. Walker and Robert W. Jensen, *The Man on the Ladder,* 161.
2. Ashley Archibald, "Where Are They Now?" *Spirit Notes,* Winter 2009, https://web.archive.org/web/20090526091307/http://www.usc.e-du/dept/band/about/spiritnotes09.pdf
3. Doug Williams, "Team may change, but Laker Band endures," espn.com, May 4, 2012, https://www.espn.com/blog/music/post/_/id/762/team-may-change-but-lakers-band-endures
4. Keith H. Walker and Robert W. Jensen, *The Man on the Ladder,* 199.

## 17. Legendary Legacy

1. The School District of South Orange and Maplewood, "Hall of Fame," https://www.somsd.k12.nj.us/columbia/our-school/hall-of-fame/.
2. USC, "The 136th USC Commencement," YouTube video, 1:55:01, https://www.youtube.com/watch?v=m32B85v_eEU

# ABOUT THE AUTHOR

Christy Stansell shares people's stories. An Emmy-nominated news producer, and now content developer for a global life coaching institute, Christy earned her broadcast journalism degree cum laude from University of Southern California (while also performing with Hollywood's Band!). Published in the paper at ten and featured in a television sports anchor challenge at twelve, Christy delivered her first live news report at sixteen. After fourteen years reporting, anchoring, and producing news in markets from L.A. to D.C., Christy landed in Idaho to publish magazine articles, lead workshops for small business networks, and be twice-named Woman of the Year. Christy now writes from home with three dogs underfoot, husband in the kitchen, one daughter upstairs, and the other at USC.

www.HollywoodsBand.com
AuthorChristyStansell@gmail.com

CPSIA information can be obtained
at www.ICGtesting.com
Printed in the USA
BVHW082128161121
621782BV00002B/72